Leon Battista Alberti

*Leon Battista Alberti, self-portrait
(National Gallery of Art,
Washington, D.C.,
Samuel H. Kress Collection)*

Joan Gadol

Leon Battista Alberti

Universal Man of the Early Renaissance

The University of Chicago Press

Chicago and London

Standard Book Number: 226–30789–1
Library of Congress Catalog Card Number: 72–75811

The University of Chicago Press, Chicago 60637
The University of Chicago Press, Ltd., London

To my parents
and to the late
Garrett Mattingly—
fine teachers all

Contents

Illustrations

Preface

The principal aim of this book is to portray Alberti's intellectual character.
I regard him not as an art theorist primarily, nor as a humanist, an architect,
a cartographer, nor even a mathematician, but as a representative of that
Renaissance type which Burckhardt called the "universal man." What I sought to
understand was the coherence of his thought, the ideas that led him from one
set of problems to another, and this is what I now seek to present. I should like
to say at the outset, then, that although this is a comprehensive treatment of
Alberti in the sense of dealing with all his varied works, it is an analysis
in terms of the basic ideas and ways of thought that unified them. It is not and
does not pretend to be an exhaustive study of each of his major undertakings.
Much remains to be done in special areas to extend our knowledge of his
particular works and of their historical influence, and in the notes I have called
attention to certain issues which I hope others will pursue. But for this book,
it is enough if it succeeds in conveying a faithful image of Alberti's world of
thought, making its many-sidedness comprehensible and disclosing its central,
unifying ideas.

   Because of Alberti's "universal" interests, he was caught up by, and he
helped determine the course of, almost all the currents of early Renaissance
culture. The aesthetic, cosmological, natural-scientific, and ethical and social
interests of his age were centered in his case in a few rather simple but seminal
ideas which appear in chapter 1 in the technical, mathematical form in which
they first presented themselves to him, as the ideas of perspective, *Prospettiva*.
I have treated them in full detail there for two reasons: first, so that those
unfamiliar with the perspectival "science" of the Renaissance might understand
its systematic core without reference to mathematical works on the topic; and
secondly, so that the evolution of these ideas might be understood, for simple as
they may seem to us now, it is nonetheless a subject of historical wonder how
they ever arose. However, I somewhat regret the disadvantages of this detailed
treatment. Some readers are apt to be repelled by a first chapter filled with

numbers and diagrams, and others, if they are mathematically minded, are apt to become impatient because of the length to which I have gone to expound the elementary mathematical ideas of the fifteenth century. I advise those who fall in either of these groups merely to skim this chapter. It is possible to do so without affecting one's understanding of the rest of the book, although I do believe that the reader who masters these few technicalities of perspective, or who simply reviews them, will be rewarded later when he discovers their bearing on further developments which are not at all as technical in nature and which would seem at first glance to have no relation to them.

This book has been long in the making and has incurred many debts, the chief of which I owe to my husband, Eugene T. Gadol. He has read the entire manuscript patiently and critically in several stages of its preparation and has helped me enormously by his intellectual sympathy, his demand for precision, and his stylistic suggestions. Aside from giving me the help of a professional philosopher, he prepared the orthographic projection which I use in Chapter 1 and took all the photographs of Alberti's buildings, with the exception of those to which other credits are attached. Professor Paul Oskar Kristeller of Columbia University has for years been most generous and helpful with his information and advice. I owe him and Professor Garrett Mattingly an incalculable debt for guiding me with scrupulous care in my doctoral work on Alberti. Among my colleagues at the City College of New York, my special thanks go to Professor Helene Wieruszowski and Mrs. Charles Kleinbaum for the benefit of many long conversations on matters dealt with in this book and for freely giving me their valuable help in a number of other ways.

My first researches in Italy were made possible by a combined grant from the Danforth Foundation and Columbia University, and by the kind assistance of my former dean at the Baruch School of the City College of New York, Dr. Emanuel Saxe. The descendants of the two Florentine families that supported and encouraged Alberti graciously offered me whatever assistance they could. The Marchesa Maria Concetta Medici de' Tornaquinci was most kind and generous with her time, and the Rucellai family courteously allowed me to view their palace and chapel and gave me a great deal of information about the family architect.

I was greatly assisted in my research by the excellent facilities and obliging staff of the libraries of the Research Division of the New York Public Library and of Columbia University. My special thanks go to Mr. Adolf Placzek of Avery Library, to Mrs. Norma Balsam and Messrs. Jefferson, Mask, and Tobin of the New York Public Library, and to the entire staff of the Photographic Division of the New York Public Library. Miss Janet L. Snow of the Art Reference Bureau, Ancram, N.Y., obligingly obtained certain special photographs for me, and Mr. Gabriel Austin, formerly of the New York Public Library, helped me considerably in the initial stages of my research.

The City College Research Fund helped to defray a considerable portion of my secretarial expenses, and my former student, Mr. George Bock, carried out a large part of those secretarial labors with exceptional helpfulness. Miss Sharyn Orlowski and Miss Barbara Rushmore were ideal student assistants who cheerfully relieved me of a number of tasks.

And last, but far from least, I wish to express my warm gratitude to Abby Kleinbaum for helping me read the proofs and prepare the index.

Leon Battista Alberti

Introduction

"In what category of learning can I put Battista Alberti?" wondered the
Renaissance humanist and poet, Cristoforo Landino. "Among the physicists,
you say; and I must admit that he seems to be have been born only to inquire
into the secrets of Nature. But then, what branch of mathematics was not known
to him? Geometry, arithmetic, astronomy, music—and in perspective he did
marvels." Alberti was a humanist, too; and an exceptional one at that. The
classical learning of his *Ten Books on Architecture* was astonishing and its Latin
elegant. He was versed in all the arts. An architect of renown, he wrote
authoritatively on painting and sculpture as well as on the art of building, and
"with his own hand . . . painted, sculptured, chiseled, and cast works." And as if
all this were not enough, his labors on behalf of the Tuscan vernacular won him
a place among the founders of Italian literature. Dante, Petrarch, and Boccaccio
deserve the credit for transforming that vernacular into a literary language,
Landino allowed, "but in prose Battista surpassed the greatest."[1]

So Leon Battista Alberti appeared to his age: he was one of those
extraordinarily versatile spirits of the time whose life seemed to bear out his own
youthful conviction that "nothing is too difficult for study and determination to
overcome."[2] It was a life spent largely in study and writing, in inventing and
building. Very few of the personal events that make up a biography in the usual
sense of the word are known in Alberti's case, but what has survived reinforces
the impression his contemporaries give us, that the character and significance
of his life is to be found in the great variety of his works. He was born in 1404
in Genoa, during the exile of his powerful merchant-banking family from
Florence, the second natural son of Lorenzo Alberti and a Bolognese widow. His
father soon moved to Venice where he brought up Battista and his elder brother,
Carlo, providing them with a Florentine stepmother whom he married in 1408.

1. *Apologìa di Dante,* quoted by Girolamo Mancini, *Vita di Leon Battista Alberti,*
p. 442.

2. Alberti, *Della pittura,* p. 107.

Lorenzo Alberti attended carefully to his sons' early education and then boarded Battista at Gasparino Barzizza's Gymnasium in Padua. Some of the leading humanists and educators of Alberti's generation received their classical training at Barzizza's. Panormita, Francesco Barbaro, and Francesco Filelfo studied there, as did Vittorino da Feltre whose own Gymnasium at Mantua was to become the best known humanistic school of Renaissance Italy.

After he left Barzizza's Gymnasium in 1421, Alberti continued to devote himself to the "new learning." Officially, he attended the University of Bologna to earn a degree in canon law, but he deepened his knowledge and understanding of ancient culture during this seven-year period, from 1421 to 1428, as his literary studies came to sustain him through a series of personal misfortunes. His father died during his first year at the University, and only a few months later the death of his paternal uncle deprived him and his brother of their guardian and their inheritance. Certain members of the family whose name, cultivated manners, and ideas of bourgeois economy Alberti was to immortalize in *De Familia* took advantage of the illegitimate birth of the two sons (and only children) of Lorenzo Alberti and, at this juncture, appropriated their legacy. Shocked, impoverished, and often sick from nervous strain and overwork, Alberti continued both his legal studies and his literary pursuits. He clung to the Stoic belief that adverse circumstances alone cannot vanquish the human spirit: "It is not within the power of Fortune, as some fools think, to overcome so easily one who will not be overcome. Fortune yokes only those who submit to her."[3] Holding up the mirror to these painful years in *De commodis litterarum atque incommodis*,[4] Alberti reconciled himself to the sacrifices and want to which his years as a student had accustomed him. His dogged pursuit of letters had rewarded him with self-understanding; and as this early work already shows, his reflections on life and destiny had come to be shaped by Graeco-Roman literature and its fundamental notions of *humanitas*.

Alberti's own career as an author began during these years when illness forced him to rest from reading. He wrote a light didactic comedy called *Philodoxeos*[5] which he palmed off as the "discovered" work of a fictitious Roman playwright, Lepidus. By the age of twenty, he was evidently a good enough classicist to pay this strange Renaissance kind of tribute to antiquity, for despite his subsequent disclaimers, *Philodoxeos* was still published by Manutius in 1588 as a "classical" Roman work. He also wrote a number of short pieces on

3. Alberti, *I primi tre libri della famiglia*, p. 9.
4. Written before 1430; in *Opera. Pupillus* was also written about the same time on the same theme; in *Opera inedita*, pp. 126–29. Rather than burden this Introduction with the requisite bibliographical information for each of the Alberti works I mention, I shall henceforth give footnotes only for direct quotations and/or works which are not discussed later in the book.
5. Written c. 1424; in *Opere volgari di Leon Battista Alberti*, 1: cxxvii–clxv.

love in Latin and the vernacular, and in verse as well as prose.[6] Some are highly
moralistic, others playful and elegant in the spirit of Ovid, but all ring with an
autobiographical note which indicates that he was coping with an unhappy
romance as well as with the loss of his father, illness, poverty, and his family's
rejection.

Just as significant for the direction his career would take, and as an
indication of his indomitable will, are the mathematical studies Albert pursued
while he was at Bologna. Whenever the nervous malady he suffered from
impaired the functioning of his memory, he turned from words to geometry for
recreation and intellectual sustenance. By the time he received his doctorate in
canon law in 1428, mathematics had become as vital an interest as literature.
It is not surprising to find that the clerical position which he then accepted was
one that would make use of his literary gifts rather than his legal training, and
one that would give him the leisure to follow his intellectual inclinations.

Like so many humanists, Alberti became a secretary. His first position may
have been with Cardinal Albergati, the influential Bishop of Bologna and
papal legate whose stolid and serious face is known to us from a Jan van Eyck
portrait. After 1428, Alberti traveled to France, the Low Countries, and Germany,
and some biographers have speculated that he may have been accompanying
the Cardinal on some of his papal missions.[7] He may also have visited Florence
after 1428. The ban of exile against most of his family was lifted in that year
as the so-called popular party to which the Medici and the Alberti belonged
began to successfully counter the influence of the oligarchical faction headed by
the Albizzi family. But there is no sure information about his whereabouts or his
doings until 1432, the year he came to Rome and entered the service of the
Bishop Biagio Molin, head of the papal chancery.

Bishop Molin commissioned Alberti to write the life of St. Potitus which
dates from this period, and he secured a post for him as *abbreviatore apostolico*,
a position which he was to hold until 1464. Alberti thus became one of the
hundred or so secretaries of the papal chancery, joining such humanists as
Flavio Biondo and Poggio Bracciolini in a "rhetorical" occupation which
required classical training and made reasonable demands upon his time. He now
took holy orders, and he received the priory of Gangalandi in the diocese of
Florence as an ecclesiastical benefice. Pope Eugenius IV had to issue two bulls to
effect this: a general one annulling the prohibition against natural children
receiving holy orders and ecclesiastical benefices, and one specifically permitting

6. "Amator," *Op. ined.*, pp. 1–18. "Ephebie," *Op. volg.*, 5: 297–322. "Deiphira,"
ibid., 3: 365–409 (with apocryphal passages). "Ecatonphila," *ibid.*, pp. 236–74.
Alberti's poetry is discussed in chap. 5.

7. In his biographical essay on Alberti in vol. 1 of the *Dizionario biografico degli
italiani*, pp. 702–9, Cecil Grayson questions this view. He has found that Alberti's name
does not appear among Albergati's followers either at the Council of Basel or at the
Peace of Arras.

Alberti to accept a prebend as a case in point. (Nicholas V later confirmed Alberti in the prebend of Gangalandi and also conferred the rectory of Borgo San Lorenzo in Mugello upon him.)

Despite his connections and obvious talents, Alberti seems to have given no further thought to advancement within the hierarchy of the Church. Once the problem of securing a livelihood was settled, it was his intellectual career that he developed; and during this first stay in Rome from 1432 to 1434, its characteristic features already began to emerge. He was at work on humanistic, scientific, and artistic problems. He wrote a dialogue *On the Family* in the Tuscan vernacular, the first of his major humanistic pieces and a landmark in the history of Italian prose. At the same time, he began to work out a method for constructing survey maps of cities and small areas, a procedure unknown in the chorography of the time. This interest in the principles of map making was to issue a decade or so later in a brief but seminal work on cartography, his *Descriptio urbis Romae,* but it also had implications for painting. Alberti was experimenting with a *camera oscura* in Rome, studying the formation of visual images by light rays and making "artificial images" (i.e., pictures) which his friends thought so natural they deemed them "miracles." This interest in the problem of pictorial projection, coupled with the surveying and mapping procedures he was mastering, provided the foundations for his systematization of painter's perspective—the great project that absorbed him in Florence where he went with Eugenius IV and the papal court in 1434.

Renaissance Florence was literally taking form when he arrived there. Brunelleschi was just completing the majestic dome which gave the church of Santa Maria del Fiore its unique and unforgettable appearance and its now commonly accepted name, the Duomo. His Sagrestia Vecchia in San Lorenzo was finished, and the nave of the church was under construction. The young painter Masaccio who died in 1428 had barely carried out his great frescoes in the Brancacci Chapel of the Carmine. Ghiberti was at work on the second (East) doorway of the Baptistery; and Donatello and Luca della Robbia were doing the reliefs of the Cantoria for the Duomo. These works had a tremendous impact upon Alberti and gave a decisive turn to his development. Florence stimulated his literary interests and reinforced his humanistic, social ideas, but most important at this stage was its art in which Alberti found that creative renewal, that "renaissance," which his humanism had predisposed him to expect.

Forming a close friendship with Brunelleschi and Donatello, he threw himself into the artistic renaissance of quattrocento Florence. He began to paint and sculpt, but the major accomplishment of this Florentine period (1434–1436) was theoretical. By bringing his humanistic and mathematical learning to bear upon the practice of painting and sculpture, Alberti furthered the new, mathematically inspired techniques of these arts and developed the aesthetic implications of this "renascent" artistic reliance upon geometry.

6 In *Della pittura* he gave the first systematic exposition (and indeed the first

written exposition) of the rules of painter's perspective, and he set forth at the same time the first theory of painting, grounding that art in visual experience and its "geometric" representation. The sculptural counterpart to the theory of perspective appeared somewhat later in *Della statua.* Treating the statue as another kind of geometric "imitation" of nature, he devised an equally ingenious method of mensuration for the sculptor and worked out the first Renaissance canon of proportions.

After leaving Florence in 1436, Alberti traveled about for some seven years as the papal court moved to Bologna, Ferrara, back to Florence, and then to Rome. His work was largely literary during this period. He wrote some of his deftest Latin in the succinct *Apologi,* a number of *Intercoenales,* and *Musca* and *Canis,* all brief pieces in which he successfully revived the form and urbane, rational spirit of classical literature. At the same time, he continued to promote the literary use of the vernacular. He sponsored a vernacular literary context when he was in Florence in 1441 and wrote two of his most important works on moral philosophy in the *lingua Toscana.* These are the vernacular dialogues *Theogenius* and *Profugiorum ab aerumna* which should rank high alongside *De Familia* in the corpus of Alberti's writings and in the history of Renaissance literature, for replete with classical references as they are, they still reveal with that poignancy peculiar to the Renaissance the personal conflicts of their author.

Theogenius, although artistically the lesser of the two works, is particularly important for reflecting a critical moment in Alberti's career. Withdrawal, solitude, a life given over to contemplation—for a moment these notions once again acquired their old force, tempting this author of a treatise on bourgeois family life, this promoter of the empirically oriented artistic and scientific innovations of his time, to assume an ethical position which blended the values of the medieval monk with those of the ancient sage. This was a work of self-doubt, yet even here Alberti's essentially life-bound vision won out. Today Alberti is rightly regarded as a representative of the "civic humanism" of Florence, but to my mind, he won that position not so much in *De Familia* as in *Theogenius,* where he had to struggle to defend his commitment to the world, and in *Profugiorum ab aerumna* (or *Della tranquillità dell'animo*), the dialogue that followed *Theogenius* and resolved whatever lingering doubts it expressed. *Profugiorum ab aerumna* represents Alberti's return to civil society and its works, and the dialogue he holds in it with a member of the Medici family and Agnolo Pandolfini, a former magistrate, symbolically unfolds under Brunelleschi's dome.

Alberti dedicated the first of these two dialogues to Leonello d'Este, the Marchese of Ferrara. In 1438, when the Church Council of Ferrara-Florence began its meetings, Alberti was made welcome at the Este court, and Leonello became both a patron and a friend. In this circle, which included the humanist, Angelo Decembrio, and the artists, Jacopo Bellini and Pisanello, Alberti's artistic side seems to have been particularly appreciated. Decembrio (a younger brother of the better known humanist, Pier Candido) later wrote a dialogue incorporating a number of the ideas of *Della pittura,* and certain drawings by Pisanello and Bellini have been shown to be based upon Alberti's perspectival construction.[8] Alberti himself probably cast at this time the portrait medallion which bears his fine and firm profile and his emblem of the winged eye (Frontispiece).[9] But most important of all, it was in Ferrara that he began his study of architecture.

Leonello had asked Alberti to judge the models submitted for an equestrian statue of his father, and Alberti devoted his attention to the task at hand with characteristic thoroughness. He not only judged the contest (Solomonlike, awarding the horse to one of the two chief competitors and the Marquis to the other); he also wrote *De equo animante*[10] for Leonello, a treatise describing the appearance and habits of horses; and he personally designed a "classical" base for the statue—a miniature triumphal arch. It was while studying the rules of classical design that Alberti began to struggle with the text of Vitruvius and, upon Leonello d'Este's urging, he resolved to reclaim this great theoretical work on classical architecture, either by a commentary or a new book.

This project preoccupied him when he returned to Rome in 1443 with the papal court, and it led him to begin a study of the ruins of ancient buildings. His literary activities persisted as always: one of his major Latin works comes from this period, 1443–1452, an allegorical satire in the style of Lucian called *Momus.* But his energies were chiefly directed towards archeological and architectural studies, and to mathematics, engineering, and mechanics. He wrote a few treatises on these matters, the most important of which are *Descriptio urbis Romae* and *Ludi matematici,* and greater works were in the making.

When Tommaso Parentucelli da Sarzana became Pope Nicholas V in 1447, Fortune provided Alberti with the opportunity and incentive to translate his absorbing interest in architecture into what turned out to be his most outstanding theoretical achievement and the most congenial artistic practice of his career. A friend since their student years at Bologna and a patron of the arts and new learning, Nicholas made Alberti his architectural adviser. Together they inaugurated the works of the Renaissance papacy. The various projects Alberti planned and carried out in Rome gave him the architectural and engineering experience necessary for the comprehensive study of the art of

8. Samuel Y. Edgerton, Jr., "Alberti's Perspective: A New Discovery and a New Evaluation," *Art Bulletin,* 48 (1966): 367–78.

9. Sir George Francis Hill, *A Corpus of Italian Medals of the Renaisance before Cellini,* 1: 18. For a description of this medallion and of another self-portrait in the Louvre, see Kurt Badt, "Drei plastische Arbeiten von Leone Battista Alberti," *Mitteilungen des Kunsthistorischen Institutes in Florenz,* 8 (1958): 78–87. In this article, Badt also argues that Alberti was the sculptor of the portrait bust of Lodovico III Gonzaga in the Kaiser-Friedrich Museum in Berlin.

10. *Op. ined.,* pp. 238–56.

building which he had decided to write, and for the first of his own buildings: the Tempio Malatestiano, which he designed in a bold "Roman" style for the Lord of Rimini. This building established Alberti as a major architect, a worthy successor of his friend, Brunelleschi. Although it was the first of his buildings, it advanced in unprecendented fashion the classical style which Brunelleschi had introduced, making Alberti the mediator between the quattrocento master and the architecture of the High Renaissance. The culminating work of these years, the book which had been growing since Alberti first began his study of Vitruvius, played a comparable historical role. In 1452, Alberti presented to the first Renaissance Pope his classic treatment of the theory and practice of Renaissance architecture, *De re aedificatoria.* Rich in all the practical knowledge needed by the builder, this first modern treatise on the art of building re-established the rules of classical architecture as well, and grounded them in an aesthetic theory of harmony which became definitive for Renaissance art.

For the final twenty years of his life, Alberti himself gave artistic expression to the artistic vision that illuminates and unifies the learning of *De re aedificatoria.* His great buildings, with the exception of the Tempio Malatestiano, all belong to the years 1452–1472. In architecture he found the mode of plastic expression that suited his artistic genius, and in Giovanni Rucellai and Lodovico Gonzaga he found patrons who encouraged and sponsored him. The Florentine merchant, Giovanni Rucellai, commissioned a number of projects, the most famous and enduring of which are the façades of Santa Maria Novella and the Palazzo Rucellai. For Lodovico Gonzaga, the humanist prince of Mantua who had been educated by Vittorino da Feltre, Alberti designed the church of San Sebastiano (at present, drastically altered) and the truly magnificent Renaissance church of Sant' Andrea.

Alberti traveled a great deal on his architectural commissions and at other times, particularly in the summers, he made visits to Florence (or to Camaldoli), and to his friend Federico da Montefeltro at Urbino, but Rome was his home after 1443 and it remained so even after 1464 when Pope Paul II drastically reduced the number of *abbreviatori apostolici* and dismissed him from the papal chancery.

Rome and the members of the papal bureacracy with whom he associated seemed to stimulate his technical, scientific interests. It was in Rome that he had begun his work on perspective and surveying, and the "learned friends" who asked him to set down the principles of constructing a survey map of the city were most probably papal secretaries. His *Regule lingue florentine,* which he wrote sometime before 1454, reflects another problem entertained by certain members of the papal chancery, the problem of the relation between Latin and the vernacular. It is a grammar book, demonstrating in an original (and irrefutable) fashion that the Tuscan vernacular is as "regular" a language as Latin and thus as fit an instrument for prose. In the 1460's Alberti undertook another highly original work at the request of another papal secretary, his long-time friend, Leonardo Dati. *De componendis cifris* is a brilliant little study of coding and decoding; it contains the first known frequency table and the first polyalphabetic system of coding by means of what seems to have been Alberti's own invention, the cipher wheel.

If his scientific writings were chiefly Roman in inspiration, the literary and ethical writings of Albert's late years belong to Florence. In the 1460's, he moved in Lorenzo de' Medici's circle, auditing lectures by Marsilio Ficino, the great Neoplatonist of the latter half of the fifteenth century, and enjoying the friendship of younger humanists like Cristoforo Landino for whom he became a model of life and learning. The humanistic side of his nature seemed to draw sustenance from the city of the Duomo, and Alberti contributed in turn to its literary and philosophical culture. For Lorenzo de' Medici, he wrote a little Latin treatise on the rules of rhetoric,[11] and for the younger members of the Alberti family, a small work on moral philosophy.[12] But it is in *De Iciarchia,* the last in the series of vernacular dialogues which began with *De Familia,* and the most artful of them all, that he paid his finest tribute to quattrocento Florence. Written just a few years before his death in 1472, in the limpid Tuscan tongue he had helped to refine, *De Iciarchia* is a classic literary affirmation of the guiding ideas of Florentine humanism and of Alberti's own life.

Faced with this array of accomplishments, finding that "at whatever discipline he applies himself, he excels with ease and rapidity," it is no wonder that Alberti's contemporaries should acclaim him as "beyond comparison."[13] "Was anything unknown to him?" asked Politian, the finest poet of fifteenth-century Italy. In a letter of 1485 introducing the posthumous printed edition of *De re aedificatoria,* Politian reviewed Alberti's mastery of poetry and prose, his classical scholarship, his restoration of the theory of architecture, his buildings, his invention of machines, his work in painting and sculpture; "it is better to be silent about him," he concluded, "than to say not enough."[14] But few chose to be silent in that very literary age. Alberti was "marvelous, divine, omnipotent in the judgment of many," and many of those who knew him recorded their impressions of the man they thought so "learned, eloquent, by

11. "Trivia," *Opuscoli morali di Leon Battista Alberti, Gentil'huomo Firentino.*
12. "Sentenze pitagoriche," *Op. volg.,* 2: 485–87. From about the same time come his "Epistolae septem Epimenidis nomine Diogeni inscriptae," "Epistola ad Cratem," *Op. ined.,* pp. 267–71.
13. Lapo da Castiglionchio in a dialogue *Sui comodi della curia pontificia,* mentioning members of the papal court says of his "coetaneo Battista Alberti il cui ingegno mi apparisce così degno di lode da non poterlo paragonare ad altri; a così ammiro che ignoro se mai passerà ai posteri un nome ugualmente grande. E talmente disposto che a qualunque disciplina si applichi, con facilità e celerità supera tutti." Quoted by Mancini, *Vita,* pp. 153–54.
14. *Op. volg.,* 1: lxxxv–lxxxvi.

nature open and liberal, the pride of Florence and Italy."[15]

It was from such recollections of his versatility and determination to excel, features which Alberti's successive translators, editors, and biographers preserved and passed on, that Jacob Burckhardt fashioned his striking image of Alberti as a representative Renaissance man, a *uomo universale*. In his brilliant essay on *The Civilization of the Renaissance in Italy* (1860), he called attention to Alberti's work in mathematics, physics, architecture, painting, sculpture, and literature (as well as to certain improbable gymnastic feats which a fifteenth-century biographer had ascribed to him); and he selected, in this bewildering diversity of accomplishments, one of the fundamental principles of Alberti's life. "That which others created he welcomed joyfully," Burckhardt wrote, quoting Alberti's anonymous biographer, "and [he] held every human achievement which followed the laws of beauty for something almost divine."[16] Placing Alberti in the context of his age and finding its forces reflected in him, Burckhardt shed new light upon his creative, comprehensive nature. In his esteem for man's creative abilities, and in his own command of so many aspects of human culture, Alberti was seen to reveal one of the dominant tendencies of the time: he captured in his own person the new reverence of the Renaissance for the formative, Promethean powers of the human spirit.

Enhanced by Burckhardt's persuasive imagery, Alberti's reputation for universal learning persisted in historical memory, but time had long since obscured the exact character and significance of his work. Some of his writings had never been published in printed editions and are still being "discovered" today. And some of his ideas and inventions were forgotten, not because they were literally lost, but because they were so completely assimilated by his contemporaries and successors. Vasari, for example, aptly describes Alberti's work in his *Lives of the Most Eminent Architects, Painters, and Sculptors of Italy* as a fusion of theory and practice; yet he had already lost sight of one of the most

15. Girolamo Aliotti, a monk and disciple of Ambrogio Traversari called Alberti "dottissimo, eloquentissimo, per natura ingenuo e liberale, decoro di Firenze e d'Italia, il cui ingegno maraviglioso, divino, onnipotente, a giudizio di molti dev'essere lodato e ammirato." Quoted by Mancini, *Vita*, p. 156.

16. Jacob Burckhardt, *The Civilization of the Renaissance in Italy*, pp. 85–87. The fifteenth-century biography Burckhardt used can be found in *Op. volg.*, 1: lxxxix–cxx. It was written in Latin and is incomplete, breaking off around the year 1437. Some scholars have attributed it to Alberti. Renée Watkins sums up the discussion on this matter in "The Authorship of the Vita Anonyma of Leon Battista Alberti," *Studies in the Renaissance*, 4 (1957): 101–12. She concludes that the work is Alberti's, but her claim rests largely upon a biographical account of why Alberti might have written the *Vita*— if indeed he wrote it. Dr. Watkins also finds the style of the *Vita* to be Albertian. I find the work too formless, naive, and immodest to be his. In my estimation someone other than Alberti wrote it, perhaps his cousin, Bernardo, as Cecil Grayson tends to believe; see his "Alberti and the Vernacular Eclogue in the Quattrocento," *Italian Studies*, 11 (1956): 16, n. 1.

remarkable products of that union. Alberti had been the first to systematize the rules of painter's perspective and set them down in writing in his book of 1435 *On Painting*. Yet even though Cosimo Bartoli dedicated his vernacular edition of Alberti's *Della pittura* to Vasari, when Vasari was writing in the middle of the sixteenth century about artists who all employed perspective, Alberti's role as an originator of perspectival art was forgotten. He appears in the *Lives* chiefly as an architect and architectural theorist; in painting he is but another "student of perspective."

The mathematical ideas and mechanical devices described in Alberti's writings suffered the same historical fate. After his death in 1472, the next few generations of mathematicians, cartographers, surveyors, engineers, and cryptographers adopted and developed whatever was of systematic value in his works, severing his original ideas from their historical roots in the process. Leonardo, who incorporated a number of passages from *Della pittura* in his own *Trattato* on painting (a legitimate procedure at the time), also studied many of Alberti's technical innovations and improved upon them. Of even greater importance, he made fully explicit the methodological rule which had directed Alberti's empirical researches. "The sciences," as Leonardo put it, "have no certainty except where one applies one of the mathematical sciences and unites them with these mathematical sciences."[17] Once Leonardo extended this fruitful principle of inquiry to the wide range of artistic and physical problems which preoccupied his genius, all that remained of scientific value in Alberti's technical writings were a few novel applications of the same basic ideas.

These ideas, belonging chiefly to surveying and and cryptography, were soon absorbed after Cosimo Bartoli published his collection of Alberti's *Opuscoli* in 1568. Bartoli himself wrote a book on applied mathematics which incorporated the surveying practices he had discovered in *Ludi matematici,* one of the treatises of the *Opuscoli. De cifris,* which Bartoli also included in this collection, was still referred to some twenty years later in a *Traicté des chiffres* by Blaise de Vigenère, but thereafter, as Alberti's rules were mastered and elaborated upon, their author was forgotten.

The bulk of Bartoli's *Opuscoli* was made up of Alberti's humanistic writings, but although they were still read with enjoyment, they had served their cultural purposes. Their classical, humanistic content was by now common property, and in the age of Castiglione and Bembo, Alberti could no longer be regarded as a model of vernacular prose. The only work that retained something of its original importance beyond the middle of the sixteenth century was *De re aedificatoria.* It continued to stand as a definitive source for the theory and practice of classical architecture, and it circulated in almost every European language until that style was rejected in the course of the last century.

By the nineteenth century, however, as the systematic importance of even

17. *The Literary Works of Leonardo da Vinci,* 2: 289, no. 1158.

this work began to wane, Alberti had become an object of the awakening historical interest in Renaissance culture and the Italian past. A professor of rhetoric, Pompilio Pozzetti, sounded the new note, appropriately enough in 1789. He appended to a traditional, typically laudatory Latin eulogy of Alberti a description in Italian of documents and notices about him that could be used to compose a genuine biography; and before the century ended, Girolamo Tiraboschi, the noted historian of Italian literature, did just that.[18] In the succeeding years of the Italian Risorgimento, most of Alberti's scattered vernacular writings, and documents pertaining to his life and works, were brought together by Aniccio Bonucci in five, still indispensable volumes of *Opere volgari.* Published in Florence between 1843 and 1849, this vernacular collection was followed by Girolamo Mancini's *Opera inedita* of 1890, a single volume containing most of Alberti's minor Latin works. Mancini also wrote the first comprehensive, critical biography of Alberti.[19] His reconstruction of the course of Alberti's life and the sequence of his works, based upon a thorough study of Alberti's writings and other fifteenth-century sources, is the standard biography to this day.

In our own time, the work of Bonucci and Mancini is being continued by Professor Cecil Grayson of Oxford University. His tireless researches in the Alberti manuscripts have led not only to the proper identification of some hitherto lost or unknown works but also to a number of emendations in the known ones, and to the beginning of a new, critical edition of all Alberti's writings. Two volumes of *Opere volgari* have appeared thus far (Bari, 1960 and 1966). This work will supersede Bonucci's when it is completed, and it will be followed by a collection of the Latin writings which will supersede Mancini's. Thus the basic task of determining the corpus of Alberti's writings and issuing sound editions of them is still in progress, but enough of a foundation had been laid by the nineteenth century for the work of historical examination to begin. Modern scholarship, turning its attention to the evolution of the various arts and sciences to which Alberti had contributed, has dealt by now with several of his accomplishments, studying them in their particulars and assessing their historical significance.

Alberti's writings on the arts attracted most attention, as they still do. They were republished a number of times in the nineteenth century, in response to the new historical interest in the Renaissance, and ultimately they were subjected to close, critical analysis in two Viennese editions: an 1877 edition (and German translation) by Hubert Janitschek of the books on painting, sculpture,

18. Pompilio Pozzetti, *Leo Baptista Alberti.* Girolamo Tiraboschi, "Vita di Leon Battista Alberti," *Della pittura e della statua di Leon Battista Alberti,* pp. vii–xxiv.

19. Mancini, *Vita.* The first edition came out in 1882, a revised edition in 1911. See also Luigi Passerini, *Gli Alberti di Firenze. Geneologia, storia e documenti;* C. Ceschi, "La Madre di Leon Battista Alberti," *Bolletino d'arte,* (1948): 191–92; and Cecil Grayson's short, up-to-date biography in the *Dizionario biographico,* 1: 702–9.

and the five architectural orders; and Max Theuer's 1912 edition (and translation) of *De re aedificatoria*.[20] The subsequent treatment of *Della pittura* and *Della statua* by the noted art historian, Erwin Panofsky, gave these works their present renown.[21] Panofsky followed Janitschek's reconstruction of Alberti's technical procedures, expanding what he said and at times correcting him, but his emphasis fell upon their historical importance. He showed that Alberti's systems of perspective and human proportions constituted the technical foundations of Renaissance painting and sculpture, introducing into these arts ideas and values which had far-reaching cultural implications for the age. Rudolf Wittkower performed a somewhat similar service for Alberti's *Ten Books on Architecture*. In his *Architectural Principles in the Age of Humanism*,[22] he demonstrated that the Pythagorean-Platonic ideas which Alberti revived in *De re aedificatoria* were fundamental to Renaissance architecture. Tracing Alberti's dominant influence upon Renaissance theory and practice, he exposed the religious and metaphysical presuppositions of what had long been regarded as a derivative, "pagan" architectural style.

The germinal ideas of Wittkower and Panofsky are still being developed in a number of highly specialized Alberti studies which have progressively clarified his contributions to Renaissance art. His humanistic and scientific writings have not been treated so extensively, but many of them have been studied, and here, too, a new appreciation of his role in these areas is gaining ground. Alberti's moral philosophy has been thoughtfully discussed in several Italian works on humanism, and his purely literary accomplishments have been evaluated.[23] The first Italian grammar, recently republished in a critical edition, is now definitely attributed to him.[24] His treatise on ciphers has been

---

20. Hubert Janitschek, "Leon Battista Alberti's kleinere Kunsttheoretische Schriften," *Quellenschriften für Kunstgeschichte.* 11 (1877). Max Theuer, *Zehn Bücher über die Baukunst.*

21. Especially in "Das perspektivische Verfahren Leone Battista Albertis," *Kunstchronik,* 25 (1915): 504–16; and "The History of the Theory of Human Proportions as a Reflection of the History of Styles," in *Meaning in the Visual Arts,* pp. 55–107. See also *Renaisssance and Renascences.*

22. Rudolf Wittkower, *Architectural Principles in the Age of Humanism.*

23. For Alberti's humanistic ideas, see especially Giuseppe Saitta, *Il pensiero italiano nell'umanesimo e nel rinascimento,* 1: 393–424; and Eugenio Garin, *L'umanesimo italiano,* 9–10, 60–61, 87–88. Valeria Benetti-Brunelli has given Alberti's moral philosophy extensive treatment in *Leon Battista Alberti e il rinnovamento pedagogico nel quattrocento.* See also Cecil Grayson, "The Humanism of Alberti," *Italian Studies,* 12 (1957): 37–56.

Cecil Grayson has also concerned himself with Alberti's literary endeavors in "Alberti and the Vernacular Eclogue," Italian Studies, 11 (1956): 16–29; and "Note sulle rime dell'Alberti," *Rassegna della Letteratura italiana,* 63 (1958): 76–78.

24. *La prima grammatica della lingua volgare,* edited by Cecil Grayson. See also Carmela Colombo, "Leon Battista Alberti e la prima grammatica italiana," *Studi linguistici italiani,* 3 (1962): 176–87.

shown to be the first modern, scientific work of cryptography;[25] and his cartographical work appears to have initiated the surveying procedures usually ascribed to the sixteenth century, and seems to have founded as well the tradition of scaled city plans and survey maps which originated in Renaissance Italy.[26]

Once again we may begin to wonder into what category of learning we shall put Battista Alberti, for in each, bearing out the judgment of his contemporaries, his work has been shown to be sound and original, giving rise to new and fruitful developments and setting new intellectual and artistic currents in motion. The truth seems to be that he belongs to all the fields Landino mentioned—and then some. We have to penetrate all of them—painting, sculpture, architecture, aesthetics, mathematics, cartography, surveying, mechanics, cryptography, literature, and moral philosophy—to get to the center of his thought; from no one discipline taken singly, nor, I would add, from all of them simply taken together, can we derive an adequate understanding of it. Indeed, the determination of this center, of this Archimedean point around which all of Alberti's activities harmoniously revolve, has become the main problem in Alberti studies today. Modern scholarship has described and evaluated a good number of his accomplishments, but because of its specialized nature, it has treated them in isolation, examining each one separately and from the vantage point of the discipline to which it belongs. Thus almost all the pieces of Alberti's world of thought are known, but not the inner logic that made them cohere in a consistent whole.

In this respect, Alberti studies reflect a difficulty which has beset Renaissance history for almost a century. A hundred years of specialized scholarship, inspired very largely by Burckhardt's synoptic view of Renaissance culture, seems to have broken down his synthesis into a multitude of complex, jarring pieces. Burckhardt regarded the Renaissance as the first stage, the genesis, of "modern" European civilization and culture. But as individual Renaissance figures were subjected to closer examination, they were found to exhibit "medieval" ideas and attitudes as well as "modern" ones; to hold "Christian" as well as "pagan" views; to espouse "metaphysical" as well as "empirical" ideas. Many of the "modern" secular and empirical features of Renaissance life were also found in the Middle Ages, and certain "medieval" characteristics were seen to survive into quite modern times. Burckhardt's general concepts, it seemed, had failed to capture the "meaning" of the Renaissance; and this criticism, which stimulated further studies of a highly specialized nature, gave rise to the idea that the quest for synthesis per se was mistaken. The very notion of a unified picture of Renaissance culture was deemed impossible by Lynn Thorndike and his successors—who went so far as to proscribe even the name "Renaissance" in the belief that it expresses no

25. Aloys Meister, *Die Geheimschrift im Dienste der Päpstlichen Kurie;* and Luigi Sacco, *Un primato italiano: la crittografia nei secoli XV e XVI.*
26. This will be shown in Chapter 4 of this book.

determinate concept and can express none.[27]

What happened to the historical picture of the Renaissance since Burckhardt's time has happened also to Alberti. His life's work has been analysed into a number of well-examined but quite disparate parts, and this has seriously affected the interpretation of certain particular works and of his thought as a whole. For one thing, specialized studies rarely attempt to comprehend the general concepts that underlie the particular work they analyse. Yet for a complete historical, as well as a systematic, understanding of any cultural work, we need to know why its content should have been delimited and handled as it was; we need to understand the fundamental concepts and theoretical orientation that led to this particular formulation rather than another. This is the task that urges the historian beyond the study of an isolated work or works of just one kind.[28] If Rudolf Wittkower's presentation of Alberti's architectural ideas is especially illuminating, it is so because he went beyond the bounds of architecture to determine its relations with the scientific, metaphysical, and religious preoccupations of the time. For these relations are what made the principles of Renaissance architecture meaningful; and they enabled Professor Wittkower to discover in the distinctive forms of Renaissance building the

27. This is Lynn Thorndike's position in "Renaissance or Prenaissance," *Journal of the History of Ideas*, 4 (1943) : 65–74. In reply to this, Paul Oskar Kristeller pointed out that the Renaissance is a period of European history which, while certainly continuous with the past, "has a distinctive physiognomy of its own, and . . . the inability of historians to find a simple and satisfactory definition for it does not entitle us to doubt its existence; otherwise, by the same token, we should have to question the existence of the Middle Ages, or of the eighteenth century." *The Classics and Renaissance Thought*, p. 4. Most of these difficulties disappear when attention is focused upon the peculiar balance which an age establishes among its divergent ideas and cultural forces, and upon the tendency or direction of its cultural development. See Ernst Cassirer's brilliant essay on this in "Some Remarks on the Originality of the Renaissance" in the same issue of *Journal of the History of Ideas* in which Thorndike's essay appears. Cassirer's own *Individual and Cosmos in Renaissance Philosophy* (English translation by Mario Domandi) constitutes a new and by now classic synthesis of Renaissance thought which in many respects vindicates Burckhardt's work. A useful discussion and bibliographical reviews of the so-called "problem of the Renaissance" can be found in *The Renaissance,* edited by Tinsley Helton.

28. As an outstanding historian has put the matter with reference to Renaissance studies: "If it is true that mental attitudes and problems are apt to spread across the separate departments of culture, and that this dissemination of new concepts often requires the span of generations, two inferences seem inevitable: first, that no estimate of the forces of 'tradition' and 'innovation' in any period is reliable if based on research in a single field; and second, that neither science, nor political thought, nor any single cultural activity can be understood in its specific evolution, unless allowance is made for cases in which essentials of progressive growth—for instance, the awareness of natural laws, or the power to make causal observations and research—are born and first elaborated in sectors of intellectual life remote from the particular field of our learned specialization." Hans Baron ,"Towards a More Positive Evaluation of the Fifteenth-Century Renaissance,"

Journal of the History of Ideas, 4 (1943) : 21–49.

cultural values those forms were meant to express.

The search for such unifying concepts remains outside the scope of most specialized studies, however; and this has reinforced the assumption that they are, for that very reason, unattainable. This notion, which is essentially a methodological one (and a false one, as Wittkower's study demonstrates), has come to function in the last few decades as a principle of interpretation. It is responsible, in fact, for one of the most distorted, yet widely accepted views of the Renaissance and the men who made it: the belief that the various currents of Renaissance culture need not or cannot be unified. This has led to a strange projection upon that age of the fragmentation of culture which is a characteristic of our own. Thus Federico Chabod, summing up almost a century of scholarship on "the concept of the Renaissance," concludes that the Renaissance failed to achieve a coherent orientation, that "having unlocked the door to various branches of human activity, [it] was subsequently unable to redintegrate them, in spite of the fact that human nature is constantly tormented by its need for a comprehensive vision."[29]

This extreme, if not eccentric viewpoint has appeared in Alberti studies, too. Paul-Henri Michel's *Un idéal humain au XVe siècle: La pensée de L. B. Alberti* (1930) was the first significant attempt to survey the entirety of Alberti's thought in the light of recent findings. It is a scholarly, and often rewarding study but Michel discovered that "medieval" and "modern" features were also hopelessly intermingled in Alberti. He could not treat Alberti as representative of either one or the other period, finding instead an irresolvable conflict between old and new in him, a conflict between "the man of the Middle Ages and the man of the Renaissance, the Christian and the pagan—these two dissimilar aspects of Alberti's person."[30] This convinced Michel that generalizations and concepts of types had to be abandoned altogether. He would "look at Alberti and forget 'the Renaissance man' "; but in his resolve to approach Alberti's thought without any general, unifying ideas, he presumed that Alberti himself had no unified orientation. Alberti struggles to bridge the "two worlds" of medieval and modern culture in Michel's study, and this made his life's work "a tragic effort towards the impossible." A medieval yearning to unite the totality of knowledge in a comprehensive *Summa* accounts for the universality of his interests, but this aim, Michel believed, had become chimerical by the fifteenth century. Systematic unification was impossible because of the increasing autonomy of the several arts and sciences; therefore no unity other than a merely personal one could underlie the variety of Alberti's works. The very reach of his thought had made it "imparfaite, inachevée, fragmentaire."

Michel has had his followers. His theme, which can also be found in the

29. Federico Chabod, *Machiavelli and the Renaissance*, p. 191. See also pp. 185–91.
30. Paul-Henri Michel, *Un idéal humain au XVe siècle: La pensée de L. B. Alberti.* The quotations are from pp. 132, 535, 138–39, 615.

literature on Leonardo, reappeared in Ruth Lang's *Leon Battista Alberti und die Sancta Masseritia*[31] where a sort of *reductio ad absurdum* was inadvertently achieved. Since Michel could not discover any unifying intellectual or moral principles to account for the development of Alberti's ideas and interests, Dr. Lang supplied a psychological "drive" of a curiously contemporary kind to fill the void. Her Alberti is beset by *Angst;* he strives desperately to lose himself in diversity, to amass ever more "merely human" values so as to fill what she regarded as his spiritual emptiness. Thus like his age, Alberti exhibits no positive features of his own. His is the disparateness, and the despair, that results from the coexistence of "medieval" and "modern" desires, from the anomaly of being a Dante at heart but a "rationalist" in practice.

More recently, and in a far sounder work than Lang's, Giovanni Santinello has conceded a "universal vision" to Alberti in *Leon Battista Alberti. Una visione estetica del mondo e della vita.* But Santinello's sympathetic study still eschews the task of uncovering the logical unity of that vision. Indeed, he maintains that the historian cannot analyze and resynthesize it since Alberti's vision "of the world and man" was not a systematic construction. That is, like Michel, Santinello continues to restrict the term "systematic" to deductive systems such as those of Scholastic philosophy, and this has led him to miss a key intellectual fact of Renaissance history in general, and one that is indispensable for an understanding of Alberti in particular: namely, that modern scientific modes of systematic thought, as opposed to metaphysical system building, had their inception in the Renaissance, in its humanistic study of culture and its artistic-technical inquiries into nature. Thus Santinello may be correct in criticizing Michel for imposing an alien set of categories upon Alberti's thought in an effort to present it "systematically"; but he and Michel are equally at fault in regarding that thought as unsystematic, and his procedure suffers as much as Michel's from this mistaken judgment. For Santinello concluded that the only way to present his subject faithfully was to follow a chronological order.[32] His study of Alberti's cosmic vision consists of a description of the contents of Alberti's books, one by one and in the sequence in which they were written.

There is a possibility, of course, that Alberti's thought was devoid of systematic coherence. This view has to be entertained, especially after the studies of Michel and Santinello, but it cannot be accepted at the outset, and neither can it be regarded as a "neutral" position open only to "the facts" without

31. Ruth Lang, *Leon Battista Alberti und die Sancta Masseritia.*
32. "Avevamo detto della necessità di seguire cronologicamente, per opere, il pensiero albertiano, sia perchè non volevamo imporgli esteriormente un'unità che esso non ha, sia perchè la sintesi ci avrebbe anche richiesto un lavoro di analisi, di separazione di problemi, cosa che pensiamo difficile a farsi nel caso del nostro autore . . ." Giovanni Santinello, *Leon Battista Alberti. Una visione estetica del mondo e della vita,* p. 190. See also pp. 11–12, 21–26, 193–94.

imposing concepts upon them. It, too, is a synthetic construction, a particular historical interpretation, and as such it is subject to the customary rules of critique and evidence. If Alberti's diverse works are essentially unrelated to each other, these works themselves should lead us to adopt this position. They should be illuminated when viewed from this standpoint, thereby substantiating the judgment that issues from it. The fact is, however, that when we view Alberti's works from another vantage point, we are struck by a cluster of certain ideas found throughout: ideas of measure, harmony, and proportion. These ideas bespeak a moral and intellectual outlook quite at variance with the conflicts, disparateness, and despair that have been attributed to him; and they point, I believe, toward a systematic unity that underlies and adequately explains the diversity of his many achievements.

One theoretical outlook is expressed by these ideas, one comprehensive view of the world and man which Alberti articulated and elaborated in the many facets of his thought. This is so much the case that no single work can be fully understood save in this context; and no single work can serve to characterize in full the nature of his thought. Indeed, what is distinctive about Alberti is that his mode of thought not only unified his artistic and technical-scientific ideas, but it bound them to certain ethical and cultural values as well. Alberti achieved a unique balance among the artistic, scientific, and moral aspects of human life and expression, a balance which was broken almost as soon as it had been attained. Leonardo, the universal genius of the following generation, did not share with his precursor the same set of "universal" interests. Applying the new, mathematical-empirical method of inquiry to the diversity of physical phenomena, he broadened and deepened the realm of artistic and scientific knowledge, but he did not venture upon cultural and ethical maters. Even in this restriction he seems to have reached beyond his age, to foreshadow the time when the moral and physical realms of experience would appear to be hopelessly sundered once the instrument of mathematical reason was found to apply to physical nature only. For Alberti, however, there was as yet no such division between the "inner" and the "outer" world. His knowledge of nature and understanding of the human spirit arose from the same theoretical source. "Science" and "humanism" were not conflicting directions of thought for him, but different aspects of one intellectual vision and pursuit.

By focusing upon his methodological precepts and the theoretical orientation implicit in them, we may therefore hope to discover the principles that gave rise to Alberti's many works, principles which fostered their very diversity while binding them in one general aim of thought. And if we succeed in this, we shall recover the "inner logic" of one of the most comprehensive spirits of the early Renaissance, a man of thought and practice who was responsible for a new and genuine unification of the various cultural currents of his age.

1

The Painter's Perspective

Among those men of genius who created the new space of Renaissance art, Leon Battista Alberti was the only one who was merely an amateur at painting and sculpture. His contributions to these arts were theoretical and technical rather than artistic, but that is exactly what constituted their unique value. After he had written his book *On Painting* (1435), those who sought to draw correctly were advised to turn "to the mathematicians and to Baptista Alberti";[1] for Alberti, believing that the natural "roots" of painting were to be found in mathematics, had fused geometry and vision in a new and powerful theory of pictorial art.

By giving a geometric interpretation to the traditional theory of light and vision called *natural perspective,* Alberti had worked out the new "science" of painter's perspective. "Practice in painting must always be founded on sound theory," Leonardo was later to write, "and to this perspective is the guide and gateway."[2] The aim of perspectival painting as Alberti defined it, and after him Leonardo, Albrecht Dürer, and everyone who has since written on the subject, is to treat the two-dimensional picture plane (the wall, or panel, or canvas) as if it were a window in which a three-dimensional scene appears. The science of painter's perspective, set forth for the first time in Alberti's *Della pittura,* consists of a series of simple "geometric rules" which show how this appearance is produced.

It was by means of these rules that the Renaissance artists constructed the new, three-dimensional space of their paintings and reliefs. But this artistic revolution, significant as it was for the future of European art, was not the sole consequence of the union of geometry, vision, and depiction brought about by painter's perspective. At the same time as the mathematically inspired concept of

---

1. Filarete, the fifteenth-century architect and theorist. He follows Alberti very closely in his own statements on painting and perspective in his *Treatise on Architecture.* This reference to Alberti is from vol. 2, bk. 22, fol. 176ʳ. Peter Tigler compares Alberti's and Filarete's ideas on painting in *Die Architekturtheorie des Filarete;* see especially pp. 172ff.

2. *The Literary Works of Leonardo da Vinci,* 1:18, no. 19.

perspectival space began to appear in art, the actual, physical image of the world came to be conceived as ordered in accordance with mathematical principles. The old Euclidean science was understood in a new light and put to new uses; and the new grasp of the principles of geometry, together with their application to problems of depiction, worked, in turn, to transform man's imaginative and theoretical vision of the world.

With the perspectival ordering of pictorial space, we stand, therefore, at the very threshold of the imaginative and intellectual world order we call Renaissance. Painter's perspective opened not merely a new phase in the practice and theory of the visual arts but a new age in which reality came to be viewed and understood in mathematical terms.

Vision: The Optical Theory of Natural Perspective

The optics of natural perspective which forms the theoretical basis of painter's perspective also leads us to the artistic antecedents of Alberti's work. As he acknowledged in the prologue to *Della pittura,* where he dedicated the book to Brunelleschi, it was Florentine art of the 1420's and early 1430's that inspired him to undertake this study of painting. Returning as a papal secretary in 1434 to his family's native city, he was struck by works of art which for the first time rivaled the monuments of antiquity. It seemed to the young humanist as though Nature were renewing her powers in the Florentine artists; the perpetual cycle of creativity and decline had begun a new round, and his response to the signs of rebirth was immediate and generous. "Especially in you, Filippo [Brunelleschi]," he wrote, "and in our close friend Donato the sculptor, and in others like Nenci [Ghiberti], Luca [della Robbia], and Masaccio, there is a genius for accomplishing every praiseworthy thing."[3] Alberti had played no part in this artistic resurgence of the early decades of the quattrocento because of his family's exile from Florence, but now that the Medici influence was in the ascendant and the ban of exile lifted, he stayed and took up as his own the problems raised by the art he so admired.

By 1435 he had written the Latin version of *Della pittura,* and by 1436 the artists had his vernacular version of it.[4] The chief technical problem which Alberti posed for himself in this work was to find correct rules of construction

3. *Della pittura,* ed. Luigi Mallè, pp. 53–54. Cecil Grayson offers some critical notes on this edition in "Studi su Leon Battista Alberti," *Rinascimento,* 4 (1953): 45–62. There is an English translation, *On Painting,* by John R. Spencer. I have occasionally used Spencer's translation, but generally I give my own.

4. The Latin text, which was dedicated to Gianfrancesco Gonzaga of Mantua, has more literary and philosophical allusions, whereas the vernacular text is more direct and "unadorned." There is no critical edition of the Latin text, but Mallè and Spencer cite the Latin in footnotes where there are discrepancies between it and the vernacular. Some further discrepancies have been noticed by Cecil Grayson who is collating a greater number of mss. than have ever been used before in preparation for his forthcoming edition of the work.

for the new and cogent kind of three-dimensional space which Masaccio had introduced into painting. In his great fresco "The Trinity" in Florence's Santa Maria Novella (fig. 1), Masaccio had created an unambiguous, receding space in which almost all the elements of figures and setting are properly proportioned to each other. He did this chiefly by means of the painted architectural setting, a vaulted niche which gave him measurable spatial units and allowed him to construct a picture space independent of the personages in it. There are some "inaccuracies" in Masaccio's picture, but on the whole it is an impressive achievement—artistically, of course, but perspectively too.[5] Vasari, the Renaissance biographer of the new art and of the men who made it, claims that Masaccio learned perspective from Brunelleschi. Unfortunely, most of the details about just what Masaccio learned are obscure. We do not yet have complete knowledge of all the techniques Masaccio employed, and we know even less about the degree of his indebtedness to Brunelleschi for them, but surely one of the things that Masaccio learned from Brunelleschi was to consciously *see* perspectically—possibly by means of the architect's famous painted panels.[6]

5. Although the architectural structure of "The Trinity" is precisely measured and appears to diminish accurately toward a single vanishing point, there is a certain spatial ambiguity to the picture taken as a whole. John White, in *The Birth and Rebirth of Pictorial Space,* pp. 139, 140, attributes this to a deliberate intention on Masaccio's part to keep the divine figures and the setting of the donors unforeshortened so as to heighten the "emotional and apparitional impact" of the work. H. W. Janson, on the other hand, in his *History of Art,* pp. 322, 323, claims that Masaccio defied perspectival law in his placing of God the Father so as to conform to iconographic tradition. I should like to add a consideration of another kind: namely, that since Masaccio's means of creating a perspectival illusion, whatever they may have been, were not those which Alberti was to work out, the "inaccuracies" we notice may stem from this fact rather than from any artistic intention.

A new and rigorous analysis of "The Trinity," showing that it is somewhat more "correct" (though still not entirely so) than had hitherto been supposed, was given in a paper delivered at a meeting of the Columbia University Seminar on the Renaissance in 1965 by H. W. Janson, "The Perspective Construction of Masaccio's Trinity Fresco—Fact and Fancy."

6. There is a large body of literature on Brunelleschi's perspectival work. A fairly recent list can be found in Robert Klein, "Pomponius on Perspective," *Art Bulletin,* 43 (1961): 211–30. Antonio Manetti (d. 1491) left a description of Brunelleschi's panels, and this report is probably what Vasari based his judgment upon, as do all modern interpreters of Brunelleschi's ideas on perspective. The most lucid presentation of Brunelleschi's role in the development of artistic perspective with which I am familiar is Rudolf Wittkower's "Brunelleschi and 'Proportion in Perspective,' " *Journal of the Warburg and Courtauld Institutes* 16 (1953): 275–91. In *Birth and Rebirth,* pp. 113–21, John White gives a good description of the panels. A clear and plausible reconstruction of Brunelleschi's procedure can be found in Richard Krautheimer and Trude Krautheimer-Hess, *Lorenzo Ghiberti,* pp. 234–45. This is the method of combining ground-plan and elevation drawings into a final, front view.

On Renaissance perspective in general, the pioneer work is Erwin Panofsky's brief "Die Perspektive als 'Symbolische Form,' " *Vorträge der Bibliothek Warburg,* pp. 258–330. Panofsky's ideas have been expanded and related to specific works by Miriam Schild Bunim, *Space in Medieval Painting and the Forerunners of Perspective,* and by John White, *Birth and Rebirth.* See also Panofsky's more recent statement of his ideas in *Renaissance and Renascences,* pp. 123–45.

1. *Masaccio,* The Holy Trinty,
Santa Maria Novella, Florence.
(*Alinari-Art Reference Bureau.*)

2. *The Duomo and Baptistery, Florence.*
(*Alinari-Art Reference Bureau.*)

According to Brunelleschi's fifteenth-century biographer, Antonio Manetti,
the first of these two panels (both of which are lost today) depicted the
Florentine Baptistery and the Piazza del Duomo (fig. 2) as seen from inside the
doorway of the Duomo. At the center of the picture of the Baptistery there was a
small hole which opened into a funnel on the back of the panel. The viewer stood
behind the panel and looked through the funnel at a mirror held at arm's length
in front of it. The mirror reflected the painting, and the results, Manetti tells us,
were astonishing. A powerful abstraction had been created whereby the painter
compelled the viewer to see nothing but what he wished him to see. With his
normal field of vision cut off by means of the funnel and eyehole, he saw only the
painting as reflected in the mirror, his entire range of vision being taken up by
the painted image of the Baptistery and plaza as it now appeared in the mirror.
Moreover, since the upper half of Brunelleschi's panel was left coated with silver,
it reflected the clouds and sunlight of the real sky which, in the mirror image,

25

appeared to surround the painted Baptistery. Altogether, it was a picture more "real" than nature, because nothing else detracted from or interfered with its sheer visual appearance.

The second panel was done without the eyehole and mirror, a fact which indicates that Brunelleschi somehow reproduced upon it the optical effect created at first by the funnel. Among other things, he probably made the orthogonal lines of the picture (all "parallel" lines in depth) converge at a central vanishing point, thereby aligning the picture with the spectator's principal line of sight so that the (virtual) space of the picture would seem to be continuous with his (actual) space.[7] This seemingly obvious use of a central vanishing point (and indeed the whole complicated funnel-and-eye-hole contraption of the first panel) was the result of a great deal of theoretical work. Brunelleschi's panels stemmed from a completely novel understanding of pictorial space in terms of the then traditional theory of optics, natural perspective.

The rules of painter's perspective which Alberti was to develop in *Della pittura* are founded upon this same optical theory. Referring to the "philosophers'" ideas which made up the "science" of light and vision in antiquity and the Middle Ages, Alberti writes:

> Surfaces are measured by rays of sight which are called "visual rays" and which bear the form of the thing seen to the sense. . . . Among these rays, there are differences which need to be recognized, differences in strength and in function. Some of these rays, hitting the outline of the surfaces, measure the quantities [of their dimensions]; since they cut the extreme limits of the surfaces, we call them extreme or *extrinsic* rays. Other rays, coming from the entire face of the surface, have as their task to fill the "pyramid of sight" [formed by these visual rays] with the colors and lights with which the surface gleams; these rays are thus called *median* rays. And here, among the visual rays is one we call the *centric* ray. This one, where it strikes the surface, makes equal right angles all around itself; *this point is called centric.*[8] (fig. 3)

Leonardo, who knew *Della pittura* and made use of a great deal of it in his own *Trattato* on painting, was to employ these same terms and ideas,[9] as did

---

7. "Virtual" and "actual" space are Susanne K. Langer's terms. Raising the question "what is created" by the various arts, Professor Langer showed, in the first part of her *Feeling and Form,* that the "primary illusion" created by the visual arts is a virtual space (pp. 45–104). In the mode of painting, this virtual space is a "virtual scene": the painting "always creates a space opposite the eye and related directly and essentially to the eye" (p. 86). Perspective sought to make this relation explicit and geometrically accurate.

8. *Della pitt.,* p. 59, italics mine.

9. *The Lit. Works,* 1: 29–34, nos. 50–54. Leonardo follows Alberti and even uses some of his phrases; see, for example: the perspectival picture is to look as if it were drawn on a glass through which the objects are seen (1: 267, no. 533); the *velo* or reticulated net is to be used to find the correct positions of objects in relation to each other (1: 260–61, no. 523); judge the accuracy of the picture by its reflection in a mirror (1: 264–65, no. 528, no. 529);

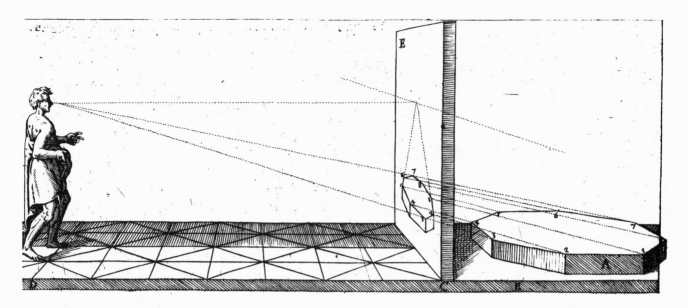

3. *Seeing by means of visual rays.*
From Vignola, La due regole della
prospettiva practica, *1611.*

Filarete, Piero della Francesca, and all writers on painter's perspective after
Alberti. These notions were originally derived from two major works on optics
which were known in late antiquity, one ascribed to Euclid and the other to the
Alexandrian Ptolemy (both attributions being rejected by modern scholars).
Around 1270 Witelo revived the theory of the visual cone (what Alberti calls the
"pyramid of sight") in the first European treatise on optics. His sources were
the pseudo-Ptolemaic text and the writings of the eleventh-century Arabian
mathematician and astronomer who was to interest Leonardo so much, Alhazen.
Soon after Witelo, John Peckham and Roger Bacon wrote on "perspective," by
which they chiefly meant the determination of visual images by means of rays
which extend between the eye and the object seen and "cause" vision. A strong
interest developed in these ideas in the course of the fourteenth century.
Following the teachings of Peckham, Biagio Pelacani, a lecturer at the University
of Padua, wrote his *Quaestiones perspectivae* around 1390, and this became a
standard work. Brunelleschi's friend, Paolo Toscanelli, is known to have brought
a copy of it to Florence in 1424 when he returned there after completing his
studies at Padua. However, "perspective" was at this stage still a theory of optics
and vision; it had no bearing upon painting or drawing until Brunelleschi, and
Alberti after him, began to establish certain relations between them.

the painter should do all parts of a painting well, and not excel merely at one kind of painting
(1: 250–51, no. 499); the painter should learn to listen to everyone's advice (1: 266,
no. 532); the only "modern" painters praised are Giotto and Masaccio (1: 331–32, no.
660); and so forth. As we go on, I shall indicate some other points which Leonardo took up
and developed. (Leonardo's *Trattato* was not composed by him in the form we have it; my
references are all to Richter's edition, henceforth called "Richter.")

To understand how they could found the practice of painting upon perspective, one has to consider not only the explicit propositions of the theory but the assumptions contained in Alberti's account of it. The metaphysical presuppositions of the theory of light and vision described by Alberti, and subscribed to by him, can be conveniently divided into those belonging to theory of knowledge and those belonging to theory of reality. In the statement that, in perception, the form of the object seen is borne to the eye by visual rays, the copy theory of truth or knowledge is taken for granted. The visual image is a "copy" of what really is. Alberti's ideas about the nature of the reality thus perceived are, therefore, fundamental; and they are the notions which enabled him to fit the abstract theory of vision naturally and neatly into the practical context of painting.

Writing "as a painter," he was concerned not with ontology, not with questions of what an object, or what reality, is in itself. He was bound to reality qua appearance or phenomenon, and here he proceeded with the momentous assumption that appearances conform to the rules of simple, plane geometry. Visual phenomena, be they objects to be painted or the visual rays by which they are seen, are all treated in *Della pittura* as sensible instances of mathematical ideas. "Mathematicians measure the forms of things by the mind alone, separate from matter," Alberti points out in the very beginning of the book, "but because we wish to treat of things given to sight, we must use, as they say, a more sensate wisdom."[10] With only this terse indication of the unprecedented step he was about to take, he set forth his primer on painting—"a subject, as far as I know, never treated before." And it had never been done before, this interpreting of the ideal figures of geometry as visual entities. He must have been sorely criticized for it, for he had to write two further works in which he clearly discriminated the geometric "point" from the painter's "point" to indicate that he knew very well, indeed, what he was about, and that it was nonsense to accuse him of trying to "see" mathematical concepts.[11]

What he did do in *Della pittura* was to systematically order visual reality in geometric terms. He used the invisible point of geometry to characterize the painter's visible dot as a "corporeal point," a figure which cannot be divided into parts. Many such dots compose the painter's "corporeal line," a figure which may be divided lengthwise but is too fine to have its width divided. And corporeal lines, woven together like threads in a cloth, make a surface, that outer part of a body known by height and breadth only, and not by depth. In the "visual geometry" which Alberti was here developing, the surface or "outer

10. *Della pitt.*, p. 55. "Noi perché vogliamo le cose essere poste da vedere, per questo useremo quanto dicono più grassa Minerva." I have followed Spencer's translation; actually *più grassa Minerva* is a version of the Latin *pingui Minerva* and means, roughly, *grosso modo.*

11. See "De punctis et lineis apud pictores," *Opera inedita,* p. 66; and "Elementa picturae," *ibid.,* pp. 47–65.

skin" of an object is the key element. "The chief work of the painter is the *istoria*," he wrote. "Bodies are part of the *istoria*, members are parts of the bodies, surfaces are parts of the members."[12] It was surfaces which he wanted to teach the painter to handle perspectively.

The kind of surface Alberti usually had in mind was a simple or flat one. In general, he thought of objects as having bounding surfaces which can be analyzed into rectilinear plane figures or their parts (as, for example, triangles), with some of these surfaces lying in planes perpendicular to the ground and facing the spectator squarely. (These surfaces he called "equidistant" to the spectator.) Thus, for example, a cube which faces the spectator squarely would be his prototype. If a surface is complex, if it has protrusions or is broken up like an inclining set of stairs, then it is thought of as analyzable into as many rectilinear or triangular plane figures as is convenient. Each subsurface lies in a distinct plane and can be treated as exemplifying such plane figures.

The visual rays which bear the form and lighting of these surfaces to the eye he also represented geometrically. They are straight lines, "like fine strings . . . all closely bound at one end within the eye where the sense of sight resides; and from there, almost like the trunk of all these rays, that knot extends its straight and fine shoots to the surface facing it." The optical theory described in these "sensate" geometric terms contains a corpuscular theory of the rays of sight which Alberti adopted, but it was not of any real importance to him. The Pythagoreans had maintained that the visual rays were rays of light which carried to the eye minute particles projected from the surface of the object seen; the Platonists spoke rather of a stream of particles emitted by the eye. Such questions about the nature of visual rays Alberti passed over as "useless" for his purposes. He confined himself to the bare statement that they extend (in a straight line) between the eye and the surface viewed, for his interest was in the faithful reproduction of visual appearances with the help of geometry, and specifically, with the geometric model of the "cone" of vision or "pyramid" of sight which visual rays were said to form.

The visual pyramid is a purely imaginary construct. It is produced by conceiving the field of vision as delimited by an intersecting quadrangle dropped in front of the eye. This "frame" limits the visual rays extending from the eye to the narrow quadrangular field it cuts out; and all visible objects behind it cast their reflections (projections) upon it where the visual rays to them pass (like strings) through this plane. Actually, it was Alberti who first used the term "pyramid" of sight, substituting it for the visual "cone" of which ancient and medieval optics had spoken. If the notion of a cone is used, the visual rays have to be thought of as extending to a circular base,[13] whereas Alberti wanted

12. *Della pitt.*, pp. 85, 55ff. Leonardo follows Alberti in defining painter's perspective as a sort of visual geometry: "Tutti i casi della prospectiva sono intesi mediante i cinque termini de' matematici, cioè punto, linea, angolo, superfitie, e corpo." Richter, 1: 27, no. 42.

13. Spencer believed that Alberti introduced the idea of the pyramid so as to make

to make the base of his "cone" rectangular, an analogue of the rectangular picture frame.

The base of the visual pyramid is coincident, then, with what modern perspectival works refer to as the "perspective plane" (in Vignola's drawing in figure 3, *E* is the perspective plane):

> A perspective drawing is a representation of the lines that would result from the projection upon a transparent plane of a plane or solid figure situated behind that plane, the lines of projection being visual rays converging from every point of the figure to the eye of a spectator situated in front of the plane. . . . The transparent plane of projection is called the *Perspective Plane.* . . . The conical projection of a figure, line, or point upon the perspective plane is called its perspective. When viewed from the station-point (the position of the spectator) the perspective exactly coincides with and covers the object itself . . . The surface upon which the drawing is made is called the plane of the paper, or *plane of the picture.* When the objects to be drawn are very small, or the picture very large, the plane of the picture and the perspective plane may coincide. But generally the objects to be drawn are many feet in dimension . . . while the drawing is to be measured by inches; and as it is always convenient, for practical reasons, to have the plane of projection as near the object as possible, and consequently of about the same size, while the picture must be small and near at hand, the plane of the picture and the perspective plane are generally nearly as far from each other as the spectator from the object.[14]

The surface "behind" the base of the pyramid need not have any point in common with the base, although it is possible for one or even all points of a surface to lie in the base. And the surface need not lie in a plane parallel to the base, although this is the prototype Alberti generally had in mind. His "visual pyramid," then, is a regular one with four equal edges. Its apex is in the eye; its base is a rectangle;[15] the centric ray of the theory of natural perspective forms

"the one-point perspective system possible," avoiding thereby "the axial perspective of the Romans and Giotto" to which, Spencer thought, "the theory of conic vision led" *On Painting*, p. 103, n. 18. This is incorrect; as White has already noted, the theory of the visual cone does not require a curvilinear projection *Birth and Rebirth*, p. 256. As long as the base of the cone (and the picture plane) is regarded as a plane figure rather than a spherical one, and as long as the visual rays are represented (as they were in antiquity) as straight lines, the system of plane perspective results. If some ancient depictions tended towards a curvilinear projection, this is due, not to the idea of the visual cone per se, but rather, as Panofsky has pointed out, to the fact that ancient optical theory and art theory held to the idea of the curvature of the visual image.

14. William R. Ware, *Modern Perspective*, pp. 255–57; italics mine.

15. For Filarete, this rectangle is a square. He draws the quadrangle defining his picture frame by means of a compass and ruler, placing four points "equidistant" to each other and joining them by straight lines. Hence his visual pyramid has not only four equal edges but four equal faces.

its height by running from the apex to the center of the base; and visual rays extending from the apex to the sides of the rectangular base complete the sides of the pyramid.

By applying these ideas about the visual pyramid and its parts to art, Brunelleschi made his panels "perspectival" and became the founder of "artificial" or painter's perspective. Drawing the Baptistery and the Piazza del Duomo on his first panel as they looked from one vantage point (the immobile eye of the theory of natural perspective), and drilling an eyehole at the (centric) point on the depicted building which corresponded to the point on the actual building that was directly across from his eye as he painted, he brought all the visual rays from his mirror image (i.e., the reflection of the depicted Baptistery and plaza, and of the natural skies reflected above) to a perfect convergence in the focus of the viewer's eye. Without moving a step, the viewer was suddenly transported to the painter's original vantage point inside the Duomo. The painter's principal line of sight (as defined by the centric ray) became his own, and its terminus at the centric point became the vanishing point for all the visual rays stretching between him and the building he viewed.

This uniform convergence at the centric point of all lines "parallel" to the principal line of sight may have been drawn by Brunelleschi on his second panel. Here he did away with the eyehole and funnel, the physical equivalents of the visual pyramid, probably to represent perspectival vision with the help of a schematic drawing over which he painted the picture, a drawing in which all lines in depth (orthogonals) meet at a (centric) vanishing point (fig. 4). A

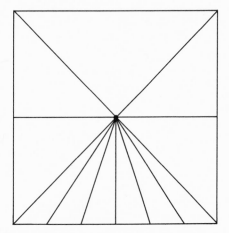

4. The centric-point scheme

schematic drawing of this kind, with the addition of horizontal lines across its face which form the squares of a checkerboard pavement, was used by Masaccio and was known to Alberti. It almost certainly had its origin with Brunelleschi and is perhaps what Filarete was referring to in his own writings on perspective

31

when he said Brunelleschi "found by reason what the mirror showed."[16]

The centric-point scheme clearly embodies the idea of the visual pyramid, and its use by artists in the late 1420's and 1430's indicates that the perspectival theory of vision which Brunelleschi had introduced into painting had begun to affect the depiction of visual reality.

Depiction before Alberti

The usefulness of the centric-point scheme is best appreciated if we consider, first, why preperspectival painting looks as "inexact" as it does to our eyes. In a fourteenth-century painting such as Taddeo Gaddi's "Presentation of the Virgin" (fig. 5), we can discern which objects are meant to be "near" and which "far," but we cannot find a viewpoint from which to make consistent sense out of the jumble of aspects of things we are given. We are shown the fronts and sides of the architectural setting simultaneously, because the painter, partly in order to capture all the privileged aspects of the things he wanted to depict, shifted his position when copying the objects of the scene. There is no "centric ray" in such works. The painter has not given any one *direction* to his line of sight to the scene, nor has he kept the *distance* constant between himself and its various objects. The gradation in the size of the figures as they "recede" toward the horizon is as inconsistent as the directions in which the parts of the temple face.

The lack of exactness which marks the preperspectival construction of a three-dimensional space is reflected in the poor and crude rules of painting which preceded those of painter's perspective. Cennino Cennini, setting down the practices of Giotto and his followers in the late fourteenth century, urged, for example, that buildings be placed in a painting this way:

> the mouldings which you make at the top of the building should slant downward from the edge next to the roof; the moulding in the middle of the building, halfway up the face, must be quite level and even; the moulding at the base of the building must slant upward, in the opposite sense to the upper moulding which slants downward.[17]

The size of buildings in relation to figures and other objects in the picture is hit upon by rule of thumb, as is the direction and degree of the "slanting" Cennini recommends. The roughness of this procedure, and the incongruities to which it led, must have gradually caused feelings of discomfort, leading to an effort to regularize the spatial pattern of the painting by means of the schematic "underdrawings" which were introduced in the course of the fourteenth and fifteenth centuries.

5. *Taddeo Gaddi,* The Presentation of the Virgin, *Santa Croce, Florence. (Alinari-Art Reference Bureau.)*

16. Filarete, *Treatise,* vol. 2, bk. 23, fol. 178[r]; also fols. 178[v], 179[r].
17. *Il libro dell'arte,* 2: 56–57.

Before Alberti's time, there were two such schemes. Both were drawings of a checkerboard pavement. The lines forming its squares or diamonds were drawn in accordance with a rule of construction, and the pavement was then used as a sort of grid over which the preliminary sketch was drawn or the picture was painted.

The bifocal rule of construction, which has just recently been rediscovered,[18] goes back to an artisan tradition and apparently had no relation to the idea of the visual pyramid or, indeed, to any theoretical ideas concerning vision (fig. 6).

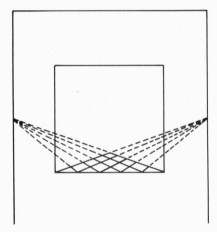

6. The bifocal rule of construction

These two sets of converging "parallel" lines were usually made by means of strings which were fastened to pegs on either side of a fresco area and stretched to points along the base line of the picture. When the strings were chalked and snapped against the wall, they left light lines, and the painter filled in his fresco over them.

Alberti nowhere mentions this scheme, either because he was ignorant of it or, what is more likely, because he regarded it as completely superseded by the other, centric point scheme which served the painter's purpose so much better.[19]

18. Robert Klein found the bifocal rule of construction described in Pomponius Gauricus' *De sculptura* of 1504. "Pomponius on Perspective," pp. 211–30. Also see Ugo Procacci on such "underdrawings," *Sinopie e affreschi.*

19. In an effort to defend Alberti's familiarity with workshop tradition, Samuel Y. Edgerton, Jr. has recently tried to derive Alberti's construction from the bifocal scheme. "Alberti's Perspective: A New Discovery and a New Evaluation," *Art Bulletin,* 48 (1966): 367–78. I disagree with this view. It is apparent from *Della pittura* that the workship tradition Alberti was familar with was the one he was correcting: namely, the centric-point scheme with the addition of the so-called two-thirds rule which we shall describe below. There is no evidence that he used the bifocal scheme. Moreover, he could not have realized how to transform it into his own *costruzione legittima* except by going through all the steps, theoretical and practical, which in fact led to the *costruzione legittima.*

For helpful as the lines of the bifocal scheme were, they could be used only for painting ceilings and pavements. They did not regulate the appearance of other objects in the picture. For one thing, they bore no regular relation to the size of people and buildings in the picture; thus the disproportion in the sizes and distances among things remained. And secondly, the two (what would later be called) "distance points" of this construction were not related to a centric vanishing point which would define the spectator's line of sight and toward which all "parallel" lines in depth could be made to converge. In pictures based upon this scheme, the extensions of such lines drawn from the depicted objects do not meet in one point. Things have been foreshortened, but without consistent consideration of the point of view of the spectator.

Some of these failings were corrected by the *centric-point construction* which evidently originated with Brunelleschi. Brunelleschi must have conceived of this scheme as a frontal view of the base of a visual pyramid or of a parallel section through it (see fig. 9C below), for the centric point is the point at which the spectator's line of sight pierces the base of the pyramid, and at this point the "perspectives" of all lines parallel with the centric ray converge. By introducing a single vanishing point for all orthogonal lines, this scheme unified the picture space. The *direction* in which objects seem to recede became unique. However, the distance of the painter (and viewer) from the depicted scene remained indeterminate. The spatial intervals which are marked off by the horizontal lines of a checkerboard pavement diminish as they "disappear" toward the horizon. The centric-point scheme at this stage of its development did not determine the degree of this diminution, as it should have, by means of a distance (given by the centric point and the eye point) from which the spectator is supposed to view the scene.

This became Alberti's chief technical problem, to find a rule of construction which relates this distance to the receding spatial intervals of a depicted pavement so that these intervals will appear to diminish in a regular proportional progression. Brunelleschi must certainly have faced this problem too; indeed, it has even been suggested that it was this idea of a proportional progression in depth which initially stimulated his interest in pictorial perspective.[20] The two arcades of the nave of his Florentine church of San Lorenzo (fig. 7), when seen receding toward the altar (or toward the door) diminish in such a perfect and definite progression that Professor Wittkower called this the first true and deliberate example of artistic "proportion in perspective." Of course the architect, working in a three-dimensional space, has only to make the intervals between the columns equal to each other to ensure this visual effect. The viewer may move closer or farther away from the altar as he likes. As long as the direction of his line of sight remains the same, that is, as long as it is oriented toward the altar (or the entrance door) as the center of vision, he will be struck

20. Rudolf Wittkower, "Proportion in Perspective," pp. 275–91.

7. *Brunelleschi, San Lorenzo, Florence.*
(Alinari-Art Reference Bureau.)

by this image of proportional diminution.

It may well have been the attempt to duplicate this effect pictorially which led Brunelleschi to construct his perspectival panels. For the painter's perspectival task is similar to the architect's. In the painting, the horizontal lines parallel to the base line of the picture (on a checkerboard pavement, for example) also mark off spatial intervals the way the columns of an arcade do, and these intervals must also diminish proportionally as they recede toward the viewer's horizon. But the painter has to construct these receding intervals as they would appear to a spectator who has taken a fixed position at a given distance from the center of vision. Since the spectator cannot actually move through the picture space, the diminution of depicted spatial intervals must be related to *some chosen distance*

36

between the spectator and the scene, and fixed according to rule.

The centric-point scheme which Alberti knew did not do this. Brunelleschi himself probably managed to regulate the apparent recession of spatial intervals by combining a number of separate views on his panels. If he composed his final picture as is generally supposed, out of preliminary ground plan and elevation drawings of the viewed objects, and drawings of his vantage point, he would have been able to measure the distance between his vantage point and the centric point and to depict it accordingly. Whatever his exact procedure, however, he did not incorporate all its steps in a schematic drawing which painters could follow. Had he done so, it certainly would have been used by Uccello, Masaccio, and others—but the fact is, it wasn't. As Manetti points out, Uccello and certain other painters tried to imitate Brunelleschi's panels, but they could not produce these perspectival views as well as he. And even Masaccio's paintings, relatively "correct" as they are, have none of the well-defined and ample spatial settings of the paintings which were to be constructed in accordance with Alberti's rules (compare figs. 1 and 16).[21]

This was Alberti's task, then: to construct a perspectivally correct checkerboard pavement. And to do this, he had to work out a pristine form of projective geometry which would give him the rules for combining frontal and elevation views in a simple, schematic drawing, relating both to the eye of the viewer.

The New Visual Geometry

In the architectural creation of "proportion in perspective" (as in views down the nave of Brunelleschi's church interiors), the ceiling, floor, and walls on either side of the viewer limit his field of vision They form an actual frame, corresponding to the perspective plane which forms the base of a visual pyramid and limits the field of vision for the painter. The painter, however, has to "create" the base of his visual pyramid. Once he turns from the theoretical description of the base of the visual pyramid, as being near to or coinciding with

21. I believe the evidence does not warrant White's statement that Brunelleschi "developed a complete, focused *system* of perspective with mathematically regular diminution towards a fixed vanishing point." *Birth and Rebirth*, p. 120 (italics mine). We have no remains of any such system, or of a rule of construction based upon it, until *Della pittura;* though certainly some of the projective techniques of this system must have been hit upon by Brunelleschi as he worked out his panels. White's position on this point obscures the historical evolution of perspectival theory and practice from Brunselleschi to Alberti, and it compels him to maintain that Alberti merely appropriated Brunelleschi's work and wrote it down, claiming all the credit for himself (p. 124). This does violence to all we know about Alberti's character and mathematical ability, and it ignores the historical evidence that points to c. 1435 as the date when artists (Donatello and Ghiberti) first began to create completely correct perspectival scenes.

a surface, to a concrete problem of painting, say a landscape, he realizes that no such "base" is to be found in the actual scene in the way that walls, floor and ceiling can be found by the architect. If the visual rays emanting from the actual scene and converging in the apex of his eye are to form an ideal pyramid, the painter must find its base indirectly. He has to delimit the scene to be depicted; and he does this by choosing a vantage point, mentally "framing" a scene, and treating this ideal frame as a plane which intersects the "trunk" of visual rays extending between his eye and the objects he sees. Alberti used a reticulated net for this purpose which he called the "intersection":

> It is a thin veil, finely woven, dyed whatever color you please and with larger threads in the parallels as you like. This veil I place between the eye and the thing seen, so the visual pyramid penetrates through the thinness of the veil. This veil can be of great use to you. First, it always presents to you the same unchanged plane. Where you have placed certain limits, you quickly find the true cuspid of the pyramid. This would certainly be difficult without the intersection. You know how impossible it is to imitate a thing which does not continue to present the same appearance.... You know that, as the distance and the position of the center are changed, the thing you see seems greatly altered.... Secondly, you will easily be able to constitute the limits of the outline and of the surfaces [of things]. Here in this parallel you will see the forehead, in that the nose.... On panels or on walls divided into similar parallels, you will be able to put everything in its place. Finally, the veil will greatly aid you in learning how to paint when you see in it round objects and objects in relief."[22]

The important thing about the intersecting *velo* or ideal frame is that it can be regarded as a "glass" which always "presents the same appearance" of the actual scene upon its surface. In perspectival painting, this is the appearance which the painter "imitates." Brunelleschi had done just this, for example, when he used the doorway of the Duomo to set the bounds of his image of the Baptistery and plaza, and thus of the picture he drew. The doorway *through* which he viewed the scene could be regarded as defining a transparent plane *upon* which the scene was projected. The picture "copied" the image of the Baptistery as that image was framed by the doorway; and thus it reproduced an actual visual experience proportionately.

How deliberate Brunelleschi was about constructing the (generally small) *picture* as a proportional copy of a (larger) visual *image* projected upon the base of a visual pyramid, we do not know. But this empirical instance Alberti picked up, recognized it for what it was, and generalized it into a theory. His construction (and all the rules of painter's perspective upon which it rests)

22. *Della pitt.*, pp. 83–84.

carries out the idea of the picture plane as a section through a visual pyramid parallel to its base. The picture plane intersects the visual field parallel to the base of a visual pyramid (as defined by the *velo*), and the picture which is drawn upon it is a smaller "reflection" of the image which appears on the *velo* (the "glass" of the perspective plane) and which is delimited by it:

> To look at a picture is to see a particular intersection of a pyramid. The picture, then, is nothing other than a section of the visual pyramid according to a given distance, center, and lighting, artificially represented on a plane by lines and colors.[23]

23. *Ibid.*, p. 65. Because of this explicit, systematic conception of the "window" of the picture plane as a section, i.e., as a cut through a pyramid of sight, I find it inaccurate and misleading to speak of the "practical" realization of this idea in trecento Italian and fifteenth-century Flemish painting. White, for example, says that this "new idea of pictorial reality" (of the frame of the picture as defining an open window) "is expressed in practice well before the evolution of a mathematical theory." *Birth and Rebirth*, pp. 107–08, *et passim.* That *a* new idea of pictorial reality is to be found in fourteenth-century Italian and fifteenth-century Flemish painting is indubitable. But it is questionable whether this is the same idea in both schools, and it is demonstrably not the case that this idea (or these ideas) is the perspectival idea of projection. The idea of the window occurs only as the theory of natural perspective is applied to painting. It is used by Alberti as a graphic example of what he means by the projection of a scene upon the base of a visual pyramid, and this is the sense in which the idea continued to be used in all perspectival treatises.

For similar reasons, I find it confuses matters to speak of Flemish paintings as "perspectival" works which were empirically constructed, by contrast with Italian ones which were mathematically constructed. Panofsky uses these terms in *Early Netherlandish Painting*, 1: 1–20, and in other works. We do not have two kinds of perspectival construction here but rather two kinds of spatial envisagement, one perspectival and the other not. After the system of perspective had ben adopted and artists had learned to see and represent perspectivally, it became possible to distinguish (as sixteenth-century theorists sometimes did) among perspectival paintings, some which were based on mathematics, some which were empirically arrived at (by rule of thumb), and some which were constructed mechanically by the aid of *graticulae* or the *velo*. By this time, all three ways of constructing the picture were really perspectival. All resulted in a focused picture unambiguously placed in strict relation to the viewing eye, all were intended to be taken as images projected upon a section through a pyramid of sight. Only the methods of producing this common effect were different.

These strictures also apply to the term "axial perspective" which is commonly used to describe Roman illusionistic painting and trecento painting. In short, I would restrict the terms "perspective" and "perspectival" to pictures which have been *constructed in accordance with a system of projection,* be that a system of plane-perspective or curvilinear-perspective or any other. If we do not do so, "perspective" becomes too comprehensive a term to be useful. If it is taken to mean merely "looking through" the picture plane to the world of appearances, all attempts to depict three-dimensional objects fall in the same category: Egyptian, Roman, Flemish, and so forth; and we lose sight of the distinguishing feature of the Renaissance attempt to represent appearances. (I find myself in agreement on this point with Decio Gioseffi, *Perspectiva Artificialis.*)

The mathematical bond between the traditional perspectival theory of vision and the newly forming theory of painting named after it was provided by the idea of the picture as a section of the pyramid of sight. This idea is what enabled Alberti to formulate the problem of depiction as one of applied plane geometry, for his rules of construction clearly stem from the connection he saw between the intersecting picture plane and the intersecting measuring rod of the surveyor (considering the surveyor's rod as an infinitely "narrow" plane intersecting the lines of sight to an object). Surveying and perspective represent two modes of seeing: seeing when measuring a three-dimensional object at a certain distance from the viewer, and seeing a three-dimensional object through a "glass" on which its outlines can be traced. The affinity between the two consists in the fact that the surveyor's sighting, the first mode of seeing, may be interpreted as a special case of the second one. The surveyor's measuring rod and the sightings obtained on it present, in fact, a profile, or one cross section of a visual pyramid when thus interpreted. Alberti made this interpretation; and by this bold stroke of mathematical imagination, he came to model the pictorial representation of things upon the methods of geometric surveying. This is why he insists that in seeing, "one makes triangles."

> The extrinsic-rays [of the visual pyramid] measure quantities. By quantities we mean any space on the surface which is between one point of the outline of the surface and another point and *the eye measures these quantities with visual rays as if with a pair of compasses.* In every surface, there are as many quantities as there are spaces between point and point; there is the height from the ground to the top, the width from right to left, the depth from near to far, and whatever other dimension or measure is made, in looking at it, one uses these extrinsic-rays. That is why it is said that in seeing one makes triangles, the base of which is the viewed quantity and the sides are the rays which extend from the points of these quantities to the eye, so surely no quantity can be seen without a triangle being formed.[24]

The paradigm for such triangles which "cut the extreme limits of a surface" and thereby measure it can be found in any work on surveying. In one of the problems of the little book of mathematical "games" which Alberti himself wrote around 1450,[25] the height of a distant tower is "measured" by two triangles formed by lines of sight from the eye to the base and top of the tower, and from the eye to the measuring rod which "intersects" the first visual triangle (fig. 8).

24. *Della pitt.*, p. 59; italics mine.
25. "Ludi matematici" is in *Opere volgari*, 4: 405–40. It is not dated but it was dedicated in 1450 to Meliaduso d'Este. The text in Bonucci's edition is marred by errors and so are the accompanying diagrams, but the "games" are easy to follow once they are reconstructed step by step. (My references to Alberti's *Opere Volgari* are to Bonucci's edition, except where I state otherwise.)

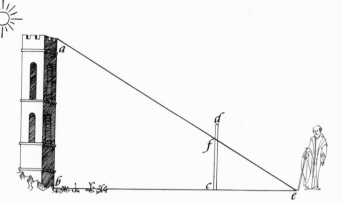

Since, in seeing, the painter "makes triangles" as the surveyor does, the "quantities" measured by his extrinsic visual rays can be proportionally reproduced on the picture plane much as they are projected upon the surveyor's rod. By transposing the surveyor's mode of sighting to the cross section of the visual pyramid that is the picture plane, Alberti thus "discovered" the rules of projection which henceforth formed the basis of painter's perspective. They are the rules which demonstrate that the "perspective" of a point (as it was later called) is found where the visual ray between the eye and that point intersects the plane of projection and/or the picture plane; that the perspective of a line is found by determining at least two of its projected points; and that the perspective of a plane figure (Alberti's "surface") is found by means of the projected line segments which determine it.

Projective geometry has its historical roots in the simple rules of linear perspective, although it developed far beyond them. Perspectival projection, arising out of surveying practice and the visual theory of the pyramid of sight, still conformed closely to the actual process of seeing. The painter's projections are formed by sight lines which meet in a focal point in the eye. The orthographic projections of descriptive geometry, on the other hand, abstract from the viewer and his visual pyramid; they are constructed in strict accordance with a Euclidean three-dimensional manifold in which all lines of sight are conceived either as parallel or at right angles to one another. Figure 9, which shows a checkerboard pavement and Alberti's visual pyramid on the three orthographic projections of descriptive geometry, illustrates these relations.

The two chief sets of rules in Alberti's "visual geometry" have to do with how, in seeing, "things appear changed in size or in outline as the position [of the viewer] changes."[26]

26. *Della pitt.*, p. 58. The following rules of linear perspective are given on pp. 58, 66–68. His (much more rudimentary) notions of aerial perspective will be touched upon in the next chapter.

8. *How to find the height of a tower, given the distance between the tower and the eye.*
From Ludi matematici, *c. 1450.*

Stick an arrow or a rod into the ground so as to form a straight, perpendicular line along which to take sightings to the tower. Mark the rod with wax where the line of sight to the top of the tower crosses it. The triangle formed by the arrow, ground, and eye is the geometric counterpart of the triangle formed by the tower, ground, and eye, hence it can be used to find the unknown quantity: ab:be = fc:ce.

The *size* of a "quantity" of an object projected upon a section depends upon *distance,* upon how far the spectator stands from the section (the picture plane), and how far he stands from the object he views (or from the plane of projection upon which its image appears). Keeping the distance between the eye and the section constant, but changing the distance between the eye and the object viewed "through" it, Alberti noted that the extrinsic rays of a visual triangle become median as this distance increases; and as this occurs, the "quantity" of the projected base of the visual triangle becomes smaller. We can illustrate this observation by means of the top view of the checkerboard pavement and visual pyramid in figure 9A (where, to simplify matters, the section and the base of the visual pyramid coincide).

At the section (or base) *ABDF,* the extrinsic lines of sight which "take the measure" of the most distant pavement line (29, 35) fall between the lines of sight to the nearest line (1,7). Hence they are "median" with respect to the rays to the nearer line; and the projected magnitude of the distant pavement line (29',35') is smaller than that of the nearer one (1',7'). Another way of putting the same rule, which is how, Alberti says, he usually explained it to his friends, is: "The more rays used in seeing, the greater the thing seen appears; and the fewer rays, the smaller it appears."

The other set of rules expresses the relations between changes in the *outline or shape* of a projected surface and changes in the *direction* of the spectator's principal line of sight (the centric ray) to the viewed object.

Stationary things present different appearances to a viewer moving about them. Take, for instance, a matchbox: facing it squarely, we get a rectangle. Moving to the left or right of it, we see some of its sides foreshortened. And when we face one of its upright edges squarely and look at the box slightly from above, its top appears as a diamond-shaped object. To correlate these different appearances with the viewpoint taken, Alberti distinguished surfaces which are "equidistant" to the section (i.e., plane figures which face the spectator squarely) from those which are not.

Surfaces which are equidistant to the section are not "distorted" as they are projected upon it; they change only in size. (The pavement line 29,30 in figure 9A may be regarded as the base line of such a surface, say for example, a wall; see its perspectives on the top view and front view).

A surface which is not equidistant to the section and lies in a plane coinciding or "collinear" with the centric ray, as Alberti put it, is not projected as a surface on the section, because the eye cannot "measure" it by a visual triangle. Only the equidistant surface of such an object will be projected (as, for example, the width of a wall which has the line 4,32 as its length). A line coinciding with the principal line of sight will be projected as a point (the line EC from the eye to the center of vision in figs 9A and 9B is projected as the point C', or E', on the front view).

42   The surfaces that are "altered" as they are projected on the section are

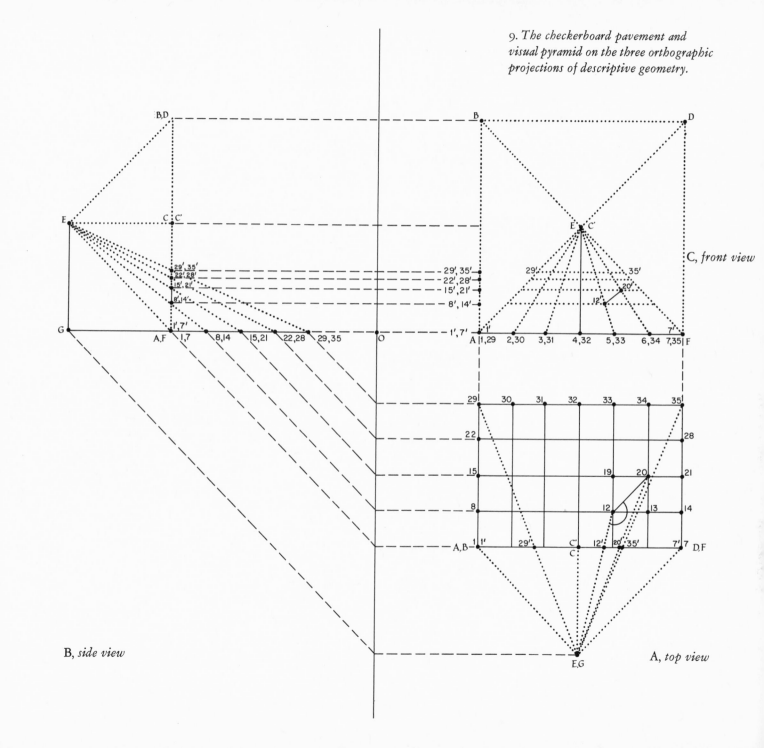

9. *The checkerboard pavement and visual pyramid on the three orthographic projections of descriptive geometry.*

C, *front view*

B, *side view*

A, *top view*

those that lie in planes which are neither equidistant to the section nor collinear with the centric ray. The degree of foreshortening varies with the greater of the two angles formed at the base of a visual triangle to such a surface. The more obtuse the angle, the greater the foreshortening (as in the diagonal line 12,20 in figure 9*A* and its perspective on the front view); for as the angle increases, the "quantity" occupies fewer visual rays and hence less space on the section.

These elementary rules at last made clear exactly what can be seen from one vantage point. By their light, Alberti was able to detect the faults in the centric-point scheme of his day and to work out a new scheme which would bind the picture of things to the viewer's distance from them and to the direction of his line of sight. Pictures based upon his construction would thereby become *pari alle vere,* presenting things "as they are"—though this meant, now, that the painting would fulfill a norm of accuracy which arose from a strictly mathematical demand: the demand for a depiction of things which is commensurable, according to geometric rule, to a visual image of those things which is also geometrically construed.

The "right" construction of the checkerboard pavement to which we now turn is the technical text that implemented this new, perspectival standard of visual truth. It "re-presents" a visual image in accordance with rules of projection; rules which rest, in turn, upon a set of theoretical notions about the nature of vision which had been seen and adopted *sub specie mathematicae,* that is, as an instance of geometric ideas.

Depiction after Alberti

Alberti's drawing of the checkerboard pavement is called the abbreviated *costruzione legittima.*[27] It combines a front and a side view of the pavement in a few easy steps (thirteen to be exact), and is thus regarded as a schematic simplification of the original "legitimate construction" which Brunelleschi had worked out on his panels.

If Brunelleschi had combined ground-plan, elevation, and frontal-view drawings of the buildings and areas which he depicted on his panels, his procedure, as we said, had not been completely schematized in a drawing.

27. The name *"costruzione legittima"* was not used by Alberti but it became common shortly after his time. Panofsky's definition is the standard one: "Dieser Name sollte nur für diejenige Konstruktion gebraucht werden, die sich unmittelbar-geometrisch aus der Definition: Bild-Schnitt durch die Sehpyramide ergab und (als zwar sehr umständliches, aber allgemeingültiges Verfahren) in der Renaissance nur bei so systematisch gerichteten Theoretikern wie Piero della Francesca ... und Dürer ... gelehrt wird." "Das perspektivische Verfahren Leone Battista Alberti," *Kunstchronik,* 26 (1915): 511–12, n. 11.

Down to Alberti's time, there was no construction which embodied the rules for combining two or more views of a scene. The centric-point scheme as Alberti knew it tried to show a checkerboard pavement in perspective, but it was no more than a rough approximation to this ideal. What Alberti did was to make this scheme exact. He superimposed upon its front view of the orthogonal lines of the pavement a second, side view which gave him the correct progression of the spatial intervals marked by the pavement's horizontal lines. This was his primary innovation, but it entailed others.

As our side view of the visual pyramid and checkerboard pavement shows in figure 9B, the determining factors in obtaining the perspectives of the lines of the pavement are the *height* of the viewer and his *distance* from the plane of projection. Alberti's schematic drawing is therefore scaled to the height of an average person and proportioned to a chosen distance between him and the base of the pyramid upon which the pavement is projected.

The idea of scaling is introduced in the first five steps of his construction which builds up the frontal view of the orthogonal lines of the pavement (figure 10):

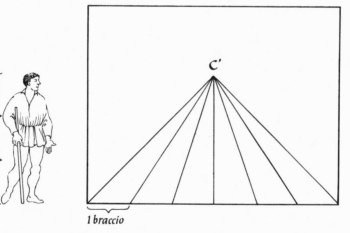

1.[28] First Alberti chose the size of his picture, inscribing "a quadrangle of right angles which is considered to be an open window through which I see what I want to paint."

28. I am following Alberti's procedure as he describes it in *Della pitt.*, pp. 70–74, 86f. I have distinguished each of its steps, however, and used modern terms to describe them.

The reader should be cautioned that Alberti's text is not self-explanatory. There are some gaps in his instructions; he may have filled them in by the demonstrations which he claims to have given *ad oculis*, but today they are the cause of differences in the interpretation of some of his operations. From the systematic point of view, most of the questions raised about these points are not important. Once the principles of the *costruzione legittima* are understood—and this was Alberti's great achievement—the construction itself can be drawn in several ways, as in fact it was by subsequent theorists and painters, and may even have been by Alberti himself. But it is of some historical

45

2. Then he chose the size of the largest (foreground) figure that was to appear in its space. This height, whatever it may be, he divided into three units, each of which represents the Florentine *braccio* (an arm's length, approximately twenty-three inches) since, he says, most men are about three *braccia* in height.

3. Using this scaled *braccio* as his module, he marked off the base line of his picture into as many such units as it would hold.

These units, and the corresponding ones of the side view, will form the "squares" of the checkerboard pavement. Thus step 3 (and its equivalent in the side view) insures that each side of a projected square will be proportional to one-third the height of a man depicted standing upon it.

Also, by dividing the base line of the picture into units which match the scaled *braccia* of the (foreground) figure standing upon it, Alberti has made the base line the perspective of the nearest horizontal line of the pavement.[29]

interest to know which of these ways is the one Alberti set down. I shall therefore give in the notes the relevant arguments on each of the disputed points.

The standard reconstruction of Alberti's procedure was given by Panofsky in "Das persp. Verfahren L.B.A.," pp. 504–16. Wm. M. Ivins, Jr. followed it in his clear account of Alberti's construction, *On the Rationalization of Sight*. Ivins tried to trace the construction to a "little box," oblong, with a checkerboard pavement drawn on its "floor," and a peephole at one end with strings (representing visual rays) stretching from the hole to points of intersection on the pavement. This is an interesting reconstruction of a model which Alberti may well have used to demonstrate his rules of projection, and perhaps even to help form them. Spencer and Mallè subsequently followed Panofsky's reconstruction in their editions of *Della pittura*, each adding certain insights and clarifications in the notes. Spencer's efforts to trace Alberti's projective technique to surveying practice I found particularly fruitful (*On Painting*, pp. 112–17.)

In "L. B. Alberti's 'costruzione legittima,' " *Italian Studies,* 19 (1964): 14–27, Cecil Grayson subsequently supplied from some Latin mss. of *Della pittura* a phrase describing an operation which is not present in the vernacular mss. and editions of the work. Alessandro Parronchi, in a series of articles, proposed a reconstruction of Alberti's procedure quite different from the traditional one to which Grayson had just added a note of clarification, and even used Grayson's discovery to bolster his own interpretation. "Il *punctum dolens* della 'costruzione legittima,' " *Studi su la dolce prospettiva,* pp. 226–312; "La 'costruzione legittima' è uguale alla 'costruzione con punti di distanza,' " *Rinascimento,* 2d ser., 4 (1964): 35–40; and "Il Filarete, Francesco di Giorgio e Leonardo su la 'Costruzione Legittima,' " *Rinascimento,* 2d ser., 5 (1965): 155–67. Samuel Y. Edgerton, Jr. summarized these recent findings and arguments in "Alberti's Perspective," pp. 367–78 and restated the traditional view.

Panofsky's reconstruction has not been altered by all this, although certain minor points have been developed and made more explicit by the subsequent writers. Parronchi's views alone constitute a novel departure, but certain difficulties (which I shall point out) prevent me from accepting his interpretation of Alberti's procedure.

29. "... et emmi questa linea medesima proportionale a quella ultima quantità quale prima mi si traversò inanzi." *Della pitt.*, p. 70. This somewhat obscure way of putting the idea has led some to believe that the text was corrupt at this point; see Mallè's note 4, p. 70. Spencer relied upon the Latin version for his translation and (correct) interpretation: "ac mihi quidem haec ipsa jacens quadranguli linea est proximiori transversae

4. Next he placed the centric point in the picture "at the place where the centric-ray strikes." And in keeping with his original idea of a scaled picture, he insisted that the centric point be placed at the height, or eye level, of the foreground figure.

That is, since the depicted figure is proportional to the actual spectator, and since they stand upon the same ground (except when one of them is explicitly placed higher or lower, as in a pit or on top of a building), he gave them the same eye level (as determined by the spectator's centric ray) to guarantee that "both the beholder and the painted things he sees will appear to be on the same [ground] plane." Simple as it now seems, this was apparently a new and difficult principle, for it was frequently violated in theory and practice at least down to Leonardo's time. Another indication of its novelty can be found below, in Alberti's criticism of the arbitrary way the horizon was then being painted, with no fixed relation to the centric point or to the height of the depicted figures.

5. To the centric point, Alberti now drew straight lines from each of the points marked along the base line of the picture. These lines form the orthogonals of the projected pavement.

To complete the pavement, horizontal lines must be drawn across the orthogonals. At this point in *Della pittura,* Alberti described and criticized the centric-point scheme as painters were then using it—thus setting off very nicely the new rules of construction which he was introducing.

Their method of drawing the horizontal lines of the pavement was "regular" enough, but it led to results which Alberti found contrary to empirical truth (figure 11). In the quadrangle and parallel to its base line AF, the painter drew a line $(8',14')$ "anywhere." Then he divided the distance between this line and the base line into three parts. At two of these "thirds" above the line $8',14'$ he placed the next horizontal line $(15',21')$; and he kept repeating this procedure to find the remaining horizontal lines—(so that $22',28'$ is at two-thirds the interval between $15',21'$ and $8',14'$; $29',35'$ is at two-thirds the interval between $22',28'$ and $15',21'$; and so forth).

As Alberti pointed out, this practice causes many inaccuracies, "because

---

et aequidistanti in pavimento vise quantitati proportionalis"; which gives him, "to me this same line of the quadrangle is proportional to the nearest transverse and equidistant quantity seen on the pavement." Our figure 9 illustrates this point. In the top view, the base of the visual pyramid $ABDF$ cuts through the pavement along its horizontal line $1,7$. The perspective of this line on the frontal view coincides with the base line of the quadrangle which represents the plane of projection.

It is true, as Cecil Grayson suggests in n. 7, p. 15 of "L. B. Alberti's 'costruzione legittima,' " that the base line of the quadrangle would be proportional to the base line of a plane dropped through the visual pyramid at the place where the viewer is standing, but I do not think this was Alberti's meaning. He was trying to express the idea of a perspective of a line without having the technical language for doing so.

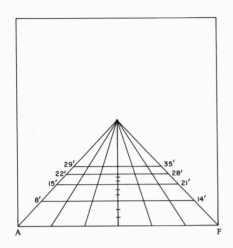

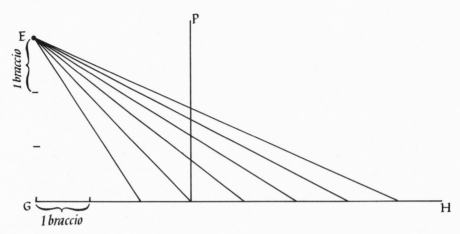

11. *The two-thirds rule for placing the horizontal lines of the pavement.*

12. *The* Costruzione legittima: *steps 6–10*

one can never know with certainty where the cuspid of the visual pyramid is." That is, the first horizontal line (which is actually the second horizontal line of the pavement) is placed "by chance." But as Alberti now knew from the perspectival theory of vision and the projective science he had built upon it, its height above the base line of the quadrangle (and hence above the pavement's first horizontal line) should have been determined by the distance of the viewer from the base of the visual pyramid upon which the pavement is projected.

His second objection to contemporary practice also reflects the new criterion of the picture as an image of things viewed by a spectator and projected upon a section of his visual pyramid. It had been the practice to place the horizon (which ought to be defined by the centric point) "higher or lower than the height of the depicted men," that is, to place it at random. As long as this was the case, the horizon was unrelated to the (imaginary) line of sight of the depicted figures and the (actual) line of sight of the beholder, and the picture failed to present the appearance of any one person's visual image.

The first of these faults was corrected by Alberti's second drawing which is, of course, a side view of the pavement—although he does not call it that, nor does he give any but the barest indication of what its points and lines stand for (figure 12):

6. Starting a separate drawing, he set down a straight line *GH*.[30]

30. This is where Parronchi's reconstruction begins to depart from the traditional one. He takes the "little space" in which Alberti says he does this drawing to be adjacent to the quadrangle, so that the line *GH* is an extension of the base line *AF*. Alberti does not say that his "little space" is adjacent to the quadrangle, but in almost all fifteenth-century diagrams of the *costruzione legittima* this, in fact, is what appears. Here I think we have to distinguish between (a) the *costruzione legittima* as actually used in painting,

7. Beginning anywhere on this line (say, at point *G*), he measured off a finite number of *braccia,* scaled to those on the base line of his first drawing.

8. Above the line *GH* (specifically, above "one end" of it),[31] he placed a point *E* at a height equal to that of the centric point from the base line in the first drawing (that is, three *braccia* high, at the eye level of the foreground figure and the beholder).

9. From this (eye) point *E,* he drew straight lines to each of the points marked on *GH* (thus constructing a side view of the visual rays to the horizontal lines of the pavement).[32]

10. Then he established the Distance by dropping a perpendicular line (representing the base of the visual pyramid) to the line *GH* (the ground), "at whatever distance I want the eye to be from the picture."[33]

Alberti did not give a rule, as Piero della Francesca would (c. 1416–92), relating the (represented) Distance on his second drawing (which is proportional to the [actual] distance between the viewer and the plane of projection) to the width of the picture (which is proportional to the viewer's range of vision).[34] Probably he decided upon it by "feel." Standing in front of

---

and (b) diagrams illustrating it. The text reads as though Alberti were speaking of the former, and that he was thinking of a panel which was to be painted rather than a wall surface. If this is the case, his side view would most likely be done as a separate drawing and then matched up with the first drawing on the panel. When the construction is drawn for purposes of demonstration, or when the quadrangle is inscribed upon a wall for a fresco, the side view can be drawn next to the quadrangle, using one of its sides as the Perpendicular of step 10.

31. This is the phrase which Cecil Grayson discovered in several Latin manuscripts of *De pictura.* The entire passage reads as follows in these versions: "Habeo areolam in qua describo lineam unam rectam. Hanc divido per eas partes in quas iacens linea quadranguli divisa est. Deinde pono sursum ab hac linea punctum unicum *ad alterum line caput perpendicularem* tam alte quam est in quadrangulo centricus punctus a iacente divisa quadranguli linea distans . . ." (italics mine). Parronchi was correct in claiming that this phrase could be incorporated in his reconstruction; and that only if it were, would Grayson be justified in asserting that this operation fixed the Distance. That is, when the side view is drawn adjacent to the quadrangle, using either one of its sides or a line down its center as the Perpendicular, the placing of this point establishes the Distance between it and the Perpendicular. When the side view is done as a separate drawing, it is not the placing of this (eye) point that establishes the Distance, but the dropping of the Perpendicular of step 10. The new phrase, however, does not decide the issue (as Edgerton thought it did) as to which of these procedures actually was Alberti's.

32. Parronchi has these lines go to the points on the base line of the first drawing, as is the case in all illustrations of the *costruzione legittima* which make the side view adjacent to the quadrangle. Alberti's text can be read either way on this point.

33. Parronchi maintains that Alberti must have made the Distance correspond to at least one-half the base line of his quadrangle; Alberti says only "at whatever distance I want. . . ."

34. Mallè pointed this out, *Della pitt.,* p. 25 and n.1, p. 73. Piero fixed the angle of vision by affirming that the eye, when focusing upon one point, embraces a horizon of ninety degrees (although he recommended an angle of sixty degrees for painting, because

49

the panel (or canvas, or wall) on which his first drawing appeared, he could
find what seemed to be the right place for viewing it—"neither too far away nor
too close," as Filarete says;[35] and this actual distance he could represent in
the scaled *braccia* of his construction.

Altogether, steps 6–10 result in the same picture as that of figure 9*B:*
a side view of a three-*braccia* figure and his lines of sight to the horizontal lines
of the pavement; the intersection of these lines of sight by the base of the visual
pyramid; and the projection of the pavement lines upon that base. To find the
proper sequence of the horizontal lines for the front view of the pavement,
Alberti combined the two drawings of the *costruzione legittima,* probably as we
did in figure 9*C.*

11. He found the perspective points of the horizontal lines of the pavement
on the side view where the perpendicular line $B(D), A(F)$ intersects the
lines of sight to the pavement.

12. Then, although he does not explicitly say so, he must have transferred
these points to the edge of the panel on which he had made his first drawing
(thus matching the Perpendicular of the second drawing with one of the sides
of his quadrangle). For, he says, he now finds completed "all the parallels,
that is, the square[d] *braccia* of the pavement in the painting."[36]

---

marked distortions appear when the angle is greater). The maximum distance from
the picture is thus somewhat less than the width of the picture. *De prospectiva pingendi,*
edited by G. Nicco Fasola, pp. 96–97.

35. Bk. 23, 177ᵛ. Alberti himself does not describe this procedure, or any other,
for determining the Distance.

36. Parronchi's interpretation of this passage is that Alberti's Perpendicular (a) is
not part of a separate drawing, (b) is not even a side of the quadrangle, but (c) is
rather a perpendicular line drawn through the centric point to the base line of the front
view. Since Alberti does not mention any operation of transferring points from one
drawing to another, Parronchi maintains he found the perspective points of the horizontal
lines of the pavement on this Perpendicular which intersects the lines of sight to
the pavement.

I do not think this was Alberti's procedure. (a) It is true that the operation described
in step 12 is not in the text; but in Parronchi's reconstruction, two operations are not
described in the text: the extension of the base line of the quadrangle for drawing a
side view which is to be adjacent to it; and dropping the Perpendicular
through the centric point. And the mere fact that no one until Parronchi has thought of
reading Alberti's text as he has, indicates how much more serious these omissions are.
(b) In Parronchi's reconstruction, the Distance is fixed as soon as the eye point of the side
view is drawn. But Alberti says he determines the Distance when he drops the
intersecting Perpendicular. Parronchi explains this statement by supposing that Alberti
moved in front of the quadrangle at this moment, and standing at the same distance
from it as was proportionately depicted on his drawing, he found the centric point where
his centric ray "pierced" the quadrangle and dropped the Perpendicular through it. This
could characterize Filarete's procedure, but not Alberti's; he had already drawn the
centric point (in step 4). Why, then, should he have to stand at any given distance from

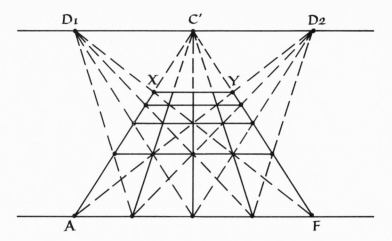

13. Alberti's pavement (unlike ours in figure 9) was a square, because his final step was to draw a diagonal line across it as a test. If the Diagonal contains the diagonals of all the squares through which it passes, the pavement is properly foreshortened.

In the special case where the pavement is a square, and the spectator views it squarely, the continuation of this Diagonal intersects the horizon at a "distance point." Piero della Francesca was to demonstrate this in his *De prospectiva pingendi,*[37] showing how the checkerboard pavement could be constructed by means of two such distance points (figure 13).

the quadrangle to mark off the points of intersection on the Perpendicular? (c) The contemporary drawings which Parronchi gives to support his views confirm, in my judgment, the traditional interpretation of the *costruzione legittima:* namely, that when the side view was drawn adjacent to the quadrangle, the side of the quadrangle was used as the Perpendicular—because that, in fact, is what Alberti's Perpendicular represented. In none of these drawings (by Filarete, Francesco di Giorgio Martini, and Leonardo) is there a central Perpendicular. Moreover, the one illustration by Francesco di Giorgio which Parronchi thinks is not related to the *costruzione legittima* is, on the contrary, a separate side view like figures 9B and 12. It shows a man whose lines of sight cross a vertical measuring rod (or profile of a picture panel) as he looks at a pavement which is divided into squares and is also seen in side view. The rod is clearly Alberti's Perpendicular, and the second drawing by Francesco di Giorgio shows that he regarded it as the side of the quadrangle or panel. See "Il Filarete, Francesco di Giorgio e Leonardo su la 'Costruzione Legittima,' " pp. 155–67.

Where I do find something resembling Parronchi's construction, however, is in the perspective reconstructions of certain drawings by J. Bellini and Pisanello given by Edgerton, "Alberti's Perspective." If these reconstructions are correct, they show a distance-point construction in which the points of intersection are marked off, not on the Diagonal as is customary in the normal distance-point construction (see below, figure 13), but on a central Perpendicular. Since Bellini and Pisanello were in contact with Alberti and were probably influenced by him, as Edgerton shows, this scheme may well have been advocated as a simpler mode of construction than the one he originally described in 1435.

37. *De pros. pingendi,* pp. 76f. See also the introduction by G. Nicco Fasola.

13. *The distance-point construction.*

Set a centric point above a base line AF, *perpendicular to its center. Connect it with the divisions of the base line and its extreme points.*

Draw the horizon through the centric point and place two points D₁ *and* D₂ *upon it at equal distances from* C'.

Draw diagonal lines from each of these two points to the ends of the base line. Where the diagonals intersect the lines AC' *and* FC', *we find points* x *and* y.

Joining the points of intersection gives us the foreshortened square of the pavement; the smaller squares are found the same way.

Although the distance points resemble the points of the earlier bifocal construction, in this construction they are related to a centric point—with all the theory and geometry which that implies. The checkerboard pavement which they were soon used to construct is the scaled and properly foreshortened one of the *costruzione legittima*. Alberti himself appears not to have known about this method of constructing the pavement. He drew his Diagonal only to test an already completed picture of it; but mathematically, the distance-point construction is a simple variant of the *costruzione legittima* and could be readily developed once Alberti's more laborious procedure had established the basic elements and operations of perspectival projection.

The logical identity of the *costruzione legittima* and the distance-point construction was demonstrated by Vignola (1507–73) in his *Due regole della prospettiva pratica*.[38] Giving the two constructions in one drawing, he showed how the horizontal lines of the pavement can be marked off on either the Diagonal of the distance-point construction or the Perpendicular of the *costruzione legittima* (figure 14).

Such were the simple steps of the *costruzione legittima*. Its pavement was now ready to serve its intended purpose as a grid; and on its scaled parallels, the painter learned to coordinate as never before the various sizes of objects, their relative heights, widths, and depths as they appear to the eye.

Drawing the horizon through the centric point, Alberti explained that this line sets the limit above which no object can appear, unless it is meant to be taller than the beholder. All average-sized men in the picture who stand on the same ground with each other have their height fixed, by the horizon, at the level of the viewing eye.

But "depicted men in the last squared *braccia* of the painting are smaller than the others"; thus all these figures who stand on the same ground and reach the same level of the horizon constitute a properly diminishing three-*braccia* standard for the painter, one by which he can measure height at any point of the pavement. And the squares of the pavement, their sides scaled as *braccia*, provide a standard for all measures of width and depth (figure 15).

Simple buildings, for example those which can be construed as boxes (i.e., solids with rectilinear plane figures as surfaces), now fit into the picture effortlessly. The new rules are at once more precise and easier to follow than

38. Panofsky first noted Vignola's demonstration of the logical identity of the two constructions in "Das persp. Verfahren L.B.A.," pp. 504–16—where he also carefully distinguished the two as different forms of the same construction. They are just that, namely two: the *E* in figure 14 (representing Alberti's eye point) is not *D* (the distance point), and the Perpendicular (the side of the panel) is not the Diagonal of the pavement. I would therefore not compound the two by calling Alberti's Eye-point a Distance-point as is sometimes done; and I see no reason why Edgerton should believe that "the whole problem of possible identity between *costruzione legittima* and *Distanzpunktverfahren* might be raised all over again."

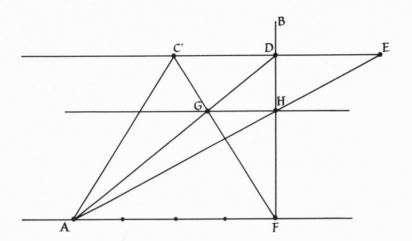

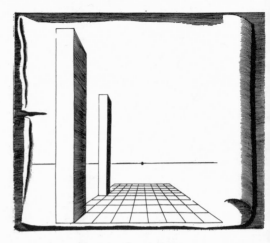

those laid down by Cennino Cennini. Take such a building with a wall parallel to the picture plane. The foundation of the building is marked off on the parallels of the pavement: the width of its face is measured, true to scale, along one of the horizontal lines of the pavement, "so that for as many *braccia* as I choose, it occupies as many parallels"; and the foreshortened side wall is measured, in depth, along an orthogonal line. For the height of the front and side walls, figures placed on the first and last horizontal lines upon which the building stands provide a three-*braccia* standard. And for the line of the roof, and the exact angle at which it recedes towards the horizon, the point of a front corner of the foreshortened wall is simply connected to the point of the corresponding rear corner.

Here, then, in the *costruzione legittima,* we have both a geometry and a novel application of geometric principles. The application is physiological, and as such, determined by the initial data of sight; but the new rules of seeing and depicting objects approximate as closely as possible the rules of constructing figures purely and abstractly. Leaning as much as he could upon a geometric model, Alberti had brought about a new kind of pictorial exactitude. The horizon of his construction and the scaled units of the pavement regulate the relative sizes of all the objects in the picture and the relative distances among them; and since the horizon is the vanishing trace for all horizontal planes as seen by the depicted figures *and* by the beholder, the "virtual" space of the picture has been made to appear as a convincing extension of the viewer's "actual" space. Properly proportioned and exactly graduated in relation to his viewpoint, the perspectival painting seems to continue his actual, visual space, an illusion which Alberti wanted the painter to heighten by having at least one of the depicted figures look directly at the viewer, as if warning him to keep his distance, or pointing out to him what is happening in the picture, according

14. *The identity of the distance-point construction and the* Costruzione legittima. *From Vignola, simplified.*

D *is the distance point. Draw* DA; *it will cut* FC′ *at point* G. *Drawing a line through* G *parallel to* AF, *we find the height of the projected square.*

The same thing can be done by dropping a perpendicular BF *to* F *and moving the distance point to* E *so that the distance from* E *to the perpendicular is equal to* DC′. *Draw* EA; *it will cut* BF *at point* H. *If we draw a line through* H *parallel to* AF, *it will go through point* G.

Thus, the distance DC′ *gives us the intersection on the diagonal at point* G; *whereas the distance from* E *to the perpendicular gives us the intersection on the perpendicular at point* H.

15. *Using the checkerboard pavement as a grid.*

16. *Raphael,* The School of Athens, *Vatican Palace, Rome. (Alinari-Art Reference Bureau.)*

to the dramatic import of its *istoria.*

The picture had indeed become "an open window through which we see what is painted"; and through this perspectival "glass" the Renaissance viewed, and construed, the world in its own distinctive fashion (figure 16).

2
The Classical Perspective

As a technique for creating pictures of the world which looked like visual images of it, perspective was immediately taken up by the artistic circles of fifteenth-century Florence, and from there it spread to all Italy and most of Europe. Wherever it was adopted, it transformed painting. Its geometric ordering of appearances started painting upon a decisively new course, and at the same time brought it into close relation with the other modes of Renaissance visual art and with the classical aesthetic tradition.

Understood as a system of projection, perspective was an original discovery, not a recovery of an ancient pictorial technique. We may debate today whether or not some rules of projection underlie the recently discovered examples of Roman illusionistic painting, but this much is certain; no such works were known to the fifteenth century. Perspective was then regarded, and rightly so, as "an invention of our age."[1] But perspective presupposed certain aesthetic ideas; it rested upon certain assumptions about nature and the artist's imitation of it, and these assumptions were also at work in the neo-classical developments of Renaissance architecture and sculpture. Alberti had drawn his inspiration, in fact, not so much from painting as from Brunelleschi's buildings and the works of Florentine sculpture. As the Prologue to *Della pittura* shows, Masaccio was the only painter he placed in the same class with the giants of antiquity and their successors in the quattrocento: Brunelleschi, Donatello, Ghiberti, and Luca della Robbia. In the new forms of Florentine sculpture, as in the metrical flow of the nave of Brunelleschi's San Lorenzo (fig. 7), in the

1. Like all humanists, Alberti liked to find classical precedents for his ideas, but he expressly remarked that painter's perspective was new, that ancient drawing and relief work was done without it, and for that reason was "incorrect." *Della pittura*, p. 74. Filarete repeated the statement that perspective was not to be found in the ancients, bk. 23, 179ʳ. In a chronicle written around 1482, Giovanni Santi referred to perspective as an "invention del nostro secul novo." In Julius von Schlosser, *La letteratura artistica*, p. 112, Pomponius Gauricus also spoke of perspective as an invention of "our time." Robert Klein, "Pomponius on Perspective," *Art Bulletin*, 42 (1961): 212, n. 11.

measure of its dark gray architectural elements, of round arch and column, of pilaster, capital and entablature, against the white walls—he had discerned the first clear echo of the vanished world of classical art.

What characterized the work of those artists whom Alberti named, what bound them to the humanistic "revival of antiquity" which he espoused, was their renewal of the classical aesthetic of proportionality. The harmonious space of Brunelleschi's church had its inception in careful studies in Rome, excavating and measuring the remains of ancient buildings. Donatello had accompanied Brunelleschi and studied the proportions of Graeco-Roman statues so as to restore to the sculpted form (as Masaccio did to the painted one) its former organic articulation. The advent of the artistic "renaissance" in the sculpture and architecture of quattrocento Florence was marked, in short, by the restoration of the classical, geometrically inspired conception of artistic space,[2] and this same spatial conception the *costruzione legittima* introduced to painting. Perspective was an independent expression of an aesthetic outlook which originally had given rise to the proportional art of antiquity. It had no direct connection with classical art, but as it imposed its proportional spatial order upon painting, it inevitably brought about a classical mode of construing appearances.

Proportion in Painting

To appreciate how perspective transformed the picture of the world, restoring to it a classical imaginative vision, one need only contrast Renaissance painting with that of fifteenth-century Flanders; for the Flemish picture was untouched by the visual geometry of Italy, although it shared with Renaissance art a

2. Thus Heinrich Wölfflin spoke of the "adoption of the antique schema" by Renaissance art, i.e., the renewal in Renaissance art of what he called the classical "mode of beholding" and representing appearances. *Principles of Art History,* p. 181 *et passim.* In sculpture, John Pope-Hennessy saw the "birth" of the Renaissance style in 1401 when "the tradition of Rome" was renewed in the reliefs submitted by Brunelleschi and Ghiberti for the competition for the second bronze door of the Baptistery. *Italian Renaissance Sculpture,* 1, 3. And H. W. Janson called attention to the development of the classical conception of organic form in Donatello's early statues, a development which "disturbed" and finally replaced motifs belonging to the International Style of the late Middle Ages. *The Sculpture of Donatello,* especially 2: 19, 29. The following description is of one of these transitional works, "St. John the Evangelist" (Florence, Museo dell'Opera del Duomo) which Donatello did sometime between 1409 and 1415: "the traditional treatment of the upper torso and shoulders [is such that] . . . they form an abstract, rounded block, to which the Ghibertesque drapery clings like an elastic skin, with little regard for the organic shape of the body beneath. . . . In the drapery a marked change can be noticed from the waist down. The ornamental system of the International Style, with its soft loops and harpin curves, remains the basic pattern, but disturbed, as it were, by an effort to adapt it to a functional relationship of body and drapery." Vol. 2: 16.

number of other notions about painting and its objectives.[3] The spatial developments of both schools meet in one fundamental respect: both "look through" the picture plane to a natural world of visible objects "beyond" it. Flemish painting took the appearances of the phenomenal world as its starting point, renouncing, as Italian painting did, the two-dimensional, hieratic symbolism of the past in order to capture the purely visual aspect of things.

In this attachment to perceptual experience, both schools were deepening an awareness of subjectivity which had already begun to affect Late Gothic art.[4] A dramatic, and at times even a sentimental interest in traditional Christian doctrine had developed in the course of the fourteenth century, and it found artistic expression in a markedly "naturalistic" tendency. Emile Mâle has shown in his studies of Late Gothic art how the moving imagery of the *Meditations on the Life of Jesus Christ,* a work of Franciscan origin, directly inspired many such iconographic changes, humanizing the personages of the Christian myths and making them more familiar and realistic in appearance. The kneeling angel of the Annunciation, for example, came to be met in fourteenth-century painting by a Virgin who also kneels. The *Meditations* had described her this way, as a tender maiden rather than the hitherto remote Queen of Heaven, kneeling as befits one "filled with the spirit of devotion, who joined her hands and said, 'Behold the handmaid of the Lord.'" This is how Giotto painted the "Annunciation" in the Arena Chapel in Padua, and it was in Giotto's dramatic pictorial world that a credible, three-dimensional space first appeared in European art.

The sense of a unified, "natural" spatial environment which Giotto's frescoes create is very largely produced by strong emotional tensions among the people in his scenes. With Giotto, everything was felt; and everything felt

3. Dagobert Frey's *Gothik und Renaissance als Grundlagen der modernen Weltanschauung* is the classic study of the Flemish and Renaissance styles, their spatial principles and the metaphysical outlooks expressed by means of them. See also Victor Wallerstein, *Die Raumbehandlung in der Oberdeutschen und Niederländischen Tafelmalerei der ersten Hälfte des XV. Jahrhunderts;* Erwin Panofsky, *Early Netherlandish Painting, Its Origins and Character;* and Wolfgang Schöne, *Über das Licht in der Malerei.*

4. See on this point Emile Mâle, *L'art religieux de la fin du Moyen Age en France.* Panofsky refers to "Late Gothic subjectivism" in *Gothic Architecture and Scholasticism,* p. 16. In another work, he wrote that the Renaissance system of perspective, its system of human proportions, and its theory of organic movement "have one thing in common: they all presuppose the artistic recognition of subjectivity. Organic movement introduces into the calculus of artistic composition the subjective will and the subjective emotions of the thing represented; foreshortening, the subjective visual experience of the artist; and those 'eurhythmic' adjustments which alter that which is right in favor of that which seems right, the subjective visual experience of a potential beholder. And it is the Renaissance which, for the first time, not only affirms but formally legitimizes and rationalizes these three forms of subjectivity." "The History of the Theory of Human Proportions as a Reflection of the History of Styles," *Meaning in the Visual Arts,* p. 98. I hope to show that not only is this the case, but that a new recognition and form of *objectivity* is also expressed by these Renaissance "theories."

he expressed in the faces and the attitudes and positions of his figures. The impact of his "Crucifixion" in the Arena Chapel (fig. 17) is conveyed, not merely by the picture of the crucified Lord, but by the creatures who actively participate in the Passion—the wildly lamenting angels who hover *behind* and *over* their dying God, the Virgin Mother on the left who faces *outward* and exposes her grief, the tender Magdalen turned towards the *center* of the terrible scene. Endowing the figures of the Gospel with a new, affective power, objectifying in them the emotional and psychological "feel" of traditional doctrinal truths, Giotto brought them to life as persons; and their new life made them and their surroundings solid, and startlingly three-dimensional. Even the schematized, Italo-Byzantine representations of landscape and architecture exhibit some of this new vitality in his frescoes, acquiring individuality and mass from his intention to make convincing "real" settings for his lifelike portrayals of the Christian *istorie*.

These pictorial innovations and the naturalistic spirit they express were absorbed by Italian trecento painting and by most European schools in the course of the fourteenth century. By 1400 they characterized European art in general, permitting us to speak of a European-wide, International Style. The two great fifteenth-century schools of Flanders and Florence had their origins here, in the International Style and its newly won vision of subjective experience and phenomenal reality. This was the vision which both schools strove to make more and more consistent.[5] Both steadily eliminated from the picture whatever a viewing subject could not actually see. Although the apparent still included angels, haloes, and what could be "seen" in mystical transports as well as in daily experience, overt, "unnatural" symbolism was made to yield to an indirect kind of reference to religious, metaphysical, or moral teachings, either by means of faithfully rendered narrative scenes which could be "read" doctrinally or allegorically, or by perceptual objects which symbolized the "invisible" while belonging to the world of other ordinary, visible things. The depiction of different narratives in one painting, or of the several events of a narrative sequence, was gradually abandoned; and as the plurality of dramatic moments disappeared from the picture, so did the plurality of its "spaces," the impossible coexistence of several independent views. The picture came to be unified as a single, visual image.

And yet, despite this common objective, despite a very deliberate effort to adhere to subjective experience and to the world of appearances, the Flemish and the Florentine painters simply did not paint the same world. Both schools took the visual image as their starting point, but they shaped that image differently. Adopting different theoretical presuppositions, each school "saw" the phenomenal world in its own way and represented it by means of a different spatial order.

5. For these developments, see Panofsky, *Early Netherlandish Painting*.

17. *Giotto,* The Crucifixion,
Arena Chapel, Padua.
(Alinari-Art Reference Bureau.)

18. *Donatello,* The Feast of Herod,
*c. 1425, Baptistery, Siena.
(Brogi-Art Reference Bureau.)*

This is where perspective played its distinctive, formative role. Wherever
the *costruzione legittima* was adopted, it introduced a new kind of regularity
into painting and relief work, stamping the perspectival scene with a
characteristic lawfulness. Donatello's two "Feast of Herod" reliefs offers a
perfect example of this development, for of the two, only the later one was
based upon Alberti's construction.[6] The earlier relief, executed around 1425 for
the Baptistery font at Siena (fig. 18), still belongs to the International Style.
The cramped space of its one-room interior is still ambiguous and "shifting,"
appearing three-dimensional and deep in some areas (the left arch) and flat in
others (the center and the right arch). As in Giotto's frescoes, the visual
coherence of the scene depends almost entirely upon the depicted figures.
By participating in a single *istoria,* they unify the virtual space of the relief;
and by their relative positions, they define its ideal, receding spatial planes, for

6. See the analysis of these panels in H. W. Janson, *Sculpture of Donatello,*
2: 65–72, 129–31.

some are apparently "next to" others, thus standing in the same plane, while others are "behind" and "in front of" these.

The space of Donatello's second "Feast of Herod" relief of 1435 (Musée Wicar, Lille) no longer depends upon the figures in this way. In this relief (fig. 19), as Professor Janson has described it, "the actors could walk off the stage, as it were, or redistribute themselves in the scene, without altering the rational clarity and intelligibility of their spatial environment." Here and henceforth, Donatello's figures, "unburdened of their space-creating responsibility, achieve a new freedom to move about, to group themselves within their vastly expanded setting"; for here and henceforth, they appear in the ample, homogeneous, and uniformly proportioned space envisioned by Alberti, a stable, lawful space which, at last, they could occupy convincingly.

The spatial effect of the 1435 "Feast of Herod" relief is exactly what Alberti sought, and true to rule (as Professor Janson has found), the base line of the panel had been divided into nine units; a single, centric vanishing point

19. *Donatello,* The Feast of Herod, *1435. In the Musée Wicar, Lille. (Giraudon-Art Reference Bureau.)*

61

(not yet present in the relief of 1425) had been put three units above it, corresponding to the eye level of a figure placed on the foreground; and a grid of intersecting parallels lines, still partly visible in the relief, had been incised over its surface. In *Della pittura,* Alberti says that he taught the rules of perspective to his friends;[7] and here, indeed, his "close friend Donato" had used his checkerboard pavement to draw to scale the figures of the scene and their elaborate setting, and to place all the architectural elements—the steps, banisters, columns, and arches—in unambiguous relation to the viewing eye (cf. figures 5 and 19). Only one part of the relief still strikes an ambiguous note, and that is the building in the rear center that stands "beyond" the pavement, "behind" the central arch. But everything that rises from the pavement is *pari alle vere,* making the virtual scene of the relief appear as a proportional extension of the actual space and natural vision of the beholder.

The first perspectival reliefs which Ghiberti designed for the "Gates of Paradise" of the Baptistery (Florence) owe their rationally coherent and continuous space to these same means. Of the "Isaac" panel of c.1435, Richard Krautheimer and Trude Krautheimer-Hess write:

> By means of the architectural setting . . . an intelligible space has been designed, continuous in depth, width and height. This space is populated by figures which diminish proportionately as the eye follows them into depth. To this end the floors of the hall and the plaza in front have been divided into a number of squares. Figures and architectural elements are placed on these squares and on their intersections. A network of coordinates has been laid out to determine the exact place and consequently the exact size of each element within the space constructed. This network is in its entirety related to the human figure. Indeed, the base of the panel has been divided into nine equal parts marking off the nine squares along the front of the panel. Each of these nine parts—that is the width of each square—measures 8.6 cm, exactly one-third of the average height, 26 cm, assigned to an adult person placed in the panel's immediate foreground. . . .

The conclusion seems to be inevitable: Ghiberti in the *Isaac* and *Joseph* panels applied verbatim the perspective construction which Alberti had expounded.[8]

Soon to shape the pictures of Uccello, Domenico Veneziano, Piero della Francesca and the rest, the *costruzione legittima* brought about a new liberation by its very lawfulness.[9] The more the artist relied upon the rules of perspective,

---

7. "Qui soglio io adpresso ad i miei amici dare simile regola" *Della pitt.,* p. 60; also 64, *et passim.*

8. *Lorenzo Ghiberti,* pp. 248–51.

9. Wölfflin very aptly applied this Kantian idea to classic art, calling attention to the new freedom it achieved by means of "strict conformity to law." *Principles of Art History,* pp. 73, 128, 145, 197, *et passim.*

the less dependent he was upon the figures of his picture to create and organize its space. The more "regular" his pictorial space became, the greater the ease with which he placed his figures in a rationally coherent setting where they could stand in proper proportion to each other and the beholder. Flemish painting, by contrast, was not bound by the rules of linear perspective. Although the Flemish painters were indisputable masters of depth-illusion, they did not seek the effect of a regular, graduated diminution in the size of things as they recede from the viewer's eye. A certain disproportion between foreground and distant objects marks their works; and since they made no attempt to fix "the measure" between man and his surroundings, their figures exceed the proportions of the structures that enclose them (fig. 20). Arches are too small and columns too slender, even for the thin and frail figures who people the Flemish scene. Were they to walk about, they would have to stoop and squeeze their way through the picture's cramped spaces.

There are, of course, vast panoramic views in Flemish painting, too, but these fail in another way to give us a genuinely perspectival image. In these impressive and beautiful vistas, filled with a multitude of sharply defined objects, distant objects appear as distinct and vivid as the nearer and larger ones. No atmospheric haze dims the intensity of their colors or blurs their outlines—as Alberti had insisted it must. He maintained that the median rays of the visual pyramid carry the color tones and highlights of surfaces to the eye, and the few rules of aerial perspective which he gave were based upon a study of these rays which, he found, have a determinate strength where they are "broken" by, and projected upon, the base of a viewer's pyramid of sight.[10]

These median rays are, so to speak, "weakened" by long journeys: the greater the distance they run from the surface to the eye, the dimmer the tone and intensity of the colors and highlights they carry. This initial observation led Alberti to consider how the "lights" of a viewed surface appear on the plane of projection when that surface is flat and when it is "spherical" or "concave." When visual rays emanate from a flat surface, the color of the surface is uniform on the projection plane; but he found that when they emanate from a spherical or concave surface, they carry characteristic highlights and shadows to the plane on which they are projected because of the way the curved surface is illuminated, and because of the way the eye views it. These variations in tone and intensity he taught the painter to capture by a judicious use of black and white. Although, according to Alberti, black and white are not colors themselves, they can be used to represent by artificial chiaroscuro nature's

10. *Della pitt.*, pp. 61–64, 98–102. Sir Kenneth Clark traced the influence of Alberti's ideas of color and light upon Fra Angelico and Domenico Veneziano in whom he found the "first passages of *plein air* painting in post-classical art." *Leon Battista Alberti on Painting*, vol. 30 of Proceedings of the British Academy. Leonardo worked out the rules of aerial and color perspective which are contained in rudimentary form in Alberti; see Richter, 1: 16–17, 143–54, 157–66.

20. *Roger van de Weyden*
Christ Appearing to His Mother.
In the Metropolitan Museum of Art,
New York, bequest of
Michael Dreicer, 1921.

shifting color values. As shadows increase, black darkens the color; and the brighter and more blinding the light that strikes a color, the "whiter" it becomes. Different kinds of light, like starlight or firelight, also affect these highlights and shadows, for in all cases, the changing appearances of color are due to variations in the kind of light that illuminates the scene, and to changes in "the reception of light" at the spectator's vantage point.

Guided by rules like these, Renaissance painting progressively developed qualities of chiaroscuro and *sfumatura.* Flemish painting, however, retained its uniform sharpness and even clarity. Regardless of distance or lighting, the finest details of buildings, clothing, and landscapes, down to petals and blades of grass, were rendered as exactly and minutely as the hairs on the head of a foreground figure. Such "unperspectival" features had, of course, an expressive function in Flemish art. They cannot be understood in a purely negative way, as mere errors, for they served to objectify a certain imaginative understanding of phenomenal reality. If the Flemish picture presents a multitude of equally distinct and visible objects which could not possibly be seen from any one vantage point at any one time; if it shows scenes through side windows and in mirrors which, given our natural vision, we could not possibly see—all this is of little consequence, for Flemish art sets forth the world of appearances as it stands in the Eye of God. This is what lends the stamp of validity to what would otherwise be regarded as technical faults. Granted, the Flemish picture is not consistently ordered by a human act of viewing, an act that imposes a specific focus and regulates the apparent relative size and brightness of things; but from His viewpoint, we *can* be led to "see around corners" and to appreciate the "fixed" reality of perceptual phenomena, no matter how far or how fine.

No wonder, then, that the centric point did not appear in Flemish painting until late in the fifteenth century; and when it did, that it was not used with any consistency to unify the picture in relation to the viewpoint of a human spectator. No wonder that the high horizon, which probably survived from the illuminator's art out of which Flemish painting developed, did tend to survive—even though it flattens the scene by forcing "distant" objects and figures to appear high in the picture (as on a manuscript page) while "nearer" ones appear lower down. The spatial effects of the medieval manuscript page lingered on in Flemish art because the Flemish painters continued to treat the world of appearances as an objective reality with enduring characteristics which lie "out there." Thus the main figures, in Roger van der Weyden's paintings, for example, generally seem to be *on* the foreground rather than *in* space; and the scene "behind" them serves more as a decorative, though naturalistic, backdrop, than as a natural continuation of their space and that of the beholder. The horizon is often placed far above the eye level of the depicted figures; and when they are "seen" as if they were on the same ground as the viewer, the horizon, which ought to be determined by the viewer's eye, is above his eye level, too. The possibilities and limitations of the human act of seeing simply had not

65

been fully analyzed, and so the Flemish painters could behold the world with an attitude of naive metaphysical realism, as if the appearances of things had some "being" in and for themselves, regardless of the way the human subject views them.

This "fixed," Godlike kind of objectivity was fated to vanish with the Flemish picture of the world. In Renaissance painting, a new, self-conscious awareness of the constructive function of the human mind and eye took hold, and it has continued to play a formative role in Western art ever since. Perspective developed and expressed this reflexive spirit for the Renaissance. It offered a "critical" appreciation of visual experience, an appreciation, not of visible things or appearances per se, but of how their structure is known and formed by the human subject.

The Renaissance painter was restricted to the perceptual form of things by perspective, to that visual aspect of reality which so affected Alberti's aesthetic imagination that his fifteenth-century biographer speaks of him as being moved to tears, and even cured of illness, by the sight of beautiful forms.[11] Here, as in Flemish art, the painter concerned himself with "accidents," leaving to others the "substances" of things which were held to transcend perceptual experiences by the contemporary Aristotelian-Scholastic theory of knowledge. But perspective made pictorially meaningful the traditional philosophical doctrine about the relative nature of these appearances and of our knowledge of them:

> Large and small, long and short, high and low, broad and narrow, light and dark, bright and dim, and all such things which are called accidents by the philosophers because they are joined to things but are not necessary to them,—these are such that all knowledge of them is arrived at by comparison . . . Comparison has this power, that it demonstrates immediately in things which things are more, less, or equal. Whence we call big that which is larger than this small thing, and bigger that which is larger than this big one; bright that which is lighter than this dark thing, brighter that which is lighter than this bright one.[12]

Visible qualities like these have no being in and for themselves. They are relative, insubstantial, mere perceptual values; and Renaissance art consciously incorporated this knowledge. It made of it a principle of composition, what Wölfflin called "composition by contrast": creating an effect of largeness by deliberate contrast with something small, building up verticals in relation to horizontals, defining distant areas by contrast with near ones, establishing brightness by contrast with shadow.[13]

---

11. *Opera volgari*, i: lxxxix–cxvii.
12. *Della pitt.*, p. 69.
13. *Art of the Italian Renaissance*, pp. 381, 407.   As Wölfflin put it, Renaissance "contrapuntal" art was the outcome "of a clear discernment of the truth that all values

It was Alberti who first directed the painter toward this end. Since the "being" of perceptual values is determined solely by their relation to each other and to the subject who compares and evaluates them, he called attention to the fact that no matter how well the painter draws small bodies, he creates an impression of smallness only by comparison with something large: "It seems to me that the ancient painter, Timantes, understood this force of comparison, for in painting a small panel of a gigantic sleeping Cyclops, he put there [as Alberti had read in Pliny] several satyrs who were measuring the giant's thumb; by comparison with them, the sleeper seemed immense."[14] Alberti also advised the painter to exhibit contrasting directions in his picture (which he classified as "up" and "down," "to the right" and "to the left," "close" and "away," and "turning around"); and the same with colors: dark colors should stand among light ones and light among dark. All this advice Leonardo summed up in a rule which the Renaissance artists adopted quite knowingly: "direct contrasts should be placed near each other and commingled, for one intensifies the effect of another, and the more so the nearer they are."[15] Although borrowed from traditional epistemology, this relational principle became so commonly accepted as a pictorial device that when Castiglione came to define the various virtues in the sixteenth century by contrasting them with their opposites, he called upon painting as an illustration and justification of his "comparative method":

> The comparison, almost the opposition, of one [virtue] with the other makes them clearly known. So good painters do who with shadows make light appear and show relief, and with light deepen the shadows of the flat areas. They place diverse colors together in such a way that each one is shown forth better by this diversity, and by placing figures in opposition to each other, each is made to realize that function which the painter intends.[16]

Perspective is undoubtedly what led Alberti (and Leonardo) to make a compositional rule out of the old Protagorean idea of relativism, for it was perspective that taught the painter to forego the attempt to represent perceptual objects per se. It turned his attention from ontically "fixed" appearances, from visible qualities in and for themselves, to the relations that constitute the structure of appearances. It turned his attention to subjective evaluations, to comparisons made by a human viewer from a particular standpoint. Essentially, perspective was a science of visual relations; but since it was a "science," its relativism constitutes only half the picture that it gave rise to. Perspective did banish the last vestiges of an absolute sensible reality from the picture. In this sense, it took painting beyond Flemish art to a more profound awareness of the role of the

---

are relative, and that all size or direction of lines is effective only in reference to other sizes or directions."

14. *Della pitt.,* p. 69; see also pp. 70, 95, 101.
15. Quoted by Wölfflin, *Art of the Ital. Renaiss.,* p. 407.
16. *Il Cortegiano,* 2: vii.

subject in forming the world of appearances. But perspective also construed the world geometrically, and because it did so, the subject's comparisons—among sizes, distances, color tones, and degrees of luminosity—led to determinations of a measurable, and hence objectively real kind.

The comparative relations formed by perspective are ratios, the kind of relations that hold among the measurable properties of things. By definition, ratios are "relative," not absolute values; and the determination of "bigger," "farther," "brighter," and so forth vary with the viewpoint taken. Considered in relation to one particular viewpoint, however, the ratios of the visual image do become constant. They vary, but they vary according to rule; and it was in such rules that the Renaissance found the new absolutes of visual experience. For Alberti's mathematical imagination, the intellectual step from the relativism of perceptual determinations to the constancy of an intelligible rule was automatic and unreflective, so much so that he even missed the sceptical import of the maxim of Protagoras which he incorporated in his discussion of the "accidents" of things.

We compare accidents, he wrote,

> chiefly in relation to things that are well known. Now since among all things man is best known to us, perhaps Protagoras, in saying that man is the measure of all things, meant that all accidents are known by comparison with the accidents of man. By this I am trying to make it understood that no matter how well small bodies may be depicted in a painting, they will appear either large or small by comparison with what is painted there. . . ."[17]

The example of the Cyclops and the satyrs follows this passage, and then the first steps of the *costruzione legittima:* the scaling of the picture by means of a module which represents one-third the height of a man. What Alberti had seen in the *measure* of Protagoras was a *standard,* a "measure" by which the painter could find and reproduce the ratios of the scene he wanted to depict! Reading the classic statement of ancient subjectivism mathematically, he had drawn from it, wonderful as it may seem, a directive for establishing the objectivity of the perspectival picture.

For scaling is what gave the perspectival picture its "truth." It was the proportional similarity between the ratios of a possible visual image and those of its picture which made the Renaissance picture *pari alle vere,* overcoming all differences of a qualitative kind or of actual size: "if the sky, the stars, the sea, mountains, and all bodies should be . . . reduced by half, nothing would appear to be diminished in any part."[18] From the standpoint of this orientation of thought, the laws by which the ratios of things are found and reproduced assumed the

17. *Della pitt.,* p. 69.
18. *Ibid.,* p. 68.

status of a new ground. The rules of perspective, which set up the *analogia* between the visual image and its picture, came to constitute the objective "being" in what was now explicitly accepted as a shifting "becoming" of appearances. They formed new, intelligible absolutes in the relativity of perceptual experience.

This kind of objectivity the Flemish painters could not realize. They continued to attribute to perceptual objects a certain invariable being, a fixed and firm reality which perspective dissolved for Renaissance art. Perspective bound the visual qualities of things to subjective acts of seeing and evaluating; but with its appreciation of the subject, of the subject who not only "sees," but in seeing takes the measure of things, the classical attitude of objective idealism emerged in painting. Perspectival art restored and expressed the theoretical outlook in which objectivity is attributed, not to perceptual experience, but to the abstract, general rules which reason discovers in it, those "first principles" which man discerns "in Nature."[19]

On the reverse of a portrait medallion of Alberti which Matteo de' Pasti did in the late 1440's (fig. 21), there are two motifs: a laurel wreath enclosing the motto of Alberti's invincible humanism, *Quid tum?* (What next?), and the hieroglyph of a winged eye that also appeared as Alberti's emblem on the earlier medallion of the Frontispiece which he executed himself. I think it is not too fanciful to take the winged eye as Alberti's symbol of this quasi-divine act of "rational seeing," a mode of imaginative vision which came to encompass all his aesthetic ideas in its gaze. The ring of laurel is the classical sign of the honor and distinction won by human deeds; the eye, associated with the Divine in the authoritative fourth-century *Hieroglyphica,* is in Alberti's own explanation,

21. *Matteo de' Pasti,
portrait medallion of Alberti,
reverse, 1446–50. From Hill,* A Corpus
of Italian Medals, *vol. 2 (London:
British Museum, 1930).*

19. Thus Alberti proposed to set down "the art of painting from its first principles in Nature." *Ibid.,* p. 55.

more powerful than anything else, swifter, and more worthy. It is the first, chief, king; it is like a god of human parts.[20]

"Rational Seeing" and "Renaissance"

All the theoretical ideas and technical devices which Alberti brought to Renaissance artistic practice served to further the revival of the classical aesthetic outlook. He, however, intended them as instruments for grasping and reproducing the appearances of the natural world. His writings on painting and sculpture are far more empirical than antiquarian in nature. Their leading ideas have a classical ring, and they promoted the classical artistic "renaissance," but they derive from ancient science just as much as they do from ancient art.

Graeco-Roman art did not furnish any models for painter's perspective, but the "natural-mathematical" principles which Alberti took as the "roots" of painting, while new to art, were hardly new to scientific depiction. In Ptolemy's *Geography* (c. 150 A.D.), the classic work of ancient cartography, the task of geography was defined as "a survey of the earth in its just proportions." Ptolemy set down the geographical knowledge of his day in coordinate tables, and his maps showed the arrangement of the points of a ground by means of proportional projections of the coordinates of each point. Like the perspectival painter, the geographer measured the horizontal and vertical distances of each point from fixed points of origin, and he plotted these distances on a reduced scale so as to represent "the exact position of any particular place, and the positions of the various countries, how they are situated in regard to one another, how situated as regards the whole."[21]

The resemblances between a scientific map and Alberti's conception of the picture are neither superficial nor coincidental.[22] Ptolemy himself had seen how

20. "Anuli," *Opera inedita,* p. 229. See Renée Watkins on "L. B. Alberti's Emblem, the Winged Eye, and his Name, Leo," *Mitteilungen des Kunsthistorischen Institutes in Florenz,* 9 (1960): 256–58. Edgar Wind saw in the winged eye a "union of supreme insight and supreme power," a meaning which an earlier version of Alberti's emblem, a falcon, conveyed. However, he also takes the Divine Eye and *Quid tum* as a possible *Dies Irae* threat, an interpretation which would seem to be ruled out by Alberti's own words on the eye. *Pagan Mysteries in the Renaissance,* pp. 186–88.

21. *Geography,* 1: 1, 19.

22. I am indebted to the late Milton Offutt, Professor of History at The City College of New York, for his suggestion that Alberti's system of perspective and his reticulated net might have had their systematic origins in the projective science of ancient geography. Dagobert Frey described the general logical relations among perspective, trigonometry, and cartography in the Renaissance. *Gothik und Renaissance,* pp. 19–30. What I hope to show are some of the specific connections, for Alberti actually applied techniques and instruments used in surveying and mapping to painting and sculpture.

Jean-Gabriel Lemoine links Brunelleschi's work in perspective to Ptolemy's *Geography* in "Brunelleschi et Ptolemée, les origines geographiques de la 'boite d'optique,' " *Gazette*

the idea of proportionality applied to both geography and painting: "As in an entire painting," he wrote, "we [geographers and chorographers] must first put in the larger features, and afterward those detailed features which portraits and pictures may require, giving them proportion in relation to one another so that their correct measure . . . can be seen by examining them."[23] But where Ptolemy's comparison between a picture and a map was a loose one, Alberti transformed the relation into a strict, technical connection.

There is no question about his familiarity with Ptolemy's *Geography* and its principles. His own "little geography" of the city of Rome owes its literary and its scientific form to this classical exemplar. Alberti probably began the studies that were to issue in his *Descriptio urbis Romae*[24] during his first stay in Rome in 1432, which would be some twenty-five years after Ptolemy's work had begun

---

des Beaux-Arts (1958) : 281–96. Lemoine states that the conic projection of Ptolemy's world map is the source of the conic projection of perspective. Unfortunately, he does not demonstrate the relation, if any, between Ptolemy and Brunelleschi's "discovery" of perspective; he merely points out that Ptolemy's projection posits a fixed vantage point for a "celestial observer" who sees this view of the earth, and that Brunelleschi's first panel likewise fixed the vantage point of the observer. The bond between the two is supplied by the purely speculative idea that Brunelleschi, inspired by Ptolemy's map, may have constructed an optical box (as Alberti is known to have done) which kept the eye fixed and determined the angle of vision, and this then led him to the construction of his panels. There may be something to these suppositions, since Brunelleschi was a close friend of the geographer, Paolo Toscanelli, and could have learned about Ptolemy through him. However, Brunelleschi's panels can be explained without any dependence upon Ptolemy. I find that the debt to Ptolemy becomes evident only when we reach Alberti. In fact, I am inclined to believe that it was precisely Alberti's understanding of surveying and mapping that enabled him to advance the "science" of perspective beyond the point where Brunelleschi left it.

    23. *Geography,* 1 : 1.

    24. *Op. ined.,* pp. 36–46. Mancini believed that Alberti wrote the *Descriptio urbis Romae* between 1432 and 1434, while he was in Rome as a newly appointed secretary in the papal chancery. *Ibid.,* p. 36, n. 1. More recently, O. Lehmann-Brockhaus pointed out that it cannot be dated earlier than the 1440's, for one of the churches named in the *Descriptio* had not yet been constructed in the 1430's. "Albertis 'Descriptio urbis Romae,' " *Kunstchronik,* 13 (1960) : 345–48. If this fact cannot be accounted for in any other way, as, for example, later additions to the mss., the work would have to be dated after 1443 which is when Alberti returned to Rome with the papal court. I am certain that it was written before the early 1450's, because Alberti had developed a somewhat different and technically superior method of surveying and mapping by then which he described in *Ludi matematici.*

    His knowledge of surveying and mapping still goes back to the early 1430's, however. Because of the projective techniques incorporated in *Della pittura,* I am inclined to retain Mancini's date, at least for the inception of the *Descriptio.* If it should turn out that *Della statua* belongs to the same period as *Della pittura,* the fact that Alberti uses in it the surveying instrument of the *Descriptio* would indicate that he had indeed done some actual surveying and might even have begun to compile his tables of measurements during his first stay in Rome.

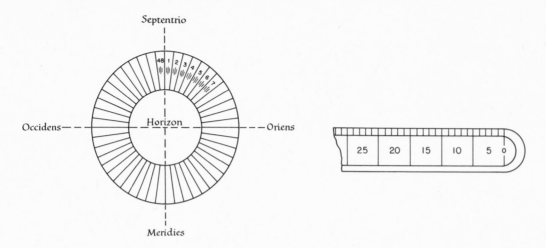

Septentrio

Horizon

Occidens — — — — — — — Oriens

Meridies

25 20 15 10 5 0

22. *Alberti's Horizon and Radius*

to circulate in Jacopo Angeli della Scarperia's new Latin translation from the original Greek. Ptolemy's *Geography* opens with a description of the instruments and methods used to construct a scientific map; Alberti was to do the same in his little treatise, briefly describing a way to survey the city of Rome and draw an accurate map of it. Ptolemy's written section is followed by coordinate tables; Alberti has coordinate tables too, giving measures which he himself took of the angles and curves of the walls of Rome, the course of the Tiber, and the positions of various buildings. (There is a further, curious coincidence which has left historians wondering in both cases whether the geographers actually drew maps in accordance with their tables and appended them to the original manuscripts, the way maps were generally appended to the various copies of Ptolemy's work; for if Alberti did draw a map, it has not survived.)

The description Alberti gives of his method shows that he did not make use of Ptolemy's rectilinear coordinates; but his map was to be drawn to scale, thus he applied the geometric principle of the Ptolemaic system of graduation in another form. He first measured the circuit of the medieval walls which surrounded Rome, then he measured the distances from the gateways in the wall to the Capitol at the center of the city. These were the actual magnitudes which would be represented proportionally on the map. Then, taking a convenient position at the Capitol, he determined the *distance* and *direction* of each object of note from this vantage point.

To measure the direction (or bearing) of objects from the Capitol, Alberti used a calibrated disk (fig. 22). He made the diameter of the disk, or "Horizon," as he called it, equal to the diameter of the circular map he intended to draw. He marked off its perimeter into forty-eight degrees (*gradus*) and subdivided each degree into four minutes (*minuta*). From the center of the disk, he pivoted a ruler called the "Radius," which meant at that time "ray" or line of sight, not semi-diameter, although Alberti made his radius a semi-diameter in length. He divided the radius, which was to sweep through the units on the perimeter of the disk, into fifty degrees (although the Horizon degrees were not multiples of them), and again he subdivided these degrees into minutes.

Standing at the Capitol with the disk held fixed and flat (i.e., parallel with the horizon), and its first-degree unit pointing north, Alberti took sightings of the things he wanted to "measure." He walked around the stationary disk until his line of sight, level with the disk, crossed its center and struck a prominent monument or landmark. Then he rotated the radius from one on the Horizon (at due north) until it lined up with his line of sight. The unit on the perimeter of the Horizon on which the radius stopped (and across which his line of sight ran to the object) gave him the *horizon degree and minute* of the object which he wrote down; and so he proceded, compiling a table of such measurements.

The distance of the object from the Capitol he probably measured by pacing. He tells us only that this "number" must also be found, but he does say that the *gradus* of the radius is proportional to a foot. Since the fifty degrees on the radial arm of the Horizon represent the maximum actual distance from the Capitol to the wall, the number of feet he paced from the Capitol to the object would give him the object's *radius degree and minute*. He set down these figures in a separate column, until each of the points of his ground had a radius and a Horizon number.

To draw the map, Alberti simply placed the Horizon over the drawing surface, letting the center of the Horizon and drawing stand for the Capitol. Then he plotted by means of his coordinate tables and the units on the surveying instrument the course of the walls of Rome, the course of the Tiber, and the positions of the major churches and monuments (fig. 23). Had he adopted Ptolemy's network of parallels and meridians, he would have had to take two sets of actual measures by pacing. His method, which amounts for all practical purposes to a system of polar coordinates, let him take one set of measures by sightings and still reach the same end that Ptolemy arrived at by the technique of rectilinear coordinates.[25] The map drawn according to Alberti's directions would show the city of Rome "in its just proportions," for like Ptolemy's maps, it was a geometric picture of an empirically measured ground.

When he came to Florence in 1434, it was this cartographic ideal that

25. Alberti could not make use of all the advantages of a polar coordinate system because no angles other than the standard Euclidean ones (i.e., 30, 45, 60, and 90 degrees, and their "proper fractions") could as yet be mathematically treated or plotted. His degrees on the Horizon were derived from the subdivisions of a 90-degree angle, and the minutes of these angles would yield only rough approximations when applied. In cases where large land areas (and hence large arcs) were involved, they would give rise to considerable errors. For the relatively small area of Rome, however, this system had a great advantage. The Horizon and radius units form one set of determinants, the relation between the Capitol and any point of the ground with respect to distance and direction; thus this system was much more practical than the rectilinear coordinate system, requiring only half as many actual measurements by pacing.

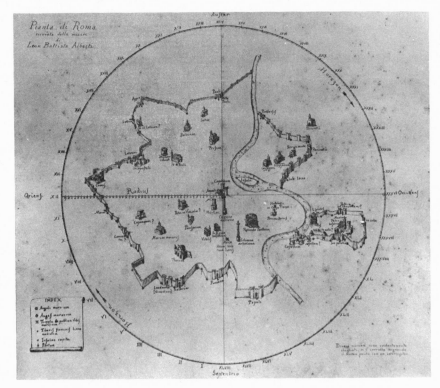

23. *Alberti's plan of Rome,*
reconstructed by D. Gnoli and A.
Capannari, 1884.
South is at the top of the picture.
From Le piante di Roma, *ed. A. Pietro*
Frutaz (Rome: Istituto di Studi Romani,
1962).

Alberti introduced into painting and sculpture. All the technical devices he developed for these arts had their source in the seminal idea of proportional depiction, or *analogia.* Taking up Brunelleschi's notion of the picture plane as a section of the cone of sight, he developed the system of perspectival projection along lines which closely followed the precedent of geometric surveying and mapping. We have already seen how he relied upon surveying practice to arrive at the rules of projection, but the scaled survey map of ancient cartography was just as essential to the perspectival picture. It is the intellectual ancestor of the scaled checkerboard pavement of Alberti's *costruzione legittima.* The Ptolemaic network of parallels and meridians (which Alberti had not used in his map of Rome) was the model that led him to transform the traditional tiled floor of trecento painting into a new kind of grid, a grid that could be used as a coordinate system by which to determine relative measures, regardless of absolute size and distance. Alberti was being quite literal when he called the squares of his pavement "parallels" and told the painter to find by means of these parallels the "latitude" and "longitude" of the surfaces he wanted to depict.[26]

26. *Della pitt.,* p. 86. "Principio comincio dai fondamenti, pongo la larghezza et la lunghezza de muri nei suoi paralleli. . . . Queste adunque metto inanzi l'altre, descrivendo loro latitudine et longitudine in quelli paraleli del pavimento."

The reticulated net or *velo* which he described as an aid for painting was a cognate device, used by painters ever since the Renaissance to help them "see" and reproduce things "in their just proportions." Looking through the net, the painter "copies" the object that appears within its parallels by sketching it in the parallels of a proportional grid (like the proportional grid that is drawn on a map); and by inscribing such a grid on a panel or wall, he can reduce or enlarge his sketch as he transfers it. This procedure is probably what Vasari was referring to when he credited Alberti with inventing an instrument for "enlarging and diminishing things."[27] Although the use of a network of squares to transfer designs goes back to Egyptian sculpture, if not further, Alberti was apparently the first, or one of the first, to use the *velo* for making a scaled picture. Moreover, he made the reticulated net stand for a section through the cone of sight; the painter who used it according to his directions "saw" how three-dimensional objects appeared upon its plane surface, and this appearance is what he transferred to his panel (or canvas) or wall by means of the parallels of the net and corresponding parallels drawn over the surface of his panel or fresco area. Thus Alberti turned the network of the *velo* into a plane of projection, using it as an instrument to bring about the perspectival *analogia* between visual image and picture.

The scientific idea of a geometric copy which the map and the perspectival picture embody also underlies Alberti's theory of the sculptural imitation of nature. Even in his book on painting, the idea of *analogia* seemed to be best exemplified by two bodies with the same proportions. After giving the geometric definition of proportionality in terms of similar triangles, he used the following example so that the reader might "understand the definition better":

> A small man is proportional to a large one when the proportions between the palm and the foot, and the foot in relation to other parts of the body, are the same, as they were in Evander and in Hercules, who was considered to be the largest of men. Nor would the proportions be different in Hercules

27. "L'anno poi 1457, che fu trovato l'utilissimo modo di stampare i libri da Giovanni Guittembergh Germano, trovò Leon Batista a quella similitudine per via d'uno strumento, il modo di lucidare le prospettive naturali, e diminuire le figure: et il modo parimente da potere ridurre le cose piccole in maggior forma, et ringrandirle." "Leon Battista Alberti," *Vite Cinque Annotate da Girolamo Mancini,* p. 32. Vasari claims Alberti made this "discovery" in 1457, but I believe he says so only to strengthen the comparison he is making between printing and Alberti's method of duplication.
  The use of a grid for transferring sketches seems not to have been known in the Middle Ages. In the thirteenth century *Sketchbook of Villard de Honnecourt,* a front face is shown within a network of squares, but it appears that Villard neither used nor recommended the network for transferring a design. See Paul Frankle on this point, *The Gothic: Literary Sources and Interpretations through Eight Centuries,* pp. 35–55.
  It is a surprising fact, but the idea of proportional reproduction by scaling seems to have no role in architectural models, pictorial sketches or cartoons, or in surveying and mapping until the fifteenth century revival of this practice.

and in Antaeus the giant, where one member is joined to the other with the same rule and ratio from the hand to the forearm, from the forearm to the head, and so on through each of the members.[28]

When he came to develop the principles and rules of sculpture in *Della statua,*[29] a little treatise on this art, this conception of the body as a proportional structure was the model Alberti had in mind. Once again he applied to art notions which systematically belong to geometric mapping, and this time he made use of the very instruments with which he had surveyed and mapped the city of Rome.

The two "rules" which he set forth for sculpture are not rules in the commonly accepted sense of the word, but are rather these instruments, and certain others, and instruction for their use. Like the rules of perspective (and of mapping), however, they did "fix" a set of ratios which the artist (like the

28. *Della pitt.,* pp. 65–66.
29. *Op. volg.,* 4: 163–86. Like *Della pittura, Della statua* is known in a Latin and a vernacular version. There are many editions of the Italian version, but they all derive from the text Bartoli published in the 1568 *Opuscoli morali.* The Latin is available in Hubert Janitschek's "Leon Battista Alberti's Kleinere Kunsttheoretische Schriften," *Quellenschriften für Kunstgeschichte,* 11.

There has been some controversy over the vernacular version, as to whether it is Alberti's or a translation made by Bartoli. Mancini believed that the vernacular was not only an original version, but that it preceded the Latin one. *Vita di Leon Battista Alberti,* p. 122. The various manuscripts and editions, and the arguments about them, are summed up in Paul-Henri Michel, *Un idéal humain au XVe siècle: La pensée de L. B. Alberti,* pp. 20–21. Michel agreed with Mancini, largely because *Della statua* was addressed to sculptors to whom Latin was generally unknown. The fact that there are no extant vernacular manuscripts weakens this position, however. I expect that Cecil Grayson will settle this issue when he publishes his forthcoming critical edition of the work. Meanwhile, see Giorgio Flaccavento's argument that the vernacular is a Bartoli "vulgarization." "Per una moderna traduzione del 'De Statua' di L. B. Alberti," *Cronache di Archeologia e Storia dell'arte,* 1 (1962): 50–59.

Della statua was not dated. Mancini set the date around 1435, about the same time, or even earlier than, the composition of *Della pittura. Vita,* pp. 122–25. One Latin manuscript contains a letter of dedication of 1464 to the Bishop of Aleria which led Janitschek to date the work around 1464. "L. B. A.'s Kleinere Kunsttheoretische Schriften," pp. xxxiif. Mancini believed that Alberti sent a Latin copy of the work to the bishop at this time for corrections (as the letter requests), not because he had just written it, but because he now wanted to have it published along with *De pictura* and *Elementa picturae.*

As Giorgio Flaccavento has pointed out, we cannot presuppose, as Mancini did, the existence of an earlier vernacular version, for none has been found. He argues for the 1464 date. "Sulla data del 'De Statua' di Leon Battista Alberti," *Commentari* 16, n.s., fasc. 3–4 (1965): 216–21.

On independent grounds, I also believe that *Della statua* is later than *Della pittura.* For one thing, it is not mentioned in the list of works given by Alberti's biographer around 1437 in the *Vita anonyma.* Also, the anthropometry suggested in *Della pittura* is fully developed in *Della statua,* to the point where the latter work corrects the former as to which part of the body should be used as the module. One consideration makes me

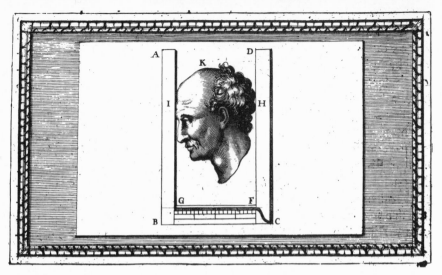

24. *The squares of Alberti's* misura,
From Della statua, *Paris edition, 1651.*

geographer) could transpose to his work. The first "rule" Alberti called the
misura, measure.[30] By means of the *misura,* the artist was to bring about a
quantitative "correspondence" among all the parts of the body to be sculptured.
That is, taking the body as the customary and unquestioned object of sculptural
"imitation," Alberti again selected the relative measures among its parts as the
basis of representation. The *misura* was the first step in this "proportional
representation": a measurement of the dimensions of the parts of the body in
terms of the length of the whole.

To find these ratios, he used two squares and a large ruler (a modification of
the surveyor's rod?). He made the ruler as long as the height of his live or
sculptured model and divided it into six equal parts which formed the "feet" of an
(apparently original) *exempeda,* or "six-foot," system of measurement. He
divided each "foot" into ten "inches," and each "inch" into ten "minutes"; and
with this ruler, he measured the length of the various parts of the body. For the
dimensions of width and breadth, he used the two squares, graduated in the
same way (fig. 24).

The ruler of the *misura* "gave the rule to the whole," as Alberti said. All the
parts of the body were measured in terms of its "foot," much as all the magnitudes
in the perspectival picture were measured in terms of the *braccio* or arm length.
Since the foot of the ruler was one-sixth the height of the body, each part of the

---

hesitant about the 1464 date, however, and that is the scant and rudimentary reflections
on the nature of beauty in *Della statua* by comparison with the highly developed aesthetic
theory contained in *De re aedificatoria,* c. 1452. It could be that Alberti left his aesthetic
ideas undeveloped here precisely because he had worked them out fully in *De re
aedificatoria*—or that he did his work on sculpture not too long after he completed the
one on painting, and that the book on architecture is the final one in this series.

A broader question which needs investigation is the use artists made of *Della statua.*

30. "Della statua," *Op. volg.,* 4: 170–74.

body was thereby related to the whole as a measureable part or proportion of it; and since the parts of the body were related to each other by this module, the relations among them could be expressed as ratios. To render a faithful likeness of his model, the sculptor (like the painter and the cartographer) had only to keep the ratios constant among the body's parts: "If you make a statue of ten braccia, make your ruler [i.e., a second ruler, one for representing rather than for taking measures] ten *braccia* long, and divide it into six equal parts which will correspond to each other as the parts of the original ruler corresponded among themselves."[31]

The second "rule" of sculpture Alberti called the "determination of bounds" *(porre de' termini)*, and this is where he placed his Horizon and radius in the artist's hands. Used in conjunction with the *misura,* the *porre de' termini* was to help the sculptor learn "the proportion that each of the parts of the members [of the body] bears to the length of the body, the proportions and correspondences they have among themselves, *and how these vary or become different.*"[32] That is, in addition to the simple measurement of proportions, the relation between changes in the proportions of the body and organic movement was here subjected to rule; and to this end, Alberti ingeniously transformed his surveying disk into an instrument he called a "Definer."

The definer consisted of three parts: an *orizzonte,* a *linda,* and a plumb line (fig. 25). The *orizzonte* was a disk like the surveyor's Horizon, now three "feet" in diameter (measured by the "foot" of the ruler of the *misura*) and divided into "inch" and minute units around its perimeter. (The problem of relating the units of the diameter of his disk to those on its perimeter may well be what drove Alberti to his efforts to square the circle.[33]) The *linda,* formerly the radius of the surveying disk, was now equal in length to the diameter of the disk (in fig. 25 it is about one and a half times the diameter of the disk), and it was graduated by the "inches" and minutes of the ruler. It pivoted from the center of the disk as before, rotating and sweeping through all the units on its perimeter; and at the same time, it extended a "foot" and a half (or more, as in the figure) beyond the disk, thus becoming a sort of ruler from which the plumb line(s) could hang, and along the units of which one or more plumb lines could be moved back and forth.

To measure the proportions of the parts of the body as it assumed any given pose, Alberti put the *orizzonte* level on the head of his model, "fastening it there," so that the entire disk could revolve about its center (how he did this on a live model he neglected to say). He placed the *linda* in the first unit of the disk, then turned the disk around until the plumb line, dropping from one of the units of the *linda,* struck a prominent part of the body, say the finger of an outstretched hand. This would give him an *orizzonte* measure of 1, a *linda*

31. *Ibid.,* pp. 168–69.
32. *Ibid.,* p. 185. This "rule" is described on pp. 174–80.
33. "De lunularum quadratura," *Op. ined.,* pp. 305–7.

measure of, let us say, 5.3, and a measure of 46.2 on the plumb line from the ground up to the finger as measured by the ruler of the *misura*.

To find, now, the angle of the left elbow, he kept the disk stationary and moved the *linda* until the plumb line touched the elbow. Then he noted, again in tables, (a) through how many *orizzonte* units the *linda* had to move from its first position, (b) how far out on the *linda* the plumb line had to hang in order to touch the elbow, and (c) how high the elbow was above the pavement. And so he proceeded, measuring the distances among the parts of the body in a particular pose, then changing the pose and measuring them again, and so forth.

Alberti boasted that he could determine the contours and proportions of the parts of the body with such accuracy by these two "rules," that if "a statue by Phidias should be covered with earth or clay," he would know "exactly where to drill to find the pupil of the eye, the thumb, etc." But helpful as they must have been for the sculptor who wanted to measure the proportions of ancient

25. *Alberti's Definer.*
From Della statua, *Paris edition, 1651*

statues (as Donatello had been doing), the primary objective of Alberti's "rules" was to "copy Nature." They led the sculptor to "set down in numbers" the dimensions of the parts of the body in its diverse and changing attitudes, thereby fastening his attention upon its organic form. Neither Italo-Byzantine nor Flemish art had been attentive to anatomy, but when Alberti urged the artist to make his figures "completely natural, like the real bodies made by Nature,"[34] it was an organic, anatomical naturalism that he had in mind. By measuring the proportions among the parts of the body, the Renaissance artists were necessarily led to consider the shapes and functions of its vital parts. They had to distinguish the body's various "members and their parts," to "learn the number of the bones and muscles, and the protrusions of the sinews," as Alberti advised;[35] and they had to understand the unifying relations among the parts of the body as well, so as to capture the proportional changes that occur with movement and muscular effort.

The classicism of Alberti's "rules" is to be found in their restoration of the practice of anthropometry, for this is what originally gave the sculptured form its classical flexibility and anatomical naturalism. Although his method of measuring by means of the definer was a novel extension of his surveying and mapping procedure, the idea itself was an ancient one. Anthropometry was the basis of Graeco-Roman sculptural practice and its theory of proportions.[36] Alberti knew of this tradition from Vitruvius, but it goes back at least to Polyclitus and perhaps to the Pythagoreans. From the classical Greek period until late antiquity, anthropometry dominated the art of sculpture. Then, however, the mathematically inspired conception of the body weakened and disappeared. As mathematical and empirical concerns were eclipsed by religious and metaphysical ones, the classical ideas of organic form and proportion gave way to systems of linear design in which the representation of the body came to incorporate various "symbolic figures."

34. "Della statua," p. 165.

35. *Ibid.,* p. 185: "Gioverà ancor molto il sapere il numero delle ossa e de' muscoli, e gli aggetti dei nervi." In *Della pittura,* Alberti had already advised the painter to notice how a man uses his body to support his head in various postures. When he rests on one foot, this foot is placed perpendicularly under the head like the base of a column; in an erect pose, the face generally faces the same direction as the feet. He pointed out how the face cannot be turned past a point where the chin touches the shoulder, and so forth; *ibid.,* p. 96. These observations on the position of the parts of the body in its various attitudes he then subjected to the "rule" of the *porre de' termini* in *Della statua.*

36. Panofsky's "The History of the Theory of Human Proportions," in *Meaning in the Visual Arts* is the fundamental work on this subject, just as his "Die Perspektive als 'Symbolische Form' " is the pioneer work on the history of perspective. According to Panofsky, Alberti was the first theorist to advance the system of proportions beyond medieval standards and beyond the classical system as well. His two "rules" and his *exempeda* system of mensuration are all original. Among artist-theoreticians, Leonardo and Dürer both incorporated and developed Alberti's *exempeda* system, and Francesco Giorgi described it in his speculative *Harmonia mundi totius.* The Byzantine system of proportions given below is fully described in this essay by Panofsky.

Medieval notions about the body belong to a philosophical outlook in which "correspondences" between empirical and spiritual realities are the dominant factor. Cennino Cennini restricted proportions to men, for example. Women and animals, having little or no spiritual significance, had no proportions.[37] The Byzantine system of proportions which Cennini had in mind was itself based, not upon a study of the physical body, but upon a desire to symbolize in the design of the body the "perfect" figure of the circle and the number of the Trinity. The module in this system was the face or head, described by three concentric circles centered in the root of the nose. These three circles gave the Byzantine and Italo-Byzantine artists all the "dimensions" they wanted. Singly, they constituted the bounds of the face, head, and halo; together, they determined the height of the body which was nine times the module—another "significant" number. With shape and number assuming this kind of representational task, the actual proportions and organic structure of the draped and flowing body could be virtually ignored. The only reference to anatomy in Cennini is his statement that man has a rib less than woman, having lost for all time the one out of which God created Eve.[38]

The head was the module in the Byzantine system of proportions because it was commonly regarded as the seat of mind or spirit. Alberti seems to have been moved by this consideration too, for he criticized Vitruvius in *Della pittura* for suggesting that the parts of the body be measured by the foot rather than by the "more worthy" member of the head.[39] When he actually set about measuring the dimensions of the body in *Della statua,* however, the purely functional, mathematical character of the module overcame his lingering feeling for qualitative and substantival distinctions of this sort. At this point, Alberti broke with medieval tradition and returned, in his own system of proportions, to the mathematical tradition of classical anthropometry. The "foot" of his six-foot *exempeda* system became qualitatively neutral, nothing more than an arbitrary "measure"; and Alberti's system of proportions, detached from metaphysical objectives, fastened once again upon the physical body and its empirically ascertainable dimensions.

The Form of the Individual

By extending the idea of proportional imitation to sculpture, Alberti set the theoretical study of this art upon the same naturalistic course that Donatello was following in practice. But no sooner had he worked out the "scientific" idea of *analogia* in sculpture, and this in a wholly independent way, when the classical aesthetic ideal seems to have struck him with all its original force. The Beautiful,

37. *Il libro dell'arte,* 2: 48.
38. *Ibid.,* p. 49.
39. *Della pitt.,* p. 89

Polyclitus had said, "comes about little by little through many numbers." In Alberti's terse treatise on sculpture, and arising directly out of its technical, mathematical considerations, this vision dawned anew. Almost all classical systems of proportion had issued in a canon of mean proportions, and now Alberti, like a new Polyclitus, set down in a table of "principal measurements" the Greek ideal of beauty as "congruity," an "apt" relation among the parts of a whole. In many numbers, in the proportions among the parts of the body as measured by the feet, inches, and minutes of his *exempeda* system, he sought, "that exact beauty" which Nature grants only in part to many bodies. "I want to establish," he wrote near the end of *Della statua,*

> not the particulars of this man or that one, but as far as possible, that exact beauty granted by Nature and given, as if in select portions, to many bodies. ... I have therefore chosen many bodies which are reputed to be the most beautiful by those who are knowledgeable, and I have taken the measures and proportions of all of these. Comparing and eliminating the excesses of the extremes, ... I have selected from many bodies and models those mean proportions which seem to me most praiseworthy.[40]

The empirical anthropometry of *Della statua* thus culminated in an aesthetic norm, but a norm which was in no way at variance with the avowed aim of Renaissance art "to imitate Nature." To be sure, the renaissance of the classical aesthetical ideal caused the paths of Italian and Flemish art to diverge even farther. Whereas Flemish painting sought to faithfully portray the individual as a manifold of its unique, sensible characteristics, apparently indifferent to beauty, Alberti's advice (and Leonardo's, too) was to make the figure beautiful as well as a faithful likeness, and to do so by studying the commonly acknowledged "best parts" of many models.[41] From the classical viewpoint, beauty was not identical with a non-mathematical arrangement of the sensible properties of a person; and as "congruity," it was something shared by many persons and in varying degrees. Yet Renaissance art did not sacrifice its imitation of the individual in order to attain the beauty it also sought; it did not produce standardized, general "types"

40. *Op. volg.,* 4: 180–81. Leonardo also worked out a canon of mean proportions: see Richter 1: 169–201, nos. 308–92. It is quite incorrect to hold, as Anthony Blunt does in *Artistic Theory in Italy, 1450–1600,* pp. 31–33, that Alberti's theory of proportions led to "academic uniformity" whereas Leonardo's emphasized the individual and the characteristic. In fact, Leonardo followed Alberti's theory and principles in every detail. He simply increased the amount of empirical data on human proportions by taking a greater number of measurements.

41. *Della pitt.,* p. 107. Leonardo wrote: "It seems to me to be no small charm in a painter when he gives his figures a pleasing air, and this grace ... he may acquire by study in this way: Look about you and take the best parts of many beautiful faces, of which the beauty is confirmed rather by public fame than by your own judgement; for you might be mistaken and choose faces which have some resemblance to your own." Richter, 1: 293–94, no. 587.

in painting and sculpture, despite the "truism" (Panofsky's term) "that northern Late Gothic tends to individualize where the Italian Renaissance strives for that which is exemplary or . . . for the 'ideal,' that it [Flemish art] accepts the things created by God or produced by man as they present themselves to the eye instead of searching for a universal law or principle to which they more or less successfully endeavor to conform.[42]

If this is taken to mean that the Renaissance artist turned his back upon the sensible individual in order to adhere to his abstract model, the general ideal of proportional form; that he falsified his representation of the person by "generalizing" it, then we should have to deny to the art of the Renaissance that vital concern with individuality which appears in almost every other facet of its cultural life. One of the strongest features of Renaissance culture, stamped upon almost all its intellectual movements and evolving forms of political and social life, is the new relation it established between the categories of the "individual" and the "universal," a relation which led to a profound, and distinctive appreciation of individuality.[43] Surely Renaissance painting and sculpture belong to this context too. It is difficult to see how a "Mona Lisa" or a "Colleoni" can be said to be wanting in individual features and characteristics, and the same difficulty arises when we examine Renaissance art theory from a standpoint immanent to the culture of the age. Its systematic aim (in the light of which isolated statements take on their intended meaning) in no way subordinated imitation of the individual to depiction of an ideal or general type,

---

42. *Early Netherlandish Painting,* p. 8. Panofsky himself seems to subscribe to this view on pp. 194–95, but elsewhere he has shown how the tension between nature and beauty came to be felt only in the seventeenth century as the neo-classicists were forced to define their position vis-à-vis the "realists" like Caravaggio whose "imitation" appeared to be unselective. This is when the idea of the imitation of an "ennobled nature" emerged. *Idea,* especially chaps. 5 and 6.

43. In my treatment of the Renaissance idea of the individual, I am following Ernst Cassirer's classic *Individuum und Kosmos in der Philosophie der Renaissance.* Cassirer did not deal with Alberti in particular, but he demonstrated in a brilliant and comprehensive way how all the categorial relations—the relation of the one to the many, of part and whole, subject and object, and so forth—underwent a marked and characteristic change during the Renaissance. With regard to the idea of the individual, he showed how the ideational or universal came to be regarded as immanent to the individual, thus elevating the individual to a new dignity. As he wrote elsewhere: "the relative emphasis placed on the 'universal' and on the 'particular' began to shift. In the scale of values the individual was now assuming another place and another station. . . . That an author [Montaigne] should dare to portray himself in all his peculiarities, particulars, accidents and idiosyncrasies—and that he should nevertheless claim for this portrait a *universal* significance: this is indeed something new with the Renaissance. The consideration of individuality thus acquires an entirely new value." "Some Remarks on the Question of the Originality of the Renaissance," *Journal of the History of Ideas,* 4 (1943): 49–56. This same shift of emphasis occurs in Renaissance art theory as Alberti's ideas on composition demonstrate.

as might be said, for example, of the aim of early Gothic statuary with its conventional "types" of prophets, saints, angels, virtues, and so forth. Thus John Pope-Hennessy, concerned only with Renaissance sculpture and not with the differences between it and Flemish figure construction, could write, "Alberti, in his treatise on sculpture . . . talks of the differences between one human being and the next. For Alberti the aim of sculpture was verisimilitude; . . . the statue, declares Alberti, must portray an individual. . . . Here we seem to sense the current of thought which culminates thirty years later in Pico della Mirandola's *De Hominis Dignitate*."[44]

Alberti was, in fact, the first theorist to caution the artist against working without models (*senza avere essemplo alcuno dalla natura*), and his contemporary biographer claims that he tested the worth of his own sketches by seeing if children could identify the people he had drawn. The imitative task of art, which the systems of perspective and human proportions alike presuppose, so dominated his artistic thinking that even when he distinguished the representation of "a man in general" from "a particular man," he spoke of both as imitations of the individual. The distinction he drew in *Della statua* between "general" and "particular" is instructive, for it is merely a distinction between a known individual, meant to be recognized as such, and an unknown one. In both cases, the statue was a "likeness" of a concrete individual; both "closely resemble a given man," and to both he offered his "rules" of sculptural imitation:

"The manner and method of representation in sculpture, if I understand it correctly, is of two kinds: one of these is the image . . . in which, no matter how closely it resembles a given man, it is of no concern whether it resembles Socrates rather than Plato or some other man not known to us. That is, it is enough that this work depict a man, even though one not known to us. The other kind is that of those who intend to represent not the image of a man in general but of one in particular, as for instance Caesar or Cato, appearing in a certain manner and dress, seated in the tribunal or declaiming to the people. Here the sculptor labors to imitate and express that entire manner or stance of the body or whatever it may be [that is characteristic] of some known personage."[45]

Clearly the individual is just as much the object of representation here as in Flemish art. No preference has been expressed for a general type as opposed to representing a particular individual—or, for that matter, vice versa. The peculiar interpretation of the "particular" and the "general" in this passage indicates, in fact, that Alberti entertained no such notion of a radical tension between the two. Somehow, he had managed to bypass this

44. Pope-Hennessy traces most of the distinctive characteristics of Italian quattrocento sculpture to this individualistic current. *Italian Renaissance Sculpture,* pp. 54–62.

45. *Op. volg.,* 4: 167.

ontologically conceived opposition which was central to Aristotelian-Scholastic logic and metaphysics. His little treatise on sculpture thus raises the question that is really germane to an understanding of the Renaissance "imitation" of nature and of the differences between it and the Flemish: namely, in what way was the particular (the sensible and concrete) set off from, and related to, the universal (the abstract and general) in Renaissance art on the one hand, and in Flemish art on the other? For if Flemish and Renaissance art both took the individual as the object of representation, their differences must be rooted in the different ways both schools "saw" the individual they wanted to represent. Their principles of figure construction, like their spatial principles, spring from and reveal two, distinct "modes of imaginative beholding."[46]

The new appreciation of the individual expressed in Flemish art reflects a theoretical appreciation of individuality which began to appear in the Scholastic thought of the late Middle Ages. Understanding the individual as a union of matter (the substrate of all beings) and form (the universal essence common to the species), thirteenth-century Scholastic philosophy had regarded individual differences in negative fashion, as limitations of the general form of the species which were due to the intractability of matter. (Each individual angel had therefore to be a species for Aquinas.) It is true that the individual "embodied" the universal in the Conceptual Realism of Aquinas, and that the individual being thereby achieved a dignity unknown in the thought and art of the earlier Realistic age which had placed universals in a transcendent realm of their own. But individuality or particularity per se, that is, the differences among the members of a species, played no positive role in thirteenth-century thought or art. Arising from matter, individual differences had no "place" in the scale of being of Scholastic ontology which was reserved for substantial forms; and in the Aristotelian-Scholastic theory of knowledge, in which knowledge (in the form of concepts or general ideas) is restricted to universals (such as the species), individual differences literally could not be "known."

Duns Scotus (c. 1265–1308) represents the first break with this view, and it is the Scotist notion of *haecceitas* which was to affect Flemish art.[47] Although neither a nominalist nor an empiricist himself, Scotus initiated a new tendency in Scholastic philosophy which was to issue, in the course of the fourteenth century, in a nominalistic theory of knowledge that discredited the ontological reality of universals, and in an empirical attitude which sought to derive knowledge from sensory experience. Scotus, who was a Franciscan, was not a consistent

46. Wölfflin meant by the "mode of beholding" the visual or spatial "schema," the form of imaginative seeing and representing, that characterizes an artistic period. See *Principles of Art History,* especially pp. 1–17. Wölfflin did not grant any *expressive* function to this purely formal spatial order, however. It is chiefly Frey, Panofsky, and Worringer who have sought to do this.

47. Edgar de Bruyne, *Etudes d'esthétique médiévale,* 3: 347–70; and Friedrich Ueberweg, *History of Philosophy,* 1: 452–57.

Aristotelian as the Dominican Aquinas had tried to be. For him, the individualizing principle was not matter, but form. And the individual peculiarity, the "thisness" of a being, which Scotus called the being's *haecceitas,* was not a deficiency in the realization of the universal essence (the species) of the being: it had a positive, formal existence and role. This *haecceitas* Scotus defined as an ensemble of real characteristics which truly individualize a being, marking it off from all the other members of its species. Only as a universal essence is completed by such a *haecceitas,* by an "individual nature," does the actual individual come about.

An artistic representation of Scotus' conception of "individual nature" would require precisely that fine discrimination of individual differences which Flemish art in fact gives us; and the theory of *haecceitas* also harbored a certain ideal of beauty which Flemish art reflects. Far from lacking an aesthetic ideal, Flemish art had its own (universal) norm to which its figures "more or less successfully endeavor to conform." They exemplify a beauty which Duns Scotus defined as an "exact relationship among all the qualities," by which he meant a completely determined set of values of bulk and magnitude, outline, luminosity and texture, etc. For the Beautiful, in Scotus' definition, is a manifold of perceptual qualities "which belong to this particular body here, i.e., its singular harmony among size, shape, and color."[48] Thus rather than depicting what is merely "presented to the eye" (as if that were ever possible), the Flemish painter had his own "mode of sight." The idea of *haecceitas* and its corresponding aesthetic ideal provided a rule which led him to "see" and represent the individual as a unique ensemble of sensible characteristics; they provided a model, in terms of which he construed what was presented to the eye.

Guided by these notions of beauty and *haecceitas,* Flemish art did, however, strive to compose the individual strictly by means of its perceptual "thisness"; and here we find the element of truth in the observation (the "truism") with which we began. Flemish art did seek to portray the being and the beauty of the individual (in accordance with its general norms) by means of its sensible particularity alone. But Renaissance composition, on the other hand, did *not* spring from an effort to grasp the abstract and the general. This would be the logical contrary of the Flemish objective, but since Renaissance art did not share the theoretical presuppositions of Flemish art, it could not assume such a position, or opposition. Rather than presenting a simple antithesis to the formal aims of Flemish art, Renaissance figure construction manifests an entirely different orientation.

Renaissance theory also directed the artist to imitate the individual, but in

48. "Pulchritudo non est aliqua qualitas absoluta in corpore pulchro sed est aggregatio omnium convenientium tali corpori, puta magnitudinis, figurae et coloris et aggregatio omnium respectuum qui sunt istorum ad corpus et ad se invicem." Quoted by de Bruyne, *Etudes,* 3 : 354.

its conception of the individual, the relation between the "particular" and the "general" was differently conceived. The classical system of proportions focused attention neither upon the sensible nor the intelligible per se, but upon a characteristic relation between them. The *misura* of Alberti's *Della statua* was oriented, as he himself noted, towards things which are "common and universal," things which "Nature makes innate in bodies . . . like length, breadth, and width."[49] That is, the *misura* singled out magnitudes, the mathematical kind of generality which is innate to the particular, sensible body and is expressed by the unique set of ratios that constitute its form. Conversely, the *porre de' termini* sought to describe particular, sensible changes, "the momentary variations of the members caused by new attitudes and movements of the parts of the body."[50] But these sensible changes, being numerically apprehensible, were expressed in the abstract, intelligible terms of the body's dimensions. The measures among all the "angles and lines" of the body, "their closeness and distance from each other,"— these constitute its singular form and its momentary attitude.

The classical aim of imitation which arose with anthropometry was directed, in short, at sensible, qualitative elements and innate, quantitative relations as well. Envisioned geometrically, the body was construed as a singular ensemble of intelligible relations, as a generality *in concreto;* and it is to this conception of the immanence of the general in the particular that the classical aesthetical ideal corresponds. Much as Duns Scotus' definition of beauty is bound to a particularistic idea of the individual, the idea of congruity is bound to the logical outlook of a visual geometry that "sees" abstract and intelligible relations in the sensible and particular individual. For beauty, understood as congruity, consists, the Stoics said, "not in the elements but in the harmonious proportion of the parts, the proportion of one finger to the other, of all the fingers to the rest of the hand, of the rest of the hand to the waist, of the wrist to the forearm . . . in fine, of all the parts to all others as it is written in the canon of Polyclitus."[51] As an ideal or model, the idea of congruity and the canons of proportion which sought to express it in numbers served the same purpose as did the Scotist idea of beauty: they fixed for mind and eye (but this time, for the Renaissance mind and eye) the object of the artistic imitation of nature.

Even in *Della pittura,* for example, where there are few reflections of a strictly aesthetic kind, the idea of congruity led Alberti to place a telling emphasis upon composition, upon the arrangement of the elements of the picture rather than the perfection of any single one of them. "Composition" he defined as the "rule" of painting "by which the parts of the things seen are put together in

49. *Op. volg.,* 4: 175. The *misura* gives us "certe cose più comuni e universali, le quali sono più fermamente e con più stabilità insite dalla natura ne corpi, come sono le lunghezze, le grossezze, e la larghezze delle membra."

50. *Ibid.*

51. Quoted by Panofsky, *Meaning in the Visual Arts,* p. 64. The quotation is from Galen who claims that Chrysippus held this view.

a picture";[52] and at each step in the composition, he saw the beauty of the picture *and* its fidelity to nature emerge as an apt relation among component parts. When he objected that it was not "fitting" for figures to be crammed in a building as if in a casket, or for vases to be painted standing and intact where the pictorial theme was one of battle, he was applying a criterion which was at once aesthetic and mimetic. The "rule" of composition demanded that everything be made to "correspond," each element to each and to the whole. Therefore whatever the depicted figures do had to be related to the entire *istoria* of the picture, to fill it out or point it up.[53]

Alberti saw his sculptural "rules" as an analogue of the pictorial "rule" of composition, for in *Della pittura* he treated the unification of the parts of the body as one of the three stages of composition: "I say that composition is that rule of painting whereby the parts of the thing seen are put together in a picture. The chief work of the painter is the *istoria;* bodies are part of the *istoria,* members are parts of the bodies, surfaces are parts of the members."[54] The apt arrangement of bodies in the narrative theme of the picture was a counterpart of the fitting disposition of their surfaces which Alberti regulated by the rules of perspective, and the members of the body also had their aesthetic-mimetic "rule." They were to "correspond to one Beauty," in size, function, and color.

Placed in the broader context provided by the theory of painting, the idea of the "one Beauty" of the body appears as something quite different from a generic ideal or type. If anything, the Renaissance meant just the opposite by this notion of "decorum," as the ancients called it, for it could be realized only by determining the distinctive form of the body. The aptness of the parts of the body was judged by the same criterion that Alberti applied to surfaces and to the composition of the narrative scene: namely, the proper relation of each of the parts to all the others in a unified, structural whole. For this, "a certain rule" had to be followed with respect to size. The body had to be anatomically differentiated, and one member taken as a standard by which to measure the others, "so that there will be no member which does not agree with the others in length and breadth." The members of the body were to be made commensurate with each other, in other words; and the "rule" which accomplished this distinguished the individual parts of the body at the same time as it made them

52. *Della pitt.,* p. 85.
53. *Ibid.,* pp. 91, 94.
54. Leonardo follows Alberti in this breakdown of the "parts" of painting: "The first part of painting is representation of objects in relief and their surroundings in perspective and the second essential is appropriate action and a due variety in the figures, so that the men may not all look like brothers." Richter, 1: 17–18, no. 17. Again: "I say that first you ought to learn the limbs and their mechanism, and having this knowledge, their actions should come next according to the circumstances in which they occur in man. And thirdly, compose subjects (*le storie*), the studies for which should be taken from natural actions." *Ibid.,* pp. 245–46, no. 490.

"correspond" in a single system of ratios.

The rule of composition had done something comparable for the *istoria*. As Alberti saw it, the narrative unity of the picture was achieved by, and expressed in, the diversity of its parts. When he selected Giotto's "Navicella" (St. Peter's, Rome) as a model of composition, he praised just this realization of unity in diversity: Giotto's depiction of the "eleven disciples, all moved by fear at seeing one of their companions walking over the waters," was remarkable "because here, each one expresses with his own look and gestures his own symptoms of inner tumult, so that each has his distinct movements and states of feeling."[55] So, too, with the function, kind, and color of the body's parts. Each member had to be given whatever was proper to it in the organic and dramatic intent of the whole. The members must "agree": the painter should "thrust out" the hands of a runner as well as his feet, he should make all the limbs of a dead body hang limp and lifeless, he should not paint hands that are gnarled and old on a young and lovely Helen. But all this aptness of parts, all this conformity to "one Beauty," far from diminishing the force of uniqueness, actually established and enhanced it. What was demanded by the rule of "one Beauty" was that each of the parts, and hence the whole they compose, be given its proper value.

> In the composition of the members, then, we must follow what has been said about size, function, kind, and color. Then will everything have its own dignity: it would not be fitting to dress Venus or Minerva in the rough wool cloak of a soldier, or to dress Mars or Jove in the clothes of a woman. The ancient painters took care in depicting Castor and Pollux to make them appear as brothers, but in the one to make a pugnacious nature show forth and in the other a sprightly one. They likewise took pains to make Vulcan's limp show beneath his robes, so great was their desire to express the function, kind, and value of whatever they depicted.[56]

The quest of Renaissance art for decorum, for "agreement among the parts," was, in other words, its expression of the general trend toward individuality that marked the age. Renaissance painting and sculpture sought to capture the individual just as much as Flemish art did, but the Renaissance artist sought the formal unity of the individual rather than its sensible particularly. The aesthetic ideal of congruity, operating as a regulative principle, held in mind a conception of the individual as a relational whole, directing him towards that unity in diversity which characterized, for him, nature's "individuals," organic forms. This

55. *Della pitt.*, p. 95. Alberti's genuine admiration for Giotto was wholly misrepresented by Schlosser: "die italienische 'Gotik' ist wie weggewischt (Giottos berühmte Navicella an S. Peter ist nur ein überkommenes rhetorisches Schulbeispiel) ..." "Ein Künstlerproblem der Renaissance: L. B. Alberti," *Akademie der Wissenschaften in Wien, Sitzungberichte*, 210, vol. 2. This remark is typical of the arbitrary pronouncements of the entire article.

56. *Della pitt.*, pp. 90–91.

is why there was no opposition between nature and beauty in the classical view of the body: the idea of congruity and canons of proportion caught and expressed the very nature of organicity for the Renaissance. The idea of proportional form, arising from the representation of the body as a structure of ratios, was the symbol and model of vital structure.[57] It conveyed an idea of the individual as a systematic rather than an aggregate whole, a unity in which the parts can never add up to the whole but are rather assigned their relative places and functions by the "rule" of the whole.

How, then, could a faithful depiction of sensible qualities alone constitute a true "imitation" of the body for Renaissance art? Along with the demand for sensible accuracy, the classical aesthetic ideal set up a demand for a "regular" arrangement of the parts of the body as an expression of the body's vital "rule." It never led any artist to make all bodies look alike (save as exemplifications of this particular style), and Alberti and Leonardo explicitly cautioned the artist against this kind of uniformity. But the Renaissance idea of beauty did teach the artist to make each part of a living form manifest a law of the whole. He who sees in the "best parts" of many beautiful bodies this lawful kind of beauty, "he will make his hand so skilled that whatever he does will seem to be drawn from Nature." Understandably, then, Alberti himself could point out that no artfully drawn figure can compete with one drawn from life; it lacks the beauty of a portrait figure because it lacks its vital force. There is no contradiction between this statement and his canon of proportions, any more than there is a contradiction in the fact that the glorious human beings in Raphael's "School of Athens" should bear the features of his associates and friends (fig. 16)—his

57. Wölfflin characterized the organicity of classic art by his formal category of "multiple unity": "The figures are developed as absolutely independent parts, and yet so work together that each seems governed by the whole. That is precisely renaissance articulation." And again, describing what "multiple unity" means: "only where the single detail seems a necessary part of the whole do we speak of organic articulation, and only where the component part, bound up in the whole, is still felt as an independently functioning member, has the notion of freedom and independence a sense." *Principles of Art History,* pp. 157, 161.

Wölfflin used several interrelated "categories" to describe the spatial features of classic art. The most convincing reason why the one of multiple unity should become particularly evident in sculpture is, I believe, offered by Susanne K. Langer's theory of the sculptural "illusion": "The source of this illusion . . . is the fundamental principle of sculptural volume: the semblance of organism. In the literature of sculpture, more than anywhere else, one meets with reference to 'inevitable form,' 'necessary form,' and 'inviolable form.' But what do these expressions mean? Nothing but vital function. . . .

"There is nothing actually organic about a work of sculpture. Even carved wood is dead matter. Only its form is the form of life, and the space it makes visible is vitalized as it would be by organic activity at its center. It is *virtual kinetic volume,* created by—and with—the semblance of living form." *Feeling and Form,* pp. 88–89.

In Renaissance sculpture, this semblance of "living form" was created chiefly by the proportionality of the figure.

Plato at the center, pointing toward the Sublime, Leonardolike in his features and flowing beard; the bald Euclid in the right foreground drawing with the compass, his friend and kinsman, Bramante; and Raphael himself looks directly at us (as Alberti would have wished) from the far right of the group surrounding Bramante. To capture the harmonious form of the individual: this was the imitation of nature as nature had come to be conceived.

"Let us always take from Nature what we wish to paint," Alberti could therefore write, "and we will always fashion the most beautiful things."[58]

58. *Della pitt.*, pp. 107–8: "Ma per non perdere studio et faticha si vuole fuggire quella consuetudine d'alcuni sciocchi i quali, presuntuosi di suo ingegnio, senza avere essemplo alcuno dalla natura quale con occhi o mente seguano, studiano da sé ad sé acquistare lode di dipigniere. Questi non imparno dipigniere bene ma assuefanno sé a suoi errori. Fuggie l'ingegni non periti quella idea delle bellezze quale i bene exercitatissimi appena discernono. Zeusis, prestantissimo et fra li altri exercitatissimo pittore, per fare una tavola qual publico pose nel tempio di Lucina adpresso de Crotoniati, non fidandosi pazzamente quanto oggi ciascuno pictore del suo ingenio ma perché pensava non potere in uno solo corpo trovare quante bellezze elli ricercava, perché dalla natura non erano ad uno solo date, pertanto di tutta la ioventú di quella terra elesse cinque fanciulle, le più belle, per torre da queste qualunque bellezza lodata in una femmina. Savio pictore, se conobbe che ad i pittori, ove loro sia niuno exemplo della natura quale elli seguitino ma pure vogliono con suoi ingegni giugniere le lode della bellezza, ivi facile loro adverrà che non quale cercano bellezza con tanta faticha troveranno ma certo piglieranno sue pratiche non buone, quali poi ben volendo mai potranno lassare; ma chi da essa natura s'auserá prendere qualunque facci cosa, costui renderá sua mano si exercitata che sempre qualunque cosa fará, parrá tratta dal naturale. Qual cosa quanto sia dal pittore a ricercarla si puo intendere ove, poiché in una storia sará uno viso di qualche conosciuto et degnio huomo, bene che ivi sieno altre figure di arte molto più che perfette et grate, pure quel viso conosciuto ad ad sé imprima trarrà tutti li occhi di cha la storia raguardi: tanto si vede in sé tiene forza ciò che sia ritratto dalla natura. Per questo sempre ciò che vorremo dipigniere piglieremo dalla natura e sempre torremo le cose più belle."

3
Art, the Mirror of Nature

In 1443, Alberti returned to Rome with the papal court. He had been moving
about with the harassed and unsettled Pope Eugenius IV since 1434, from Rome
to Florence, Bologna, Ferrara, and again to Florence as the long Church Council
of Ferrara–Florence wore on. Now he took up what turned out to be a rather
permanent residence in Rome, and the papal city began to act upon his artistic
imagination as Florence had some nine years earlier. In Florence he had
responded to the vigor and excitement of a new beginning; Rome affected him
by its sad and evident air of decline. The city that had housed the gods, the rulers,
and the people of a mighty civilization had become a rude and semi-lawless
place, and Alberti, like so many before and since, brooded over the spectacle
of its ruins.

Rome's visible mortality, and the sense of ineluctible passage which it
induced, was all the more poignant for him who was keenly aware that its
neglected, crumbling works were the remains of a more civilized, sophisticated
age: "from these works, temples and theatres, as from the most skillful masters, a
great deal was to be learned; but these I saw, and saw with tears, mouldering
away daily."[1] When Tommaso Parentucelli, a fellow humanist and a friend
since their university days, mounted the papal throne in 1447 as Nicholas V,
Alberti and the Pope together resolved to halt this mindless wear of time.
Captivated by a grandiose and intensely human dream, they made the impossible
resolve to reverse its process,—a resolution that turned Alberti toward the
practice and theory of architecture and made of Nicholas V the first papal patron
of a renascent Rome.[2]

1. *De re aedificatoria libb. X,* bk. 6, chap. 1. (The book and chapter numbers are
from the 1512 Paris edition, *Libri de re aedificatoria decem.*) Valerio Mariani gives an
interesting description of the role of Rome in Alberti's thought, particularly in shaping his
architectural ideas, in *Incontri con Roma nel Rinascimento. L. B. Alberti, Donatello,
A. Mantegna, Raffaello,* pp. 1–22.

2. Nicholas V's construction program was described by his fifteenth-century

With Alberti as his adviser, Nicholas V undertook the first of the grand projects which were ultimately to restore the visual majesty of the Eternal City. Alberti drew plans for churches which the Pope wanted to have rebuilt, and he and Nicholas V initiated the reconstruction of St. Peter's and the Vatican Palace, a program that was to engage the genius of the greatest artists of the Renaissance. Alberti even intended to rebuild an entire section of the city, something that had not been envisioned since the decline of the Empire. His bold design for a new Borgo Leonino, the quarter that runs from St. Peter's to the Castel Sant'Angelo, is significant as one of the earliest examples of the geometric spatial plans of the Renaissance. In addition to the customary walls of fortification which were to be built around the quarter, Alberti wanted to have a plaza at both ends of the long, rectangular area. The two plazas were to be connected by three broad avenues, and the entire scheme was to be given formal emphasis by the great obelisk which he wanted to set in the center of one of the plazas, in front of St. Peter's. Alberti's design was not carried out in its entirety, but it was a conception worthy of the impressive piazza that Bernini finally put there.

The general project of restoration also included works which involved a more strictly technical engineering skill. One was the series of attempts Alberti initiated during this period to raise a large object which was submerged in the Lake of Nemi. This task was not to be brought to a successful completion until the twentieth century, but Alberti managed, at least, to raise the sunken object high enough to reveal a prow, which showed that it was a Roman state barge.[3] With the Acqua Vergine, which he put back into working condition, he was more fortunate. The channels of this old Roman aqueduct were reopened, and Alberti guided its fresh water to a fountain at the Piazza del Trivio.[4]

---

biographer, Giannozzo Manetti, and by Vasari. A recent study of the projects of the Pope and Alberti's role in developing and carrying them out is Torgil Magnuson's "The Project of Nicholas V for Rebuilding the Borgo Leonino in Rome," *Art Bulletin,* 36 (1954): pp. 89–115. It is largely a re-examination of Georg Dehio's "Die Bauprojekte Nicolaus V," *Repertorium für Kunstwissenschaft,* 3 (1880): 241–57, which is still the standard work on the subject. There has been no new examination of papal accounts which, as Magnuson suggests, might yield more data for the accurate dating and authorship of the various works begun in Nicholas' reign.

3. Cardinal Prospero Colonna commissioned this task. Actually, there was not one state-barge but two, both from the time of Caligula. The larger one was over two hundred feet in length and almost eighty feet in width. Alberti proceeded by chaining together a row of empty barrels and stringing them across the lake as a sort of bridge. On the barrels, he placed windlasses which carried ropes with large grab hooks. Divers attached the hooks to the hull of one of the ships, and the prow was lifted high enough for Alberti to judge that his object was a barge, and that it was too great to be raised. On this project, see Mancini, *Vita di Leon Battista Alberti,* pp. 278–80; and V. Malfatti, "Le navi romane del lago di Nemi," *Rivista Marittima,* (1926): 693–700.

4. Arturo Uccelli, *Storia della tecnica dal Medio Evo ai nostri giorni,* p. 334.

But of all the works, plans, and ideas of the late 1440's and early 1450's, of all these new archeological, architectural, and engineering labors which the ruins of ancient Rome inspired him to assume, Alberti's two truly outstanding accomplishments were the Tempio Malatestiano, which he designed around 1450 for the ruler of Rimini, and the great book on architecture which he presented to Nicholas V in 1452, *De re aedificatoria*.[5] These two superb works were closely interrelated, one as a theoretical embodiment of the vital meaning of "renaissance," and the other as an implementation of it.

In the Tempio Malatestiano, Alberti created the most imposing of the three "classical" monuments which the town of Rimini possesses. A little bridge of Tiberius still runs its modest but sturdy arches over the Marecchia River, and some distance away, a majestic arch, erected in 27 B.C., commemorates the triumph of Augustus (fig. 26). In remodeling the medieval church of San Francesco for Sigismondo Malatesta, Alberti recaptured the spirit of these works and even drew the motifs for this, the first of his buildings, from Rimini's Arch of Augustus. He incorporated the triumphal arch, the Corinthian columns, and the ornamental disks of the Arch of Augustus in the new, classical shell which he built around the church of San Francesco, transforming it, in accordance with Sigismondo's commission, into a unique, Renaissance memorial (fig. 27).

Here the arch of antiquity was reborn to celebrate another kind of triumph, the humanistic triumph of fame over time.[6] From the ground of

5. Alberti began *De re aedificatoria* around 1443, at the request of Leonello d'Este. However, Leonello died in 1450, and so Alberti did not dedicate the work to him. The version that he presented to Nicholas V in 1452 was probably the complete work, much as we know it today. See Cecil Grayson, "The Composition of L. B. Alberti's 'Decem Libri De re aedificatoria,' " *Münchner Jahrbuch der Bildenden Kunst*, ser. 3, 11 (1960): 152–61.

The Latin edition printed in Florence in 1485 was reprinted many times and translations of the work also came out in almost all European countries. The standard English translation has been that of Giacomo Leoni, a Venetian architect who worked in England and published translations of Alberti's *Ten Books on Architecture, Three Books on Painting,* and the *Book on Sculpture* in one volume in 1726. His *Ten Books on Architecture* has been reprinted by Alec Tiranti Ltd., London, 1955. A new translation is a desideratum. Leoni's translation was from the vernacular by Cosimo Bartoli, not from the Latin; moreover, his eighteenth-century English tends to import into Alberti's text later ideas of sensibility and pleasure which do not really belong there. For these reasons, I have departed from Leoni's translation occasionally.

There is a new, critical edition of the Latin text and an Italian translation from it which came out too late for me to use—*L'Architettura (De re aedificatoria)*, edited by Giovanni Orlandi, 2 vols. For a list of the various editions of *De re aedificatoria*, see vol. 1, pp. xlvii–l; for a bibliography of secondary literature on Alberti as an architect and theorist, see 1: li–liv.

6. See Rudolf Wittkower's account of Alberti's "Triumph-over-Death" idea as he calls it, and the artistic and technical problems it posed. *Architectural Principles in the Age of Humanism*, pp. 37–38.

26. Arch of Augustus, Rimini

Alberti's white marble façade, a great central arch rises to frame the rectangular door, with its beautifully severe pediment, which leads into the nave of the church. Each of the two side bays holds a smaller, blind arch flanked by Corinthian half-columns. The great columns rest upon a ledge that runs around the entire building, carrying in its generous band a scroll design with Sigismondo's insignia; and upon this ledge, in the niches formed by the two blind arches of the façade, Alberti intended to place the sarcophagi of Sigismondo and his wife, Isotta.

Down the sides of the building, the arches are separated by severely plain piers which rise from the unbroken ledge of the first story so as to form seven round-headed niches (fig. 28). As on the façade, only the ornamental disks placed on either side of the arches decorate and emphasize the simplicity of the commemorative architectural design. And each of these niches (at least on the completed right side of the building) contains a sarcophagus for the remains of one of the scholars or philosophers of Sigismondo's Renaissance court.

The construction of the Tempio Malatestiano was forced to a halt by Sigismondo's wars, and the building was fated to remain incomplete, but had it been finished according to Alberti's design, it would have become one of the most beautiful and coherent structures of the Renaissance. The incomplete

27. *The Tempio Malatestiano, Rimini*

28. *The Tempio Malatestiano, Rimini, right side.*

29. The Tempio Malatestiano. From a medal by Matteo de' Pasti, 1450, as pictured in A. Calabi and G. Cornaggia, Matteo dei Pasti: La sua opera medalistica *(Milan: G. Modiano, 1927).*

second story gives little hint today of the effect of an articulated, organic structure at which Alberti aimed. The two stories are set off from each other by a broad entablature, but what cannot be seen is how they were to be related to each other by having the forms of the second story "respond" to those of the first. We know of this intention from a medal cast by Matteo de' Pasti in 1450 depicting the façade as Alberti planned it (fig. 29). The Corinthian columns that flank the central arch of the main story are continued above the architrave on the medal by pilasters; and the pilasters flank, in turn, a single, central arch on the upper story. As the dominant arch of the entrance holds the portal of the church, the arch of the upper story holds a large window, and a low, curving tympanum springs from the architrave to "disappear" behind it.[7] The main story of the Tempio Malatestiano would thus be bound to an upper one, and its side bays to the center; and the entire work, with all its subtle variations on the theme of the triumphal arch, was then to be crowned by a cupola. Rising majestically behind the tympanum and arch of the upper story, the figure of a Roman dome would have unified the whole.

A comparable aim of renewal, again inspired by a Roman model, prompted Alberti to undertake his "ten books on architecture." A manuscript of Vitruvius' *De architectura libri decem* had been recovered by Poggio Bracciolini in 1414 from the monastery of St. Gallen, but although this comprehensive survey of the architectural theory and engineering knowledge of the age of Augustus was saved from "the general wreck of time" which Alberti deplored,[8] Alberti

7. From a letter which Alberti wrote to Matteo de' Pasti, it appears that he intended to mask the covering of the roof, not with this curving tympanum, but with a scroll design similar to that which appears on his Santa Maria Novella (fig. 32). See Cecil Grayson on this, *An Autographed Letter from Leon Battista Alberti to Matteo de' Pasti, November 18, 1454.*

8. Vitruvius was known and studied in the Middle Ages, but his work aroused no

found the work to be "maimed by age, so that in many places there are great chasms, and many things imperfect in others." Moreover, Vitruvius had retained the original Greek terms for many of the architectural elements and practices he described. Alberti had to examine the remains of innumerable ancient buildings, comparing them carefully with the text to learn what it meant in many instances. He complained that Vitruvius wrote "in such a manner that to the Latins he seems to write Greek, and to the Greeks, Latin: but indeed it is plain from the book itself, that he wrote neither Greek nor Latin, and he might almost as well have never written at all, at least with regard to us, since we cannot understand him."[9] His judgment was a little harsh here, for he did profit immensely from the storehouse of Vitruvian knowledge, but the various deficiencies of Vitruvius' work convinced him that a new architectural compendium ought to be made for his own time. His *De re aedificatoria* became that work.

The first book of its kind since antiquity, *De re aedificatoria* became a bible of Renaissance architecture. The soundness of its technical and engineering knowledge, its archeologically correct rules of classical construction (within the limits of an age which did not know Greek temple construction at first hand), and its coherent aesthetic theory,—all earned for its author a just reputation as the "Florentine Vitruvius."[10] To be sure, some of its archeological and engineering information was destined by its very nature to be developed and superseded in manuals that followed *De re aedificatoria* (and emulated it), but the theory of architecture which it contains remained definitive for Renaissance building. These central theoretical ideas, which gave direction and meaning to the entire book, were to be reiterated for over a century, from the 1450's down through the great Palladio, but never were they more methodically developed or comprehensively expressed than here. Alberti's aesthetic reflections,

strong or pervasive interest until the fifteenth century. Only in the Renaissance did he become an "authority" on architectural theory and practice. For the mss. of Vitruvius and their diffusion, see Lucia A. Ciapponi, "Il 'De Architectura' di Vitruvio nel primo Umanesimo," *Italia Medioevale e Umanistica*, 3 (1960): 59–99. To appreciate some of Alberti's difficulties in understanding Vitruvius, see Richard Krautheimer, "Alberti and Vitruvius," *Acts of the 20th International Congress of the History of Art*, 2 (1961): 42–52, and "Alberti's Templum etruscum," *Münchner Jahrbuch der bildenden Kunst*, ser. 3, 12 (1961): 65–72.

9. *De re aedif*, bk. 6, chap. 1.

10. Rabelais, for example, called him the modern Vitruvius (Julius von Schlosser, *La Letteratura Artistica*, p. 121); and Raphael du Fresne, Alberti's seventeenth-century biographer, wrote: "In his days the study of Architecture was in a manner lost; or if any notices of it remained, they were so corrupted and different from the greatness and politeness of the ancient *Roman* times, that the works produced by them were very mean. *Leone Battista Alberti* was the first that endeavoured to bring back this art to its ancient purity, and that clearing it of the barbarisms of the *Gothick* ages, restored it to order and proportion; insomuch that he was universally called the *Florentine Vitruvius*" (*Ten Books on Architecture*, p. xiv).

which confirmed and grounded the artistic aims of the age, completely clarified the rational vision of nature that lay at the heart of the "renaissance" of classical architecture.

Renaissance Art Theory

The theory of art as an imitation of nature began the course of its modern development with the writers and scholars of fourteenth-century Italy. They revived the ancient Platonic idea of artistic imitation, although they used it to justify a new, and very unPlatonic esteem for the visual arts. The Florentine historian, Filippo Villani, praised Giotto's painting because of its "naturalistic" character, and Boccaccio took Giotto's "realistic" depiction of natural things to be the historic and happy sign of a return to both nature and antiquity. "Giotto," he explained, "painted all natural objects and artifacts in a completely lifelike manner, so that many persons considered them to be real. In this way he brought to light again the art that had been buried for centuries."[11] Disregarding the Platonic evaluation of art as two steps removed from the abstract Ideas exemplified in physical things, the trecento restored and adopted the Platonic conception of art as a sensible copy of physical things, an imitation of all "natural objects and artifacts." But Renaissance art theory could not rest at this point. It had to find a path whereby architecture could be made to join painting and sculpture in their return to nature and antiquity, and this was to be accomplished by means of a distinctive development of the idea of artistic imitation.

If, theoretically, a building were to imitate nature, it could not do so by sensibly "copying" a physical object as painting and sculpture could be said to do. The building would have to imitate by "symbolizing" an intelligible object,[12] even though this notion was fraught with difficulties for the Renaissance. The idea of artistic symbolization, which belonged historically to the Neoplatonic world of late antiquity and the Middle Ages, was entangled in a

11. Paul Frankl, *The Gothic: Literary Sources and Interpretations Through Eight Centuries,* pp. 240–43. See also Lionello Venturi, *History of Art Criticism,* pp. 77ff. The naive naturalism of trecento art theory has its counterpart in the painting of the fourteenth century; on this, see Heinrich Wölfflin, *The Art of the Italian Renaissance,* pp. 324ff.

12. I am here adopting Bosanquet's distinction between "imitation" and "symbol" which accords with the traditional meaning of these terms in ancient thought. The "imitative" work was an image, considered to be a sensible duplication of sensible appearances. The "symbolic" work presented an ideational reality in a sensuous medium. *A History of Aesthetics,* pp. 47ff., 16–17.

For Plotinus' theory of the symbolic function of art, see *ibid.,* pp. 113ff., 131, 148–49; and Erwin Panofsky's *Idea,* ch. 3. *Idea* is the fundamental work on the history of the idea of beauty and the related ideas of artistic imitation and symbolization. Panofsky has also described Alberti's debt to Cicero with regard to aesthetic theory in this work.

35455

theoretical outlook that was both unclassical and anti-naturalistic in its emphasis upon transcendent "realities."

Cicero had actually taken the first step in antiquity in rejecting the simple copy theory of artistic imitation. In his tolerant, eclectic fashion, he allowed the artist a vision of the transcendent Idea of beauty, but not until the great Neoplatonist, Plotinus (c.205–c.270 A.D.), was art systematically re-evaluated and grounded in a new metaphysical, epistemological theory. Plotinus placed the art work on the same ontological level as the physical object, letting them both directly imitate the supersensuous Ideas. "If anyone condemns the arts because they create by way of imitation of nature," he wrote,—explicitly arguing against the classical theory of imitation—"we must first observe that natural things themselves are an imitation of something further, and next we must bear in mind that the arts do not simply imitate the visible, but go back to the reasons [*logoi*] from which nature comes."[13] What the artist "sees" is the intelligible reality that underlies, forms, and shines through the visible objects of the material world; and by representing this intuition in the perceptual forms of art, he makes of the art work a true symbol. The artist creates images which are informed by, and which reflect, the same *logoi* or "reasons" that constitute the ultimate reality of nature.

Neoplatonism in this way imparted a new dignity to art, but by the same token, it fanned the desire of the late Roman world to reach "beyond" the nature which classical art had striven to imitate. It was in the Neoplatonic milieu of the Late Empire that the anagogic mode of thought emerged, a way of thinking which directed the mind to "rise" from the visible to the invisible, from the physical objects of nature and sense to the ultimate intelligible Ideas— which were soon to be understood as Ideas in the mind of God.

As a hermeneutic technique, the anagogic mode of thought was an extension of the allegorical method of interpreting literary texts, a method which originally stemmed from rationalistic motives. The Sophists and the Stoics had read Greek mythopoeic literature this way, hoping to uncover by allegorical explanations what they thought must have been the rational, didactic meanings of the ancient myths. In the hands of the Christians of the ancient world, however, the symbolic method of interpretation became an instrument for extracting "spiritual" truths which were contained in, and yet transcended, the literal words of Scripture. As the Neoplatonic theologian, Origen (d. 254 A.D.) "argued"—employing the very form of reasoning by analogy which constitutes the structure of anagogic thought and allegorical interpretation: just as there are three components of man, the body, its vital principle, and the spiritual soul, so there are three meanings in Scripture, the literal meaning corresponding to the body, the moral meaning corresponding to the vital

13. *Ennead* 1: 6, 3; quoted by Bosanquet, pp. 113–14 from Creuzer's edition, p. 1002.

35455

principle, and the mystical meaning corresponding to, and nourishing, the soul.

The allegorical interpretation of Scripture treated the stories and concrete imagery of the Bible as mere indices of such superior, moral and mystical "truths." The personages and events of the Old Testament were "read" by Augustine, for example, as prefigurements of the spiritual content of the New Testament. The Old Testament was "nothing but the New covered with a veil," just as the New Testament was "nothing but the Old unveiled."[14] But it was not only Scripture that was made to yield a glimpse of moral and mystical realities. What began as an exegetic procedure soon broadened into a general intellectual orientation, a way of thinking about any and all things. Any sensible object could be regarded from the Neoplatonic viewpoint as an analogue of spiritual realities, of ideal entities which were believed to lie "beyond," but to partly reveal themselves in, concrete symbolic representations. Thus a dove could disclose the mystical entity of the Church for the twelfth-century monk, Hugh of Saint Victor:

> The dove has two wings, just as, for the Christian there are two sorts of life, the active and the contemplative. The blue feathers of the wings signify thoughts of heaven. The wavering nuances of the rest of the body, colors as changeful as an agitated sea, symbolize the ocean of human passions on which the Church makes its way. And why does the dove have eyes of such beautiful yellow gold? Because yellow, color of ripe fruits, is the color of experience and maturity. The yellow eyes of the dove symbolize the look, full of wisdom, with which the Church considers the future. Finally, the dove has red feet, for the Church advances through the world, her feet deep in the blood of martyrs.[15]

Presupposing the existence of a spiritual realm which is at once hidden from our understanding by the physical world, and hinted at by the physical world that "corresponds" to it, the anagogic mode of thought sought in all objects of sense the higher, spiritual objects they symbolize. It accustomed the mind to think in terms of "correspondences," to consider the mystical "meanings" of the properties of things, of their number, position, color, and so forth, so that any physical object could be made to disclose an intelligible one by means of the "significant" qualities they shared. In the case of the work of art, these correspondences were built into it from its moment of conception. The famous Gothic choir at St. Denis was raised by twelve columns at the order of the Abbot Suger to signify the Apostles by sharing their number. In the side aisles, Suger had twelve more columns placed to represent (again by number) the minor prophets. The entire fabric of the church was built in

14. *De civit. Dei,* 16: xxvi; in Emile Mâle, *Religious Art in France, XIII Century,* p. 134. See also pp. 135ff., 29ff. for Origen.

15. *Ibid.,* p. 65.

this way, in accordance with the words of "the Apostle who buildeth spiritually," Suger explained: " 'Now therefore ye are no more strangers and foreigners,' says he, 'but fellow citizens with the saints and of the household of God; and are built upon the foundation of the Apostles and prophets.' "[16]

Like the world itself, the Gothic cathedral thus came to be constructed as an intricate symbolic system. The medieval conception of the art work, born of the Neoplatonic, anagogic mode of thought, was that of a referential symbol, or an assemblage of such symbols which refer by convention to abstract, transcendent realities. The Gothic cathedral, in its structural and decorative elements, referred to a whole universe of such intelligible truths. Every abstract entity, every "truth," natural, moral, and mystical, had some features which could find representation in concrete counterparts. Even the Augustinian notion of the relation between the Old and New Testaments found expression in the church, in the statues of the patriarchs and prophets placed in the central bay of the north portal at Chartres. Standing where they are, these representatives of the Old Law became the "pillars of the portico" that leads into the New Law of the Church; and each one further symbolized by prefigurement the sacrifice of Christ: Melchizedek by bearing a chalice, Abraham by holding the head of the sacrificial child, and so on.[17]

Referential symbols of this kind continued to play a role in art even after the theoretical outlook which gave rise to them lost its vitality. In Flemish painting, commonplace visible things were often used to refer to "invisible" truths and entities. Jan van Eyck's wedding portrait of "Giovanni Arnolfini and Jeanne Cenami" (National Gallery, London) is perhaps the best known, but by no means the only example of this double use of sensible objects in Flemish art. Panofsky has shown how almost every domestic detail in the picture symbolically signifies and testifies to the sacrament of matrimony: the dog as the traditional symbol of fidelity, the slippers as an admonition that this is "holy ground," the marriage candle as the symbol of the all-seeing Christ.[18] In Renaissance art, the referential conception of art also lingered on, although here it assumed its classical, allegorical sense once again. Alberti, for example, suggested a number of didactic allegories for the *istorie* of painting. But even though conventional symbols persisted to some extent in Flemish and Renaissance painting, it is clear in both cases that the anagogic conception of art had yielded precedence to a representational one. By the fifteenth century, the primary artistic aim was no longer to refer to something that transcends

16. In Erwin Panofksky, *Abbot Suger on the Abbey Church of St. Denis and Its Art Treasures,* p. 104. This entire book is a classic demonstration of the relation between Gothic art and the anagogic mode of thought.

17. Mâle, *Religious Art in France,* pp. 51–52, 73–77, 140–58. In his works on Gothic art, Mâle has read in painstaking and poetic fashion the "symbolic code," as he called it, of medieval iconography.

18. Panofsky, *Early Netherlandish Painting: Its Origins and Character,* 1: 201–3.

experience, but to represent visual experience itself; and in Italy, this development was reflected in the revival of the classical idea of art as imitation of nature.

In the literature of art theory (which was itself a renascent genre), Alberti gave the first modern development to the ancient idea of an empirical artistic "truth." He confirmed the theory of art as imitation of nature, and in *Della pittura* and *Della statua* he made the notion of imitation more precise by defining it in terms of perspective and anthropometry. It was only in *De re aedificatoria,* however, that his theory of art, and the art theory of the Renaissance, became fully explicit and revealed its distinctive features. Here, to account for architecture, he restored the idea of symbolic imitation to art, but he did so without suppressing the sense of empirical truth which had so recently been regained. Between the two, between the Platonic idea of art as a sensible copy of phenomena and the Neoplatonic idea of art as a symbol of transcendent realities, the mathematical conception of artistic form now provided a bridge. By focusing upon proportions, upon a "reality" that was at once natural and ideal, Alberti made explicit what classical art, in fact, had sought; and thus he brought the theory of imitation to a new stage. The Renaissance owes to his theory of architecture its novel conception of art as symbolizing by direct embodiment the purely structural form of phenomenal reality.

Only from the vantage point of the new visual geometry could the notion of an architectural "imitation" of nature appear as a plausible idea, and one which was also consonant with the theory of pictorial and sculptural "truth" which Alberti developed. Indeed, Alberti's sculptural theory is closely related to his theory of architecture, for the building is another instance of his idea of organic form. The building was "a kind of body" for him; and it has the same relational and rational kind of unity that the body has in *Della statua.* It consists of matter (*structura*) and design or form (*lineamentum*), and again Alberti conceived of the form of this "body" as a proportional arrangement of its material parts: the design of the building relates "things which are different but proportionable to each other"; it regulates "the situation of the parts and the disposition of their lines and angles."[19]

Understood as the embodiment of a rationally constituted form, the building could not, of course, imitate, as a sensible copy, any object of sense; but like the perspectival painting and the measured statue, it could present in the proportional arrangement of its parts the intelligible "reasons" of nature. This is why Alberti insisted, in the introductory passages of *De re aedificatoria,* upon the ideational character of the building's design.[20] Whereas the physical material of the building is given and needs only to be chosen and prepared, its form, he pointed out, must be produced by the mind. And although it is

19. *De re aedif, Preface;* bk. 1, chaps. 1, 9; bk. 9, chap. 5.
20. *Ibid.,* Preface; bk. 1, chap. 1.

articulated in the material, it is not bound to it, for the architect conceives
the design "separately," in thought and imagination. Only by means of an ideal
form could he ground the imitative task of the building. On this point,
Renaissance architectural theory was at one with the medieval understanding of
the art work as symbolic of an intelligible reality. Where the medieval and the
Renaissance views parted ways was in their understanding of *how* the artistic
image symbolizes the ideal. Symbolization now came to be understood in a
novel, immanent sense. The Renaissance building is not an aggregate of symbols
which point in anagogical fashion to transcendent, substantival truths; it
exhibits directly as a proportional structure the newly conceived, relational
"reasons" of nature.

This fundamental idea of the artistic embodiment of a "natural" order is
what justified the renaissance of the classical orders in architecture. "As the
members of the body correspond to each other," Alberti said, "so one part
should respond to another in a building, whence we say that great edifices
require great members."[21] How could this "natural" commensurability be
achieved in a building, if not by the module system of classical architecture?
As Vitruvius had explained, the Greeks took the semi-diameter of a column at
its base as a module in terms of which they determined the dimensions of the
"members" of each of the orders, and the significance of this procedure lay in
the fact that the proportions they thus established were understood to be
nature's own. "The Doric order first arose in a temple to the Pan-Ionian
Apollo," Vitruvius claimed,

> When they wished to place columns in that temple, and not having their
> proportions, seeking by what method they could make them fit to bear
> weight, and in their appearance to have an approved grace, they measured
> a man's footstep and applied it to his height. Finding that the foot was
> the sixth part of the height in a man, they applied this proportion to the
> column. Of whatsoever thickness they made the base of the shaft, they
> raised it along with the capital to six times as much in height. So the Doric
> columns began to furnish the proportions of a man's body, its strength
> and grace.[22]

Vitruvius also held that the harmonic ratios of Pythagorean musical theory
were, like the proportions of the body, "natural"; and Alberti's archeological
investigations confirmed the fact that classical buildings also exhibited these
ratios. Following Vitruvius, he therefore demanded that the metrical system of
classical architecture be restored to the art of building, and he did this in the
belief that the proportions among the elements of classical buildings reflected
the intention of the ancients "to discover the laws by which Nature produced

21. *Ibid.*, bk. 1, chap. 9.
22. *De architectura*, bk. 4, chaps. 1, 6.

her works so as to transfer them to the works of architecture."[23] Alberti was more systematic than his Augustan predecessor, however. He wanted to establish the connection between the "natural" proportions which architecture incorporates and the "approved grace" which Vitruvius claimed these proportions achieve, and to do this, he picked up the theory of artistic imitation at the point to which Cicero had brought it. Bridging one of Vitruvius' "great chasms," he took Renaissance art theory along an explicitly idealistic path. He adopted the Platonic theory of the status and role of Ideas and attributed to the architect a vision of the Idea of beauty, making of it the norm of his imitation of nature.

In *De re aedificatoria*, the idea of beauty has all the characteristics of a Platonic Form.[24] Alberti defined Beauty in the usual, classical sense as congruity or *concinnitas:* "a Harmony of all the parts, in whatsoever subject it appears, fitted together with such proportion and connection that nothing could be added, diminished, or altered but for the worse." But beauty was now a purely ideational object for him, something "conjoined to the spirit and reason." Whenever a beautiful object offers itself to the mind through one of the senses, it is this *concinnitas* that is "recognized," yet the Idea of *concinnitas* cannot be derived from sensory experience alone. Beauty does not arise from, nor is it bound to, the sensible things in which it is found; it proceeds, rather, "from itself and from Nature"—or *da per sè,* as Galileo would later say to describe the a priori character of the laws of nature which never fully realize themselves in any natural phenomenon. Beauty was regarded by Alberti exactly like such laws, as universal yet never completely achieved in any one instance. It extends its sway over all human and natural products, but "it is very rarely granted to anyone, or even to Nature herself, to produce anything in every way perfect and complete"; in everything real there is something "deficient or superfluous" which is incompatible with "the perfection of Beauty."

Here, then, illuminating art as it would later illuminate physical knowledge in Galileo's reflections, is the idealistic awareness of the nature of an "idea" which at once determines and transcends the objects that participate in it. For Albert and for the Renaissance, however, this was more than an epistemological insight; it seemed to entail an ultimate metaphysical reality, too. Having characterized beauty as an Idea, Alberti could follow Plato and disentangle it from its many perceptual instances. He could be certain that the judgment that a thing is beautiful is something quite different from subjective matters of taste or mere opinion: personal inclinations may lead us to prefer one object to another, but the evaluation of the beauty of either of them springs not from feeling but from "a certain reason innate to the mind" (*ut vero de*

---

23. *De re aedif,* bk. 9, chap. 5.

24. Alberti developed his ideas on Beauty chiefly in book 9, chapter 5. On the "transcendental" nature of his idea of beauty, see W. Flemming, *Die Begründung der modernen Aestetik und Kunstwissenschaft durch L. B. Alberti.*

pulchritudine iudices non opinio: verum animis innata quaedam ratio efficiet).
But the very objectivity of this criterion in mind raised a further, more
difficult problem, the problem of grounding the Idea. Alberti acknowledged that
this issue was "too subtle for this place." The question "whence this sense of the
mind arises, and how it is formed," was not his to handle; and yet, what his
critical reflection appreciated as too obscure to pronounce upon, he nonetheless
disposed of—in an uncritical, metaphysical fashion. The Idea of beauty, which
Kant would later describe as a pure form of thought, Alberti conceived as a
Final Cause of Nature.

Alberti's empirical attitude seems to have led him to the same sense of
discomfort that Kant was to express with regard to the semi-mystical character
of Plato's Ideas, but lacking a functional theory of the nature of knowledge,
such as the development of science would give rise to with Kant, Alberti
grounded the Idea of *concinnitas* in a teleological conception of nature. In the
Kantian system of critical idealism which Renaissance thought anticipates in so
many ways, the Platonic Ideas were to be de-ontologized at last, and understood
as epistemological principles. The a priori principles became either categories of
thought for Kant, or pure Ideals of reason. Kant understood the categories as
rules of synthesis of sense-contents, rules that are *constitutive* of both human
knowledge (of objects) and of objects themselves (as they appear to the
knowing subject). The categories were no longer to be thought of as aspects or
traits of things existing in themselves, apart from human understanding; and on
the basis of this theory of the correlation of subject and object in the
constituting of natural knowledge, the Ideals of reason (like Beauty, the Good,
etc.) ceased to be seen as transcendent, self-subsisting Archetypes and came to be
understood as merely higher, more abstract functions than the categories of
understanding. For Kant, such Ideas became *regulative* principles, the leading
ideas in accordance with which ethical and artistic choices can be made
rationally. But for Alberti and the Renaissance, the Idea of beauty was still
a law of nature. Beauty was the primary and absolute *telos,* the goal toward
which nature "strives" in all her creations: "All Nature's works are governed by
the law of Beauty (*omne ex concinnitatis lege moderatur*); nor does Nature
seek anything greater than to make all her works perfect, which they could never
be unless they had *concinnitas.*"[25]

Beauty thus assumed an ontological and constitutive status in *De re
aedificatoria* and in Renaissance aesthetic thought generally. Its objectivity
could apparently be explained in no other way; but in this form, it made
possible a conception of art which kept the artist true to experience and at the
same time elevated the theory of his imitation of nature far beyond the
classical notion of a sensible copy of physical things. Understood as a Final
Cause of Nature, the Idea of beauty imparted to nature the same rational,

25. *De re aedif,* bk. 9, chap. 5.

creative activity that gives rise to human art. Architecture's "imitation" came to
be rooted in this dynamic moment, the moment of rational forming when the
artist and nature alike obey the same, supreme law. It was in this sense that
the Renaissance building was to be "like an animal, so that *in the formation
of it* we ought to imitate Nature."[26] Architecture was to bring about in its
"bodies" what nature strives for in hers.

The Theory of Renaissance Architecture: Numerus, Finitio, and Collocatio

In Alberti's theory of architecture, the imitation of nature takes place within
three categories: the number, measure, and arrangement of the parts of the
building. Having bound the Idea of beauty to Nature and Reason, Alberti
discarded the numerous and overlapping aesthetic norms which Vitruvius had
applied to architecture, preferring to order his own rules around the idealistic
notions of Beauty, Nature, and Reason which he had come to accept. Vitruvius
had taken his categories from ancient rhetoric: *ordinatio, dispositio, eurythmia,
symmetria, decor, distributio;* and he neither grounded them in a theory of art
nor set them in logical order. Alberti's categories flow from the Idea of beauty
which he proclaimed to be the primary and absolute law of nature and of art.
His definition of *concinnitas* corresponds to Vitruvius' *symmetria:* an aptness of
the parts within a whole so that nothing can be added or taken away, be
decreased or enlarged, or be differently placed; but taking this Idea as the
objective of architecture, he drew from it the novel concepts of *numerus*
(number: so that nothing can be added or taken away), *finitio* (measure: so
that nothing can be decreased or enlarged), and *collocatio* (arrangement: so that
nothing can be differently placed).[27] An agreement among the parts of the
building brought about in each of these categories would give rise to that
Harmony which Alberti saw as the *telos* of the architectural and the natural work.
 Of the three categories, the second was the most important to Alberti and

---

26. *Ibid.,* italics mine.
27. Flemming believed that Alberti was using the Aristotelian categories of quantity,
quality, and relation when he made these distinctions; *Die Begründung der modernen
Aestetik,* p. 33. However, everyone who has adopted Flemming's idea has seen *finitio* as the
qualitative category, perhaps because it is so misleadingly translated as the "finishing" of
the work; hence the usual claim (e.g., in Paul-Henri Michel, *Un idéal humain au XVe siècle:
La pensée de L.B. Alberti,* pp. 361ff.) is that *finitio* refers to harmonious, qualitative
relations, as among old and new parts of a restored building. But *finitio* is actually the
architectural equivalent of the sculptural "rule" of the *por' dei termini* for which Alberti
used the instrument he called the Definer, the *finitorium* in Latin. If in fact he did have the
Aristotelian categories in mind, *finitio* would therefore have to be a relational category,
the one that has to do with the ratios of the building. *Collocatio* fits the category of quality
somewhat better, for here Alberti wanted "a correspondence in kind."

$$\underbrace{1 \cdot 1 \cdot 1 \cdot 1 \cdot 1 \cdot 1}_{6}$$

$$\underbrace{1 \cdot 2 \cdot 3}_{6} \qquad \underbrace{1 \cdot 5}_{6}$$

$$\underbrace{2 \cdot 2 \cdot 2}_{6} \quad \underbrace{2 \cdot 4}_{6} \quad \underbrace{3 \cdot 3}_{6}$$

was destined to play a central role in Renaissance architectural theory and practice in general. The number and arrangement of the parts of the building were factors which the Renaissance architect surely considered, but their measure was the very heart of the new Idea of beauty. Alberti's consideration of *numerus* and *collocatio* is nowhere near as fully developed as his treatment of *finitio*. In fact, under the heading of number,[28] he continued to cling to the medieval conception of symbolization, setting up arbitrary analogies between the number of certain parts of the building and certain parts of what the building purportedly represents.

He declared, for instance, that the supports in ancient buildings were even in number because animals support themselves on an even number of feet. Apertures, on the other hand, were generally odd in number, just as the mouth is a single opening in the face. The only difference between him and the Abbot Suger on this point is that Alberti's numbers ostensibly correspond to numbers found in nature whereas Suger's correspond to the Trinity, the Apostles, and so forth. Alberti merely substituted for analogies with "divine" Forms analogies with organic forms, and he replaced the "correspondences" of Christian myth with the "significance" attributed to numbers by ancient myth—such as the perfection accorded to the number six by the Pythagoreans, because six consists "of all its own entire parts" (fig. 30).

If Alberti's numerical symbolism is only remotely related to his new aesthetic ideas, he did not relate it to artistic practice at all. There are no rules of application in this section. It is almost as if he did not really expect his remarks on number to be carried out. He set down everything he had learned about the evaluation of the various numbers in antiquity, but in a way that would baffle anyone looking for specific directives: "architects have most

28. *De re aedif*, bk. 9, chap. 5.

frequently made use of the foregoing numbers [5, 7, 9, 4, 6, 8] upon these accounts, but in their apertures they seldom have exceeded ten for an even number, or nine for an odd one."

Under his third heading of *collocatio*,[29] he again gave no rules. Explicitly leaving the arrangement of the parts of the building to the architect's aesthetic judgment, he made only two suggestions to guide him. One was that he should seek "a correspondence in kind," that is, that qualitative "decorum" which he had required for the parts of the body in *Della pittura* and which in architecture became "symmetry" in the modern sense of the word: what is on the right should be made to respond to what is on the left, the high should respond to the low, the similar on the one hand to the similar on the other. In this way, Nature herself would seem to order the building, setting its diverse parts in their "natural" places. And secondly, the architect could follow in his arrangement of the parts of the building some of the rules which Alberti had set down for its *finitio*—for here, in his second category, he had concerned himself with the metrical correspondence of the parts of the building. Under this heading, as we might expect, he made a thorough, and a thoroughly absorbing, study of the ways in which Nature's works reflect the universal law of Harmony.

The *finitio*[30] of the building is the building's "measure." It has to do with "the correspondence of those several lines whereby proportions are measured, namely the length, the breadth, and the width," hence it brings us to the geometric form of the architectural "body" and to that aspect of art which Alberti consistently regarded as the really imitative one. Only proportional structures captured and represented Nature's order for him, and this was the case in building, too. The proportions of the work of architecture were to be determined "not confusedly and indistinctly, but in such a manner as to be constantly and in every way comfortable to Harmony." That is, the proportional form of the building was to set up its *analogia* with nature through the mediation of the Idea of beauty, and this is what led Alberti to adopt for architecture the Pythagorean musical ratios.

He found himself "persuaded," he explains, "by the saying of Pythagoras, that Nature is sure to act consistently and with constant proportion in all her operations." Whether it be through sight, hearing, or any of the other senses, it is always the same Beauty that is conveyed to the mind. The harmonic ratios that produce the beauty of sound must consequently be "the very same that please our eyes and mind"; and since the "measure" of the interval between harmonious tones is given spatially, in terms of the length of the strings that produce them, harmonic ratios can be spatially expressed in the dimensions of the architectural design. What creates an audible Harmony can create a visual Harmony as well.

29. *Ibid.*, bk. 9, chap. 7.   30. *Ibid.*, bk. 9, chaps. 5, 6, 7.

For the *finitio* of plazas and open areas, where only two dimensions need be considered, Alberti accordingly recommended the 1:1 ratio of the perfect square and the ratios of the simple consonances given in the Greek system of musical harmony. To determine the relation of length to width, the architect should use the Fifth (a 2:3 ratio), the Fourth (3:4), the Octave (1:2), and the Tone (8:9)—the consonances which are shown in the left foreground of Raphael's "School of Athens" (fig. 16), on the tablet held before the figure of Pythagoras.[31]

To work in three dimensions, the architect could adopt certain progressions which relate three numbers to each other in accordance with the laws of Harmony. These progressions, which form the harmonious order of the cosmos in Plato's *Timaeus,* arise, as Alberti shows, from the compound consonances of musical theory, the Duple, the Triple, and the Quadruple.

The Duple yields sequences in which the third number is twice the first number. To form these sequences, the simple consonance of a Fourth is "added" to the simple consonance of a Fifth. Starting, for example, with the number two, the Fifth of two (or that number which stands in a 2:3 relation to it) is three; and the Fourth (3:4) of three is four. The progression or compound consonance of the Duple is, in this case, 2:3:4; and the final number, four, is the double of the first number, two. Again, starting with the number three and adding a Fourth (3:4), and then a Fifth (2:3 or 4:6), we find the Duple sequence 3:4:6, and so forth.

The progressions of the Triple are formed by a Duple and a Fifth, so that the third number of the sequence is the triple of the first. And the Quadruple combines two Duples, or a Fourth, a Fifth, and a Duple, so that the final number of the sequence is four times the first number (fig. 31).

These ratios of the musical consonances were to be used by the architect in such a way as to bring about a unified system of proportions in the building. If the parts of the building were to have "that proportion among themselves so that they may appear to be an entire and perfect body, and not disjointed and unfinished members," they had to bear such proportions to each other as belong to an integral set of harmonious ratios. Should the height of a room be twice as great as its width, for example, only dimensions derived from a Duple could be used in the room. Or, where the length of a room was three times its width, only numbers belonging to Triple progressions could be used for the *finitio* of the other parts of the room. Thus when Alberti used a musical metaphor to protest certain suggested changes in the design of his Tempio Malatestiano, he had a quite literal meaning in mind: "You see whence the measures and proportions of the pilasters arise," he wrote to the acting architect at Rimini;

31. For Raphael's tablet and the role of the musical consonances in Renaissance art, see Part 4 of Wittkower's *Arch. Principles,* "The Problem of Harmonic Proportions in Architecture."

		2:4:6
The Triple	oo	
	oooo	Doubled
	oooooo	Sesquialtera (a Fifth)

		2:3:6
The Triple	oo	
	ooo	Sesquialtera (a Fifth)
	oooooo	Doubled

		2:4:8
The Quadruple	oo	
	oooo	Diapason (doubled)
	oooooooo	Disdiapason (Duple doubled)

		2:3:4:8
The Quadruple	oo	
	ooo	Sesquialtera (a Fifth)
	oooo	Sesquialtertia (a Fourth)
	oooooooo	Doubled

Fig. 31.—Harmonic Progressions in *De re aedificatoria*.

31. *Harmonic progression in De re aedificatoria.*

"what you would change brings discord into all that music."[32] By giving spatial embodiment to the musical intervals in a regular fashion, that is, in progressions consistent with the laws of Harmony, congruity would be realized on a grand visual scale in the medium of the building. This was the "music" of the whole that could not be disturbed.

This artistic intention is made transparently clear in Alberti's second church façade, that of Santa Maria Novella in Florence (fig. 32). Designed in the late 1450's, it completed the exterior of a medieval church, and yet it has been rightly described as a "great Renaissance exponent of classical *eurhythmia*," for its dimensions are all bound to each other by the 1:2 ratio of the musical Octave.[33] The marble panels, which produce a mosaiclike effect of discrete color patches on medieval Italian church exteriors, such as Santa Maria del Fiore's (the Duomo), here contribute to a sense of rhythmic, geometric unity, and Professor Wittkower's reconstruction of Alberti's design shows us why.

32. *An Autographed Letter.* The music of San Francesco was understood to be that of the golden section by Guglielmo de Angelis d'Ossat, "Enunciati euclidei e 'divina proporzione' nell'architettura del primo Rinascimento," *Atti del V Convegno internazionale di studi sul Rinascimento,* pp. 253–63. This author is correct when he points out that Alberti recommended the use of irrational numbers as well as rationals, but I cannot agree with him when he claims that Alberti used the golden section and maintained an "arcano silenzio" about it in *De re aedificatoria*. There was no mystical reason for him to suppress this knowledge in the pages which purport to disclose the lawful ratios of Nature. Gerda Soergel has made a more sober analysis of the ratios used in San Francesco in a work which Professor Wittkower kindly called to my attention, "Die Harmonien in Leone Battista Albertis Tempio Malatestiano," *Untersuchungen über den theoretischen Architekturentwurf von 1450–1550 in Italien,* pp. 8–22. See also the excellent study of the proportional form of the Tempio Malatestiano given by Carlo L. Ragghianti, "Tempio Malatestiano," *Critica d'Arte,* 12, fasc. 71 (1965): 23–31; fasc. 74 (1965): 27–40.

33. Wittkower, *Arch. Principles,* pp. 41–47. I am here following his analysis of the façade of Santa Maria Novella.

He has found that the entire façade of Santa Maria Novella can be circumscribed by Alberti's preferred form of the perfect square; and that "a square of half the size of [this] large square defines the relationship of the two stories." That is, the main story can be divided into two such imaginary squares, and the upper story fits into one such "square" (if we exclude the scrolls and extend the imaginary square to the height of the pediment). The height of each of these imaginary squares is thus half the height of the greater "square" of the entire façade, and the width of the upper story beneath the classical pediment is half the width of the whole.

The sense of balance and "aptness" which the spectator experiences

32. *Santa Maria Novella, Florence. (Alinari-Art Reference Bureau.)*

113

at his first glance at Santa Maria Novella persists and deepens as these "regular" proportions of the square (1:1) and the Octave (1:2) are gradually appreciated. The "sub-units" comprised by the three dominant imaginary squares of the façade are subtly but clearly interrelated, in their turn, by the same proportions on a smaller scale. To give but a few examples: the width of the decorative scrolls at their base is half the width of the imaginary square of the upper story. If we inscribe imaginary rectangles about the scrolls and the pediment, the "rectangle" of the pediment would be made up of two squares of the same size as the "square" of either scroll; and the "square" of the scroll is the same size as the "square" of the central bay formed by the two inner pilasters of the upper story. All these "sub-squares" stand in a 1:2 relation to the imaginary square of the upper story, and they are twice the height of the attic between the two stories . . . A single system of proportions made "one Beauty" indeed out of the many parts of the façade of Santa Maria Novella.

In addition to the musical ratios, Alberti urged the architect to "discover" other progressions for the *finitio* of the building by using the figures of the square and the triangle.[34] He could find the sequence 2:4:8 (or 3:9:27), for example, by taking the ratio of the "root" or side (2) of a "square number" to the area of the square (4), and to the cube (8) of the side. Other sequences could be found by using a right-angled (Pythagorean) triangle, with its constant proportion among the squares of the sides. The ratios arrived at by the "rules" of these geometric figures (which are also in the *Timaeus*) were, Alberti maintained, "natural proportions of bodies." But what made them "natural," and why should they be appropriate for the "body" of the building?

In the case of the musical ratios, there was at least a direct connection between the consonances and Nature's law of Harmony. There is no relation between these geometric ratios and Beauty, except for the feature which gave them a cosmos-building role in the *Timaeus:* their regularity. At this point, then, Alberti's conception of "natural" (and hence beautiful) proportions had imperceptibly broadened: from ratios governed by the laws of musical harmony, it had come to include *any* ratios that are generated by rule. This shift in meaning is borne out by the third and final set of proportions which he recommended for the Renaissance building. They, too, bear the stamp of Nature

---

34. Alberti seems to have been following the *Timaeus* here, but he could also be leaning in part upon a Gothic tradition of construction. In *The Gothic,* pp. 71–74, 702ff., and in "The Secret of the Medieval Masons," *Art Bulletin,* 27 (1945): 46–60, Paul Frankl has shown how the medieval architects used the square and right-angled triangle to reproduce the angles of their models and/or designs in their buildings. Ignorant of the method of plotting to scale by proportional numerical units, they determined the dimensions of the structure *ad quadratum* or *ad triangulum,* by transferring to the building the *angles* of square and triangular figures drawn over their designs. For the Gothic builder, however, these geometric figures were a purely technical expedient for transferring proportions which had already been decided upon by independent aesthetic considerations. For Alberti, the square and the triangle were to furnish proportions for the design itself.

and Nature's supreme law in the sense of *regulae.* They are the mean proportionals, and although they have a more immediate relation to Harmony than the "rules" of the square and the triangle, it is only their character as rules that Alberti fastened upon.

Alberti would have known from the *Timaeus* that the simple consonances of the Pythagorean musical system can all be generated by the mean proportionals, but he overlooked this fact entirely, choosing only to point out that in the sequences arrived at by the means, the middle ("mean") number corresponds with the two extreme numbers "in a certain determined manner," as he put it, "or, to use such an expression, with a regular affinity."[35]

> Our business in this inquiry is to consider three terms, where of the two most remote, one is the greatest of the three terms, and the other is the least. The . . . mean number must answer to these other two *in a just relation or proportionate interval,* which interval is the equal relative distance between this number and each of the other two.

To arrive at the *arithmetic mean,* the two extreme numbers are added together and the sum is divided by two. The mean number thus "stands at an equal distance" from the two extremes:

$$8 \quad 4$$
$$12$$
$$6$$

The *geometric mean* was so called because the geometrically minded Greeks and their Renaissance heirs thought it easier to ascertain it "by lines," that is, by drawings, than by arithmetic computation. Here, the small extreme number is multiplied by the great one. The mean is the square root of the product ("or the number of its side"):

$$4 \quad 9$$
$$36$$
$$6$$

The geometric mean, when multiplied by itself, is equal to the product of the two extremes.

The *musical mean* was the most complicated of the three means. Here the interval between the two extreme numbers must be the same as the sum of the intervals between the small extreme number and the mean, and the mean and the great extreme number.

$$30 \quad 60$$
$$1 \quad 2$$
$$3$$
$$\underline{10 \quad 10 \quad 10}$$
$$40$$

35. *De re aedif,* bk. 9, chap. 6.

To find the musical mean, we first find the ratio of the two extremes. The numbers expressing this ratio are added together, and the sum is used to divide the interval between the extremes into so many equal parts; for example, the interval between thirty and sixty is thirty, and thirty divided by three yields three units of ten. One of the "parts" (i.e., a unit of ten) is added to the small extreme number, and the sum obtained is the musical mean. The interval between thirty and sixty (namely, thirty) is equal to the sum of the interval between thirty and forty (ten) and the interval between forty and sixty (twenty).

Like the progressions generated by the laws of Harmony, the progressions generated by the mean proportionals acquired an aesthetic value in the Renaissance. They were governed by law, and lawfulness had become the sure indication of natural order. Alberti believed, for this reason, that the proportions of the classical orders must have been arrived at by the means, even though Vitruvius traced them to the human body. The ancient builders who found the width of a man to be one-sixth *(sic)* his height, and his breadth from the navel to the back one-tenth, raised their columns sometimes six times as high as the diameter of the column at the base, and sometimes ten times as high, but the "truth," Alberti pointed out, lay in some mean between the two. Hence they must have calculated the arithmetic mean between six and ten to arrive at the measure they called Ionic, wherby the column is raised eight times its diameter at the base. The Doric measure of seven they found in the arithmetic mean between six and the Ionic eight; and the Corinthian nine they found in the arithmetic mean between the Ionic eight and the original ten. By the rule of the arithmetic mean, the ancients avoided the "vicious extremes" of six and ten, and found the proportions of Nature in the means.[36]

This conception of the classical orders is the counterpart of the Renaissance canons of human proportions which sought in universally accepted, beautiful proportions the "rule" of the mean. In *Della statua,* taking the measures of the generally acknowledged "best parts" of many bodies, Alberti thought he would arrive at those "mean proportions" (*mediocrità*) that avoid the defects and excesses of the extremes. Just as the ancient architects found the beautiful ratios of their orders by using the rules of the mean proportionals, so he set down beautiful ratios which had, perforce, to be "means." The fifteenth-century architect, Filarete, was to make this fundamental bond between the classical orders and canons of proportions explicit by giving the proportions of what he called a "Doric man," an "Ionic man," and so forth in his canon. Canons of proportion and the classical orders were thus thought to exhibit the same regularity of Nature, so that even the organic analogy between the building and the body came to be mediated, in short, by the idea of a universal and lawful proportional order. The ratios of the building and the body alike were

36. *Ibid.,* bk 9, chap. 7.

governed by rules, rules which human reason discerned in individual examples, but in which it recognized a supreme cosmic law.

The idea of natural law which emerged in aesthetic thought thus bound the empirical impulse of the time to the revival of classical forms. As Vasari put it (assuming that same identity of the classical and the natural which Boccaccio had glimpsed two centuries earlier at the dawn of the new art), Alberti "investigated the world and measured antiquity";[37] because in antiquity as in nature, Alberti and his age thought to discover the universal, rational order of things. Classical art became authoritative because it had made the order of nature its own, and this same rational, natural order is what the Renaissance hoped to reproduce in its statues and in the "body" of its buildings.

The Practice of Renaissance Architecture[38]

Antiquity provided instances, and even exemplars of Nature's intent and rules, but Reason remained the ultimate norm in Renaissance architectural theory, and this encouraged the independent spirit with which Renaissance art treated the classical forms it revived. "I believe more in those who built the thermae, the Pantheon, and all those great works, than I do in him," Alberti wrote about the critic of his design of the Tempio Malatestiano; "and I believe much more in Reason than I do in any person."[39]

It was, after all, by reason, the innate Idea of beauty, that the Renaissance judged what nature's order was, whether it "recognized" it in organic forms or in those of art; and by reason it discovered those "natural" proportional regularities of the musical and mathematical domains. Thus Alberti could be the finest archeologist among fifteenth-century architects, the one most appreciative of the rules of classical design, and still be "incorrect" in practice. His art was consistent not with the buildings of the past but with the rational view of the world which the Renaissance had come to share with classical architecture.

37. Vasari, *Vite Cinque Annotate,* p. 24.
38. I am omitting from my consideration of Alberti's architectural practice works which cannot be attributed to him with certainty as well as those which depend entirely upon the scholarly reconstruction of architectural historians in order to be appreciated. Such works do not affect the argument of this section, in which I seek only to show how Alberti's buildings exemplify the ideas set forth in *De re aedificatoria.* For this purpose, it is naturally preferable to refer to buildings which are known without a doubt to be his and in which the original design has not been obscured by later additions.
The works I am not considering are the following: The Rucellai Chapel and the loggia across from the Rucellai Palace (Florence); his modification of Michelozzo's Rotonda in the Annunziata (Florence); the apse of San Martino at Gangalandi; San Sebastiano (Mantua); his role in restoring San Stefano Rotondo (Rome); and the Palazzo Venezia (Rome).
39. *An Autographed Letter.*

It was Alberti, for example, who made the Roman triumphal arch an integral element of Renaissance and hence of European architecture, but his first use of the arch was completely "unclassical": he used it to form a base for the statue raised in memory of the Marchese of Ferrara, Niccolo III d'Este[40] (fig. 33).

A classicizing intention is patent in the statue as well as in the Arco del Cavallo, as it is called. It is one of the earliest Renaissance revivals of the Roman equestrian form which Donatello's "Gattamelata" in Padua, and Verrocchio's "Colleoni" in Venice would make so famous, and its conception probably stems from Alberti's humanistic learning. When his friend, Leonello, became the new Marchese of Ferrara in 1441, Alberti undoubtedly advised him about the statue the Este prince was proposing to erect for his father, for in 1444 it was Alberti whom Leonello called upon to judge the competition for the work. If the idea of an equestrian statue was boldly "renascent," however, to raise the proud statue above a classically executed arch, as Alberti then did, was even more so. Thoroughly classical, and yet thoroughly "incorrect," the arch is delightfully carried out in perfect harmony with the dignity and bearing of the princely rider it supports. Laurel rings decorate the entablature as the mark of his distinction, and the equestrian Marchese of Ferrara is literally borne up by "triumph."

The modest arch of Ferrara foreshadowed Alberti's great architectural effort, to revive the forms of classical architecture while transposing them to unclassical structures, particularly to the Christian church.[41] In this respect, Alberti did for the exterior of the church what Brunelleschi accomplished for the interior. Brunelleschi, who died in 1446, left the exteriors of San Lorenzo and Santo Spirito unfinished; and his completed Pazzi Chapel, although an architectural gem, does not give much of an idea of how he might have conceived the outside of a church finished in the Renaissance style he had created. Surely there would be no more towers, turrets, and pinnacles, no more of the spires and pointed arches which conveyed the vertical movement of the Gothic cathedral. Nor would the striped marbles dear to medieval Florence be used, those panels without volume which take their tints from the changing light. Instead of the soaring Gothic frame and the presence of color and light, the rhythmic effect of classical forms would dominate church building now, as Brunelleschi had used the round arch and column to produce the metrical quality of his loggia of the Ospedale degli Innocenti. But someone had to show how this could be done for the exterior of a church.

What made Alberti's Tempio Malatestiano "one of the most famous

---

40. On the arch for the equestrian statue, see Adolfo Venturi, "Un opera sconosciuta di Leon B. Alberti," *L'Arte,* 17 (1914): 153–56.

41. Wittkower's study of Alberti's application of the classical orders to the church is indispensable, *Arch. Principles*, pp. 33–56.

33. Arch and equestrian statue of Niccolo III d'Este, Ferrara.

temples of Italy," to quote Vasari,[42] was that its "classical" design did just that. The three arches of the main story of its façade and the arch of its (incomplete) upper story are arranged like the three doorways and rose window of the typical Gothic façade, marking on the walled exterior of the church the interior relation of nave to aisles. But the form of the arches Alberti so disposed is that of the rounded triumphal arch; and the relation of aisles to nave, and of main story to upper one, which the classical arch expresses is reinforced by his use of the Corinthian column and architrave. The dome (which was not constructed) also carried out, and furthered, a classical tradition which Brunelleschi had restored in the Duomo. Brunelleschi had been inspired by the dome of the Pantheon, but where his polygonal cupola still betrays a trace of the pointed Gothic form, Alberti's hemispheric dome swells in the rounded Roman manner.

42. Vasari, *Vite*, pp. 31–32.

Thus transposed to the walled structure of the Christian church, the classical orders and the triumphal arch and dome came to constitute the dominant features of Renaissance ecclesiastical architecture. Yet even this integration of classical forms with the requirements of the exterior of the Christian church does not exhaust Alberti's accomplishment in the Tempio Malatestiano. The design of the building carried out in all its details (or as many of them as can be reconstructed) his own renascent ideal of composition.[43] Outside, a system of squares defines the façade (as in his later Santa Maria Novella). Two imaginary squares inscribed over the main story and meeting in the center of its doorway correspond to a single, central square inscribed over the window and arch of the upper story; and the 1:2 ratio of the Octave binds the width of the two "squares" of the main story to that of the "square" of the upper story. The major areas inside the church were evidently meant to bear the same 1:1 and 1:2 proportions to each other—though here, too, we are faced with an incomplete realization of Alberti's original plan.

The most recent studies of the Tempio Malatestiano point to the fact that inside and out were conceived as belonging to a single system of ratios; and as the exterior design rested upon the square, so that of the interior was to rest upon the circle. As reconstructed by Carlo Ragghianti, Alberti's interior design consisted of a centrally planned chapel which he intended to join to the already existing basilican church. The chapel, with an altar at its center, would have been surmounted by the cupola; and the height of the cupola was to match the diameter of this little "circular temple"—as it does in the Pantheon and in Diocletian's Baths. If Alberti used the classical orders and triumphal dome and arch as never before, adapting them to the alien purposes of the Christian church in the Tempio Malatestiano, the design of the church manifests the fully classical intent of embodying the proportional regularity of Nature.

Even more than the Tempio Malatestiano, the façade of Santa Maria Novella eloquently refutes the usual (and mutually contradictory) criticisms of Renaissance architecture as subservient to antiquity and incorrect in its use of classical forms.[44] From either standpoint, the intent and effect of the Renaissance building is inevitably missed. Had Alberti wanted only to "copy" classical buildings, he would never have undertaken a work in which he would have to retain the Gothic elements of a partly constructed façade. And they are prominently placed in this church (see fig. 32): six pointed arches over the marble coffins placed just above the base of the façade, two small fourteenth-century doors under their pointed arches, and a great circular window. Nor would he have carried to completion the Romanesque marble incrustation as

43. I am here following Ragghianti, "Tempio Malatestiano."
44. These opinions spring from certain mistaken notions about the "original" and the "functional" nature of art respectively. Geoffrey Scott traced the history of these and similar ideas and exposed their fallacies in *The Architecture of Humanism.*

he did, thereby making Santa Maria Novella blend with the medieval façades of Florence's San Miniato and Santa Maria del Fiore. On the other hand, the fact that he took the entrance to the Pantheon as his model for the fine classical doorway of Santa Maria Novella; and that he crowned its façade with a classical pediment and set off the areas of the main story by giant Corinthian columns—all this is certainly an indication of a classical intent.

The architectural "meaning" of Santa Maria Novella evidently cannot be found in any of these elements taken singly, but the spirit and significance of the work speaks out clearly in the arrangement of its parts. The formal relations among what would seem to be the jarring elements of three different styles, Romanesque, Gothic, and classical, produce Alberti's unmistakeable kind of unity. His façade is a "harmony," achieving what Philolaos (fl. 470 B.C.) defined as "the unification of the composed manifold and the accordance of the discordant."[45]

By adding the four great Corinthian half-columns to the lower story, and four striped pilasters to the upper, Alberti broke up the wall of the façade into the distinct areas which he then related rhythmically to each other. The horizontal demarcation was carried out by the broad attic between the two stories, and by the entablatures that run above the columns of the main story and pilasters of the upper one. The pediment is the final horizontal touch; it lifts the upper story, and it creates the impression of the three matching imaginary squares of the front: the two "squares" into which the main story can be divided, and the "square" of the upper story between the two decorative scrolls. The scrolls, in turn, bind the upper to the lower story, just as the attic and the pediment distinguish them. With all these areas defined, the proportional rhythm of the entire façade could come to life.

The classicism as well as the originality of Santa Maria Novella consists in this metrical relation of the parts of the façade to each other and the whole. As an architectural expression of Nature's congruity, it restored the aesthetic vision of classical antiquity, yet it did so in a manner consonant with the medieval Christian context in which the classical outlook was once again emerging. With its black and white marble designs, Santa Maria Novella retains its Florentine character, just as the Tempio Malatestiano echoes the monuments of Rimini; and in both buildings, the column, the arch, and the pediment were used to bring a new and "fitting" design to the structure of the Christian church.

To restrict the use of the column and entablature to purely structural purposes would have required a peculiarly pedantic kind of classicism in the fifteenth century, an archeological attitude alien to the imaginative spirit of the time. Why should the architect reconstruct the Christian church as a pagan

45. H. Diels, *Die Fragmente der Vorsokratiker*, (Berlin, 1934) 1: 410, frgmt. 10.　　121

temple or refrain from using the classical orders altogether when, as ornament, they could articulate those intelligible harmonies which architecture had come to seek? Alberti not only made free use of the column and entablature to delimit wall areas so as to relate them proportionally to each other; he even regarded the column, composed as it is of parts exactly proportioned to each other, as the most perfect kind of ornament.[46]

Under the heading of "ornament" in *De re aedificatoria,* he included windows, the designs of pavements and ceilings, the interior decoration of cupolas, statues and paintings,—and the column and its members. Accepting the dubious Vitruvian distinction between beauty and ornament, he defined ornament as an auxiliary luster and complement to beauty. The beauty of the building, which consists in the formal relations among its parts, was inherent in the building, he thought, whereas ornament was "added on." When it came to the use of ornament, however, Alberti's recommendations coincided perfectly with his organic conception of the beauty of the building as nothing superfluous and nothing wanting. In practice, if not in its theory of ornament, Renaissance architecture was sound. From the vantage point of a theory of architecture more general than Alberti's notion of the building as a kind of "body," the organicity of the building can be seen to belong to the aesthetic effect created by it, and not to the physical structure itself. The "work" that the architect creates is this effect or "semblance," and whatever contributes to it is an integral part of it.[47] Renaissance architecture used ornament, and particularly the column, in this compositionally integral sense, to contribute to the total artistic illusion of organicity as the Renaissance saw it, namely as proportional form.

46. Alberti discussed the relation of ornament to beauty in book 6, chapter 2. Ornaments, including the column, he treated in chapters 11–13 of book 6. Book 7 is concerned with sacred ornament; book 8 with ornaments of secular and public works; book 9, chapters 1–4 with ornaments of secular and private buildings.

47. It is not the actual structure of the building but the image, the "virtual world" created by that structure that is the artistic work. Consequently, the artistic merit (or demerit) of ornament is to be judged in relation to this image. As Susanne K. Langer put it in *Feeling and Form,* "the created 'place' is essentially a semblance, and whatever affects that semblance is architecturally relevant," p. 95.

"As *scene* is the basic abstraction of pictorial art, and *kinetic volume* of sculpture, that of architecture is *an ethnic domain.* Actually, of course, a domain is not a 'thing' among other 'things'; it is the sphere of influence of a function, or functions; it may have physical effects on some geographical locality or it may not. Nomadic cultures, or cultural phenomena like the seafaring life, do not inscribe themselves on any fixed place on earth. Yet a ship, constantly changing its location, is none the less a self-contained place, and so is a Gypsy camp, an Indian camp. . . . Literally we say the camp is *in* a place; culturally, it *is* a place. . . .

"A place, in this non-geographical sense, is a created thing, an ethnic domain made visible, tangible, sensible. As such it is, of course, an illusion. Like any other plastic symbol, it is primarily an illusion of self-contained, self-sufficient, perceptual space. But the principle of organization is its own: for it is organized as a functional realm made visible—the center of a virtual world, the 'ethnic domain,' " pp. 94–95.

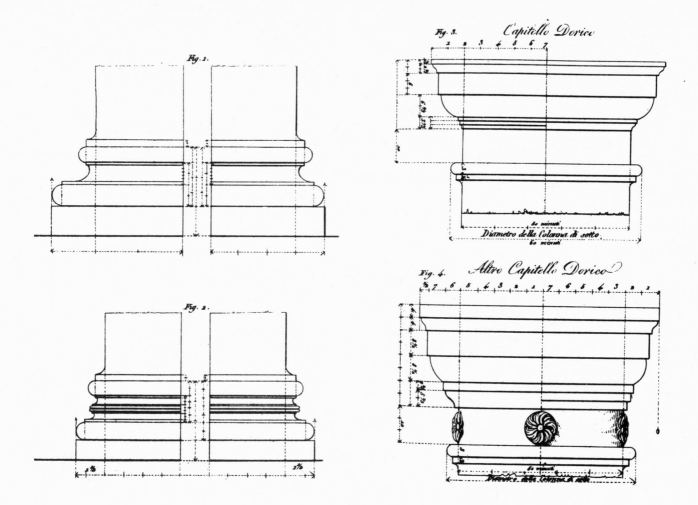

Even the sequence of the major topics covered in *De re aedificatoria* reveals this characteristic conception of the column. The book proceeds from structural to ornamental issues without incurring any break in logical and aesthetic continuity: Alberti first considered the relation of the building to its site; then the relation of the units of the building to each other and the whole; then the relations within each unit of height, width, and depth; and finally his thought moved quite naturally to the "members" of the classical orders. The theme is ever the same, the relation of parts within the whole they compose:

The Dorians made their Capital of the same Height as their Base, and divided that Height into three Parts [fig. 34]: The First they gave to the Abacus, the Second to the Ovolo which is under the Abacus, and the Third they allowed to the Gorgerin or Neck of the Capital which is under the

34. *The Doric Order in* De re aedificatoria.

Ovolo. The Breadth of the Abacus every Way was equal to one whole Diameter, and a twelfth of the Bottom of the Shaft. This Abacus is divided into two Members, an upright Cymatium and a Plinth, and the Cymatium is two fifths Parts of the whole Abacus. The upper Edge of the Ovolo joined close to the Bottom of the Abacus. At the Bottom of the Ovolo some made three little Annulets, and others a Cymatium as an Ornament, but these never took up above a third Part of the Ovolo. The Diameter of the Neck of the Capital, which was the lowest Part of it, never exceeded the Thickness of the Top of the Shaft, which is to be observed in all Sorts of Capitals. Others, according to the Observations which I have made upon ancient Buildings, used to make the Height of the Doric Capital three quarters of the Diameter of the Bottom of the Shaft, and divided this whole Height of the Capital into eleven parts, of which they allowed four to the Abacus, four to the Ovolo, and three to the Neck of the Capital. Then they divided the Abacus into two Parts, the uppermost of which they gave to the Cymatium and the lowermost to the Plinth. The Ovolo they also divided into two Parts, assigning the lowermost either to the Annulets or to a Cymatium, which served as an Edging to the Ovolo, and in the Neck of the Capital some cut Roses, and other Leaves with a high Projecture. This was the Practice of the Dorians.[48]

The column in itself is a perfect proportional form, exhibiting the order of of nature as did the entire building, and this is why the Renaissance could adopt it as ornament. For this same reason, Alberti wanted the designs in the pavements of churches to express "musical and geometric proportions," for while Renaissance decoration was thought of as "added on," it was nonetheless "natural" and "apt" in number, in symmetrical placement, and in its proportions. A delightful example of this theoretical precept is provided by the inlaid marble designs which Alberti composed for his imaginative version of the Holy Sepulcher.[49] He constructed this little tomb, which stands in the Rucellai Chapel of San Pancrazio in Florence, for his Florentine patron, the great merchant Giovanni Rucellai; and he covered its exterior with ornamental roundels, each one of which is an original motif formed by a sure proportional order (figs. 35, 36).

For one design he used the Rucellai crest, a full sail fastened by flying ribbons. This design, incidentally, he had occasion to repeat; it also runs along the entablatures of Santa Maria Novella and the Palazzo Rucellai, since it was Giovanni Rucellai who commissioned Alberti to renovate both buildings *al*

48. *De re aedif,* bk. 7, chap. 8.
49. There is an interesting article on the Holy Sepulcher and the Rucellai Chapel by Ludwig H. Heydenreich, "Die Capella Rucellai von San Pancrazio in Florenz," *De artibus opuscola XL: Essays in Honor of Erwin Panofsky,* pp. 219–29. Heydenreich maintains that the chapel must also be attributed to Alberti, and that the proportions of the Sepulcher are related to the proportions of the chapel.

35. *The Holy Sepulcher in San Pancrazio, Florence.*

36. *The Holy Sepulcher in San Pancrazio, Florence.*

modo antico.[50] The decorative roundels of the Holy Sepulcher are neither more nor less *al modo antico* than these buildings, or, for that matter, than the entire tomb itself, with its fanciful crested cornice, its "oriental" tower, its corner pilasters, broad entablature, and symmetrically placed marble designs. Again we meet novel forms which are "classical" by virtue of their geometric character, fresh perceptual images which spring at once from Euclid and from the empirical attitude of the quattrocento.

This stylistic feature of the roundels has been caught so well in the description given by the art historian and critic, Adolfo Venturi, that I should like to quote him on at least one of them, the circle inscribed in a star: "The rays of the star," he points out, "are eight leaves of chestnut gathered in the center by a black ring. The motif has been lovingly copied in the undulations of the festooned contours, but each festoon is placed in symmetrical relation with the festoon of the next leaf, and the distances between are studied with a noble sense of proportionality."[51]

Once the aesthetic function of Renaissance ornament is understood, we can easily follow Alberti's artistic reasoning as he applied the classical orders to the façade of the famous Florentine palace which, to this day, is the home of the Rucellai family (fig. 37). The Romans had already combined the Greek columnar design with walled structures by superimposing the classical orders on the walls of public buildings. The Colosseum is perhaps the best known and finest example of this decorative "Arcade order," as it came to be called. The adaptation of columnar architecture to private dwellings, however, was unknown in antiquity, but this was the way Alberti finished the façade of the already existent Rucellai Palace.

Designed around 1460, the façade of the Palazzo Rucellai cannot compete with the sense of power and might generated by the impressive, still fortresslike palaces of fifteenth-century Florence such as the Strozzi Palace designed by Benedetto da Maiano, or Michelozzo's Palazzo Medici-Riccardi (fig. 38). But the Rucellai Palace humanized and civilized this harsh, militant genre to a remarkable degree. Using flat masonry planes with beveled edges, Alberti smoothed out the rugged rustication of the Florentine palace; and by his novel treatment of the façade as a harmonic unit, he created a palatial style which was unclassical in its use of the orders, yet was surely *al modo antico.*

Again the orders serve no structural purpose in the engineering sense of the word. Their "function" is purely compositional in the Rucellai Palace (and in the whole class of palaces which soon boasted this use of the orders). In this aesthetic sense, however, they serve a genuinely architectonic purpose, for the orders make a proportionally articulated whole out of the building's façade. Elegant pilasters, Doric on the ground floor, Ionic on the first, and Corinthian

50. Filarete's phrase, describing the Rucellai Palace. See Peter Tigler, *Die Architekturtheorie des Filarete,* pp. 86ff.

51. "Intarsi Marmorei di Leon Battista Alberti," *L'Arte,* 22 (1919): 34–36.

37. *The Rucellai Palace, Florence*

on the upper floor, break up the front of the Rucellai Palace into seven vertical bays; and the three horizontal stories of the building are demarcated by classical entablatures which carry the Rucellai emblems in their frieze. The varied, rhythmic spacing of the rusticated blocks keeps each of these areas "alive" and bound to all the others, creating an effect of dynamic unity which is enhanced by elements that seem to "respond" to each other in their geometric forms. The bench that runs along the ground floor is mirrored in the projecting cornice of Roman derivation which crowns the work; and like bench and cornice, the level architraves of the doorways and windows emphasize the rectangular form of the entire façade and each of its bays.

This is Alberti's most graceful work, and it belongs nowhere else in the world but in Florence. Like the façade of Santa Maria Novella, the Palazzo Rucellai echoes an erstwhile Florentine tradition and transforms it at the same time by "a certain consensus and agreement of the parts of the whole in respect to number, measure, and arrangement, just as Congruity, the absolute and primary law of Nature, requires." For in the Renaissance, as the Florentine Vitruvius had decreed, "this is what architecture chiefly aims at."

Nature and Genius

With striking consistency, Alberti carried out his aesthetic vision in a variety of ways: in his theory of architecture, in the classical program of *De re aedificatoria,* in his buildings; and in each of these facets of his architectural work, the clarity of his theoretical ideas enabled him to bring about significant, original developments. This is also true of his reflections on the nature of artistic activity. Down to the Renaissance, the practice of art had been subordinated to to the "higher" cognitive activities of the mind. The Beautiful, which had been assimilated to the Good since the time of Socrates, served only an appetitive purpose; it awakened the desire of the soul for a transcendent Good in which the beautiful, sensible object somehow participated. Aesthetic theory therefore tended to look "through" the artistic work rather than at it. The value of art was explained in terms of moral or intelligible realities that lay "behind" or "beyond" its pleasing appearance, and the practice of art was regarded as mere craft. Whereas the "liberal arts" yielded knowledge of the intelligible, the visual arts were denied any such cognitive function—until Renaissance art theory severed the bond between the Beautiful and the Good to set up a new one between the Beautiful and the True.[52]

52. For the general relation of Beauty and Truth in Renaissance metaphysical and aesthetic thought, see Ernst Cassirer's *Individual and Cosmos in Renaissance Philosophy*. For the history of the classification of the arts, see Paul Oskar Kristeller, "The Modern System of the Arts: A Study in the History of Aesthetics," *Journal of the History of Ideas,* 12 (1951): 496–527, and 13 (1952): 17–46; reprinted in *Renaissance Thought II: Papers on Humanism and the Arts.* See also Rudolf Wittkower, *The Artist and the Liberal Arts.*

38. *Michelozzo, Palazzo Medici-Riccardi,*
Florence.
(Brogi-Art Reference Bureau.)

One of the odd features of the metaphysically inspired system of the arts which the Renaissance inherited was that music was treated as a theoretical study while the visual arts were classified as manual pursuits. Because of its theory of harmonic ratios, music was one of the seven liberal arts, belonging (along with arithmetic, geometry, and astronomy) to the mathematical sciences of the quadrivium. Classical architecture, with its harmonic ratios and regular proportions, provided no bridge as yet whereby the rational character of the musical art of harmony could be extended to the visual arts. For this, a mathematical theory of knowledge and of art was required, so as to bind art to cognition, and such a viewpoint, although not alien to ancient or medieval thought, was not consistently developed in either period. In the Middle Ages, the classical systems of architectural and sculptural proportions fell into disuse; and in antiquity, when Vitruvius sought to establish architecture's claim as a liberal art, he did so by assimilating it to the literary or rhetorical arts rather than to the mathematical ones.

Vitruvius recognized that the concept of *ars* was not always exhausted by "craft." An art, he believed, consists not only in the technical skill required for its proper execution, but also in abstract knowledge insofar as its practice is founded upon rational principles which can be "set forth and explained" in words.[53] Architecture was one of the arts that could be rationally demonstrated in this way. It could be shown to follow from linguistically expressible principles or "reasons." Vitruvius therefore required a liberal education for the architect, so that he would, in fact, be able to give a literary "demonstration" of his practice. The cognitive content of architecture depended upon the architect's general, liberal education; and conversely, only those persons were true architects "who from boyhood have mounted by the steps of these various studies and, being trained in the knowledge of the liberal arts and sciences, have reached the temple of architecture at the top."[54]

---

53. *De architectura,* bk. 1, chaps. 1, 15: "Ex duabus rebus singulas artes esse compositas, ex opere et eius ratiocinatione."

In the beginning of the first book, Vitruvius speaks of the *scientia* or knowledge of the architect who must have both manual skill and a literary education (i.e., he cannot be *sine litteris*) so that he may "set forth and explain" the works he makes. "Both in general and especially in architecture are these two things found; that which signifies and that which is signified. That which is signified is the thing proposed about which we speak; that which signifies is the demonstration unfolded in systems of precepts (hand autem significat demonstratio rationibus doctrinarum explicata). Wherefore a man who is to follow the architectural profession manifestly needs to have experience of both kinds." Bk. 1, chaps. 1, 2, 3.

Galen's classification of the liberal arts, which was occasionally adopted in the fourteenth century, included architecture (and medicine); but again the theoretical content of architectural knowledge was not regarded as mathematical in kind, and the status of architecture did not affect that of painting and sculpture.

54. *Ibid.,* bk. 1, chaps. 1, 11, 12.

The first modern reaction to the Vitruvian idea of art as a combination of theory and practice was Alberti's, and it was one of glad acceptance. In sympathy with the new feeling for the dignity of art that accompanied the flowering of Italian culture in the late Middle Ages, Alberti wrote his first work on the visual arts as a literary "demonstration" in this Vitruvian sense. He deduced the art of painting from its natural-mathematical principles, thus setting forth its *scientia*. This is undoubtedly what he regarded as the great novelty of his work, for he claimed that he was "the first to have commended the art of painting to writing."[55] He surely knew of the medieval tradition of technical studio books like Cennino Cennini's *Libro dell'arte,* and he was familiar with the ancient histories of art and the artists; but such works had not established the rational principles of painting. *Della pittura* contained more than practical rules; it deduced the practice of painting from its "roots in nature." And this kind of deduction was quite different from tracing the history of the art from its presumed genesis: "We do not recite histories like Pliny," Alberti wrote, calling attention to the distinctive, systematic aim of his work. "We are building anew an art of painting which, as far as I can see, is not to be found in writing."

As befits the newly founded "rational" character of the art, Alberti required a general, literary education for the painter. Vitruvius had demanded that the architect be given a general education; Alberti now urged the painter to be literate and to study all the liberal arts and sciences. The painter, a humble craftsman until now, was told to associate with literary men, with poets and humanists; and just as the painter was to become a liberally educated man, so painting was to become part of the liberal educational program, as contributing to the cultivation of the free, noble mind.[56]

This dissociation of painting from the crafts, as it was first attempted in *Della pittura,* did not yet express any new theoretical development. It was more indicative of the new feeling for artistic import than of any new theory of it; and the fact is, that while the "liberal" virtues of painting were soon extolled, and the sisterhood of painting and poetry became a prevalent theme, the cognitive value of painting was not to be generally acknowledged for another hundred years.[57] The fifteenth century offered no stronger argument than the one given by Alberti, and because Alberti was following the precedent of Vitruvius, he, too, rested his case upon the literary cultivation and allusions of the painter. Instead of basing the rational claims of painting upon its

55. *Della pittura,* pp. 78, 114.

56. The novelty of this demand for literacy on the part of artists is reflected in a contemporary, anonymous *Vita del Brunelleschi.* In Brunelleschi's time, the biographer writes, "a chi non s'aspettave d'essere o dottore, o notaio, o sacerdote, pochi erano quelli che si dessono, o fussino dati alle lettere. . . . Per alcuno autore nel tempo dei gentili s'è dato precetto, come ne' nostri dì fece Battista degli Alberti." Cited by Mancini, *Vita,* p. 333, n. 1.

57. Schlosser, *Lett. Art.,* pp. 106–17, and Anthony Blunt, *Artistic Theory in Italy, 1450–1600,* pp. 48–57.

mathematical, perspectival *scientia,* he cited passages from Pliny and other ancient authors to show that antiquity held the visual arts and artists in the same high esteem as he did, and for the same "humanistic" reasons—namely, the liberal education of the artist and the literary "ideas" expressed in his works. *Ut pictura poesis.*[58]

The supposed similarity between poetry and painting was not the notion that was destined to raise painting from the ranks of the manual arts, however. It did contribute to the growing sense of the painter's dignity, making his relations with poets and princes easy and familiar, but it was the inclusion of painting and sculpture among the mathematical sciences in the sixteenth century that marked their arrival, along with architecture, as *arti di disegno,* or "fine arts." Mathematics, not literature, accounted for the common features of the three arts of design in the Renaissance, and mathematics gave those features their theoretical import and worth.

Although Alberti failed to take this step with respect to painting, the acceptance of painting as a fine art came only as Alberti's ideas on nature and artistic imitation gained ground. Actually, it was perspective, rather than any of the visual arts *per se,* that first forced its way into the company of the cognitive disciplines. Perspective boldly appeared as the tenth liberal art on Pollaiuolo's Tomb of Pope Sixtus IV, signifying the right of the art of proportional vision and depiction to joint the seven traditional arts, Philosophy, and Theology as a theoretical pursuit (fig. 39). As a theory of regular, visual proportions, of spatial ratios governed by law, Prospettiva put painting on a par with music and its "science" of harmonic intervals. Leonardo was probably the first to express this idea when he called painting the sister of music because it studies the laws of spatial intervals.[59]

58. On this theory, see Rensselaer W. Lee, "Ut pictura poesis: A Humanistic Theory of Painting," *Art Bulletin,* 30 (1940): 197–269.

59. Richter, 1: 72, 76.

In "Pollaiuolo's Tomb of Sixtus IV," *Journal of the Warburg and Courtauld Institutes,* 16 (1953): 239–74, L.D. Ettlinger argues that the figure of Prospettiva represents Natural Perspective (Optics) and has no relation to painting. But Pollaiuolo has Prospettiva hold not only Peckham's book on natural perspective but the astrolabe (or Alberti's Horizon) as well. Since Prospettiva is clearly not Astronomy, who is also shown on the tomb, what can the presence of the astrolabe signify but that science of vision *and representation* which the fifteenth century brought into being in painting, in cartography, and in sculpture—using the astrolabe in all three instances so as to ascertain and proportionally represent "measures." Prospettiva unites all the arts that seek to *depict* the ratios among objects in space. She is no longer the theoretical science of Optics (which still belonged to Philosophy, also shown on the tomb); she became an applied mathematical science in the course of the fifteenth century, and as such drew painting into the circle of the liberal arts.

For the medieval iconographic tradition of the arts, see Adolf Katzenellenbogen, "The Representation of the Seven Liberal Arts," *Twelfth-Century Europe and the Foundations*
of Modern Society, pp. 39–55.

39. *A. Pollaiuolo,* Prospettiva.
A detail from the tomb of Sixtus IV in
the Grotte Vaticane, Rome.
(Anderson-Art Reference Bureau.)

But perspective (even "artificial perspective") was not a term, or a "science," which the Renaissance restricted to painting. The rules of proportional depiction came to form the *scientia* of all three visual arts in the Renaissance, and in this broad sense, Prospettiva made possible a new understanding and evaluation of them all as rational pursuits. Alberti saw this by the time he wrote his work on architecture, and there he carried this direction of thought through to its completion. He required learning, even genius, of the architect, but not a proficiency in all the branches of liberal learning. In open opposition to Vitruvius, he now declared that the artist need master only what pertains to his art, and "the arts which are useful and indeed absolutely necessary to the architect are painting [viz., perspective] and mathematics."

> I do not require him to be deeply learned in the rest; for I think it ridiculous to expect, as does a certain author, that an architect should be a profound lawyer, in order to know the right of conveying water or placing boundaries between neighbors. . . . Nor need he be a perfect astronomer to know that libraries ought to be situated to the north and stoves to the south; nor a very great musician to place the vases of copper or brass in a theatre for assisting the voice [acoustics]. Neither do I require that he should be an orator [i.e., a humanist, trained in rhetoric], in order to be able to display to any person that would employ him, the services which he is capable of doing him; for knowledge, experience and perfect mastery in what he is to speak of will never fail to help him to explain his sense sufficiently. . . . [In all these sciences] there is indeed no harm in his being more expert, but painting and mathematics are what he can no more be without than a poet can be without the knowledge of feet and syllables.[60]

In *De re aedificatoria,* Alberti's ideas on art had developed to the point where the *scientia* of achitecture alone was sufficient to ground the liberal character of the art and the dignity of the artist. His liberal education was all to the good, of course, but the architect's rational task was defined by and limited to the principles of his art; and this, because those principles were mathematical in kind. Until now, art had been readily distinguishable from knowledge: its end was a "work" whereas the end of knowing was truth. But the consistently mathematical treatment of artistic form in *De re aedificatoria* blurred this distinction. "Painting" (perspective) and the theory of musical proportions opened up to the architect a vision of the universal "reasons" or rules of Nature and its supreme, universal law; and they taught him to incorporate this vision of the ideal in the sensible "body" of his buildings. This is what made architecture a noble undertaking for Alberti, leading him to place it among the pursuits that yield disinterested knowledge rather than those which yield utility.[61]

Magna est res architectura, he confessed; and its practitioner is a man of genius as well as application, of judgment as well as experience. "To run up anything that is immediately necessary for any particular purpose . . . is not so much the business of an architect as of a common workman; but to raise an edifice which is to be complete in every part, and to consider and provide beforehand everything necessary for such a work, this is the business of that comprehensive genius." The mind as well as the hand, judgment as well as skill, and a sure knowledge of painting (perspective) and mathematics were necessary

60. *De re aedif.,* bk. 9, chap. 10.
61. *Ibid. Also,* Preface; bk. 1, chap. 9; bk. 6, chap. 4; bk. 9, chap. 8; bk. 10, chap. 1.

for the architect, because the aims of knowledge and of art had become fused in his work. Only by recognizing the supreme law of Nature as his own, and by discovering how that "marvelous artificer of things has composed . . . her beautiful bodies," could the Renaissance architect design his buildings. In the structure of his artificial bodies, he sought to catch and reflect the theoretic plan of Nature.

The architect could thus be said to create a second nature, but no longer in the Platonic sense, as a purposeless duplication of the first, an artifice leading us ever further from the Ideas in which all natural objects participate. In the perceptual form of the building, he "re-presented" the universal, ideal relations that bind the world, setting them forth in a visible medium so that they, and the Harmony they comprise, could be immediately "seen" and understood. The architect served the cause of knowledge, of Truth, by serving that of Beauty. He discovered and embodied in his buildings only the regular patterns of Nature, effecting a unification of Truth and Beauty in his works which profoundly changed both the conception of the building and of the builder. "The little temples we make," Palladio was to write, "ought to resemble this very great one, which, by His immense goodness was perfectly completed with one word of His."[62] By making the "body" of the church exemplify the necessary *ragioni* that constitute the Beauty of the cosmos, the Renaissance architect brought about a "resemblance" between his temple and the great House of the World.

In artistic practice, this meant that the church was no longer to be built as a sort of "arc" in which all the intelligible Forms of Nature, History, and Revelation could find their symbolic representation and their place. The Renaissance church ceased to be universal in this encyclopedic sense in order to exhibit, instead, the rational universality of law. This avowed architectural aim, to schematize in the spatial form of the church the immanent, harmonious order of the world, found majestic realization in Alberti's own church of Sant' Andrea in Mantua (fig. 40). This was his final architectural work, designed around 1470 for Lodovico Gonzaga, and it carries out these theoretical ideas with perfect artistic clarity.[63]

The great triumphal arch that opens the façade of Sant' Andrea and supports the deep, coffered barrel vault of the porch is once again the basic form

62. Preface to bk. 4, cited by Wittkower, *Arch. Principles,* p. 23.
63. The construction of Sant' Andrea was not completed until the eighteenth century, but the work was carried out largely in accordance with Alberti's plans. Alberti's nave terminated in an apse; the dome, transept, and choir were all later additions to his plan. Also, the painted decoration of the interior violates his preference for Brunelleschian, unpainted walls. Like Brunelleschi, Alberti wanted architectural elements alone to provide decoration within a church. For plans and detailed drawings of Sant' Andrea, see Ernst Ritscher, *Die Kirche S. Andrea in Mantua.* For the dates of construction, and a study of the rhythmic proportions of the church, see Erich Hubala, "L. B. Alberti's Langhaus von Sant Andrea in Mantua," *Festschrift Kurt Badt zum siebzigsten Geburtstage,* pp. 83-120.

40. *Sant' Andrea, Mantua, façade*

of the building. It reappears inside where it supports the enormous barrel vault
of the nave, bringing a new, and truly Roman amplitude to the Christian
church (fig. 41). A novel spatial image was created in Sant' Andrea, an image of
fullness and completion which would characterize the art of the High
Renaissance, of Bramante's St. Peter's, for example, and Raphael's "School of
Athens" which takes Bramante's design as its setting. For Alberti's rounded arch
and barrel vaulting supplanted not only the pointed arch and ribbed, groined
vault of Northern Gothic which rises with systematic lucidity to fearsome
heights; it supplanted the unvaulted nave as well, the level ceiling which
Brunelleschi used (fig. 7), as did the early Christian basilicas and many Italian

41. *Sant' Andrea, Mantua, interior*

137

Gothic churches, to give emphasis to the longitudinal movement of the Latin cross plan, directing the worshipper towards the single, sacred focus of the altar.

A self-contained, completely uniform space fills the arching shapes of Sant' Andrea, a vastness which extends in all directions alike and which absorbed the traditional aisles of the basilican plan. Here there are no aisles which give, by their distinctive space, a tripartite form to the nave,—not even those aisles which Brunelleschi formed by the classical column and rounded arch of his nave arcades. Alberti hollowed chapels out of the walls, but they belong to the one domain of the interior, a domain which is entirely visible and can be fully comprehended from any given point within it.

The interior space of Sant' Andrea is that of a cosmos held in dynamic equipoise, and the relations among the multiplicity of its forms manifest the one Final Cause of Harmony. Not only do the forms of the façade reappear in the interior of the church, but so do the relations among them, their relative positions and proportions.[64] On either side of the triumphal arch of the façade, a rectangular bay is set between two giant pilasters. The pilasters run to the height of the arch and carry the simple entablature of the façade. Inside, the height of the wall of the nave up to its entablature corresponds exactly to this measure. And on both sides of the nave, the three broad, arched chapels are flanked by narrower, rectangular areas which hold smaller chapels within them (fig. 42). On either side of these rectangular areas of the interior, giant pilasters rise once again to bear the main entablature which runs through the church at the level of the arch of chapels.

Arches, rectangles, and circles, too, appear and reappear in a complex variety of sizes and positions. Rectangular doorways are set in the arched walls of the interior, and high above the doors, circular windows "respond" to the great circle of the dome and the single, circular window that dominates the entrance wall (fig. 43). Three smaller circular windows are set in the three smaller arches that make up the great concave arch of the chancel wall behind the altar. These lucid and simple geometric forms are met with everywhere, and everywhere they bear the same dominant ratios to each other, building up by their diverse but proportional interrelations the vast, harmonious design of the whole.

Inside the church and out, broad arch and rectangular wall area alternate rhythmically; and the arched and rectangular areas of the interior are themselves made up of smaller arches, rectangles, and circles related to each other in the same subtle, but unmistakeable proportions. All these echoing forms and ratios, sounded as the dominant motifs of this beautiful church and recapitulated in each of its minor developments, create exactly the effect that Alberti sought: a lucid impression of unity in diversity, a "triumphant," intelligible harmony

64. See Wittkower's *Arch. Principles* on this, and also for his study of San Sebastiano in Mantua, interesting for its Greek cross plan.

42. *Sant' Andrea, Mantua, interior, chapel.*

which binds a manifold of relations in a perfect whole.

The multifarious world caught in this mirror of art was one governed by a majestic design which the form of the church reflected. As in nature, so in the building,

> everything is to be measured and put together with the greatest exactness of lines and angles, that the beholder's eye may have a clear and distinct view along the cornices, between the columns on the inside and without, receiving every moment fresh delight from the variety he encounters, so much so that after the most careful and even repeated views, he shall not be able to depart without once more turning back to take another look, nor, upon the most critical examination, be able to find in any part of the entire structure any one thing unequal, incongruous, out of proportion, or not conducive to the general Beauty of the whole.[65]

And the world, like the building, also had its designer. The mere idea of two such matching realms of being, of the little temple which is analogous to the very great one in its formal structure, called forth the notion of two formative powers: the rational, creative spirit of man, and the ultimate creative power of nature which came to be regarded as the original model and source of artistic genius.

This is the aesthetic outlook that gave to the artist his *divinità*, elevating him for all time from the ranks of the craftsmen. The reverence with which art and the artist came to be treated in the Renaissance arose from the conviction that the resemblance between Art and Nature was a complete one, penetrating to the very springs of creation. The age that viewed its architectural works as bodies which imitate the bodies "created by Nature," the age that recognized in artistic form the ordering power of reason—that age discovered in its own creativity a further, dynamic analogue with "Nature, the greatest artist of all forms."[66] Most of Alberti's references to God are couched in terms of his creativity, "God, the Creator of all things" being a typical phrase. When he uses the terms "Nature" and "God" synonymously, foreshadowing Spinoza's *Natura sive Deus,* it is the creative force of Nature he is referring to, the creative power which, for him, is divine: "Fece la natura, cioè Idio, l'uomo composto parte celeste e divino, . . ."[67] And because the artist imitates this creative

---

65. *De re aedif,* bk. 9, chap. 10.
66. "Naturam optimam formarum arteficem sibi fore imitandam," *ibid.,* bk. 9, chap. 5. Similarly, in *Della pitt.,* p. 88: "in questa compositione di superficie molto si cerca la gratia et bellezza delle cose quale, ad chi voglia seguirla, pare amme niuna più atta et più certa via che di torla dalla natura, ponendo mente in che modo la natura maravigliosa artefice delle cose, bene abbia in bei corpi conposte le superficie."
67. *I primi tre libri dell famiglia,* p. 195.

43. *Sant' Andrea, Mantua, interior, entrance wall.*

process which Alberti and the Renaissance took to be the divine power of Nature, the artist became another god.[68]

By art, the spirit of man itself became an image of the Divine, for what the artist had come to imitate was the rational, formative process of *natura naturans,* the creative genius of "Nature, that is, God."

68. "Dipigniendo animali, se porgiesse quasi uno iddio"; and, "in sé tiene queste lode la pictura che qual sia pittore maestro vedrà le sue opere essere adorate e sentirà quasi giudicate un altro iddio." *Della pitt.,* p. 77.
Thus Leonardo called the artist the grandson of God (Richter, I: 326–29). And Cesariano, the editor of the first Italian edition and commentary on Vitruvius, wrote in 1521: "quelli Architecti che sano producere li sollerti effecti pareno come semidei perche cercano che larte si assimiglia et supplisca a la natura" (quoted by Wittkower, *Arch. Principles,* p. 15). In *The Artists as Creator* (Baltimore, 1956), Milton Nahm has a chapter on this "Great Analogy" between the Creator – God and the creator – artist. He does not deal directly with the rise of this idea in the Renaissance, but his general observations hold true for the Renaissance period.

4
The Rational Cosmos

Art and Cosmology, Medieval and Modern

As the Renaissance applied its rules of proportion to painting, sculpture, and architecture, the world picture of the Middle Ages began to lose its hold upon the imagination. The aesthetic intuition of an immanent, rational world order steadily gained ground, weakening and finally supplanting the forms of medieval intuition and expression. Flemish painting had been very popular in quattrocento Italy, but to the fully developed classical vision of the High Renaissance, the Flemish works seemed to be composed "with a view to external exactness" only. Michelangelo complained that those glowing representations of the medieval view of reality were executed "without reason or art, without symmetry or proportion, without skillful choice or boldness."[1]

Of course, the Flemish painters were not impelled to seek a dramatic unification of the "abundance and variety" of elements in a picture. For Flemish art, the picture was an occasion to present the multitudinous details of the sensible world. For the Renaissance, details had to serve the *istoria,* "to fill it out or point it up." Facial expressions, gestures, the movements and positions of the body—all were to reveal the inner "movements of the spirit." Only thus could the painter achieve "composition and not lawless confusion."[2]

This conception of immanent law the Renaissance also sought in the well-proportioned body. The classical body which requires a nude representation to fully exhibit its principle of organic unity, this body which, even when draped, is built up as a system of bones, muscles, and sinews, was unknown to Flemish art. There is nothing organically convincing about Flemish figures,

1. Michelangelo, in Anthony Blunt, *Artistic Theory in Italy, 1450–1600,* p. 61. Alberti also spoke of the work of art as a product of reason (i.e., theory, mathematical rules) and art (technical skill): "il lavoro o una opera che sia mediante la ragione e la arte perfetta" ("Della statua," *Opere volgari,* 4: 180). The meaning of "symmetry and proportion" should be clear from the description of Renaissance architectural theory given earlier.
2. *Della pittura,* p. 92.

44. *Hugo van der Goes,* The Fall of Man. *In the Kunsthistorisches Museum, Vienna. (Bruckmann-Art Reference Bureau.)*

enveloped as they are in heavy, richly-worked robes, or masked by crisp cloth.
Even where the nude is present, as in Hugo van der Goes' "Fall of Man" (fig.
44), it is the living effect of flesh tones (which reproduce poorly) that strike
the viewer rather than the body's anatomical form. Eve's arms, hands, and feet are
particularly "out of proportion" in the van der Goes panel. In other portrait
panels, another kind of disproportion commonly appears where the hands and
body seem smaller than they "ought" to be by Renaissance standards, heightening
a certain disparity in expressiveness between face and figure. In such portrait
studies, as in Hans Memling's "Portrait of an Old Man" (fig. 45), the head
dwarfs and dominates the body, and whatever is animate and moving
comes to be concentrated in the fine, introspective faces of the paintings.

The Flemish picture simply does not wish to "compel us" (as Wölfflin
thought the spatial schema of Renaissance art did) to an organically conceived,
"united perception of the manifold."[3] It is not dramatically cohesive, and it lacks
the architectonic symmetry of Renaissance art, because in place of the
proportional values and conception of immanent law which the Renaissance
took as the standard of "reason and art," the Flemish painters continued to
direct their gaze toward the light and color that dominate the glass painting and
illuminated work of Gothic art. Light played the role in their outlook that
proportionality assumed in the aesthetic vision of the Renaissance.[4] The Italian
painters treated light as a physical, optical phenomenon, using the perspectival
"science" of visual rays to enhance the proportional and plastic values of their
work. But for the Flemish painters light remained of the greatest metaphysical
significance.

Light forms an intricate pattern in the Flemish picture, a pattern which
emerges with striking clarity when we detach ourselves from the representational
significance of the picture and look at it upside down. Then we can readily see
how the Flemish quest for particularity took place within its own kind of
universal scheme. Those fine distinctions among material things are distinctions
among innumerable qualities of light, light which streams through clear and
colored window glass, light reflected from shutters and sills and cloths, light
glowing in jewels, and in hands and faces. Every sensible thing has its luminous
uniqueness; and every color and tone, every shade and degree of brightness and

3. Heinrich Wölfflin, *Principles of Art History,* p. 156.
4. Alberti, for example, advised the painter to concentrate not on color per se but
rather on the use of black and white by which he could imitate the natural effects of
light, shade, and atmosphere. By this "artificial" light and shadow, he was to model the plastic
form and create the perspectival impression of objects receding in space, diminishing in
clarity and intensity as they recede. Jan van Eyck, on the other hand, used color as "a
qualitative and connective principle," as Panofsky describes it. His painting which "is
'jewellike' in a quite literal sense, meant to recapture that glow of pearls and precious stones
which for him, as for Suger, still symbolized 'celestial virtues' and seemed to reflect the Light
Divine," *Early Netherlandish Painting, its Origins and Character,* 1: 70.

opaqueness, has its place within a luminous whole. The phenomenal world that Flemish art represents is not governed by the rational universality of proportional law. It is a world that echoes the age old mythical-religious motif of Light and Creation. Here radiance manifests the creative force of God, and differing intensities and hues of light indicate the degree to which corporeal things participate in the Divine.

In the aesthetic thought of the High Middle Ages, which was based upon the metaphysics of Dionysius the Areopagite, the recognition of Divine Beauty is aroused by light, for things reflect by means of their luminous form the Beauty of God, the *Pater Luminum*.[5] Light, which was the first creation, came to be regarded as both the second cause of the world and the most fitting symbol of the First Cause. As a symbol, it possesses the "creative" property of instantaneous diffusion, a mode of activity which the Creator possesses in a transcendent state. But it was by means of this luminous energy, this fundamental energy of the cosmos, that the corporeal world was formed out of prime matter. Thus all things owe their perfection to the active principle of light. The Spiritual Light is the Final Cause of the beauty of a being (to use the thirteenth-century Scholastic terminology of Ulric of Strasbourg);[6] and the Formal Cause of beauty is the conformity of that being with its "luminous form," the ideal after which it aspires and in which its goodness or perfection consists.

Proportion, in this context, came to mean a congruous "match" between an object and its "ideal," between an individual and its (universal) form, and it was in this altered sense that the notion of proportion persisted in medieval aesthetic thought. The classical idea of congruity, thus bound to the idea of light or luminous form, constituted the medieval notion of Beauty only in conjunction with the idea of light. Aquinas held, for example, that the Beautiful has three objective characteristics.[7] Light is one; the other two characteristics—integrity or perfection, and consonance or proper proportion—are obviously derived from the ancient idea of congruity, but for Aquinas, as for Ulric of Strasbourg, proportion meant the approximation of the real object to its ideal, its realization inspired neither by nature nor by art, but by his mediations upon the idea of the (following the Gospel of John) is the resplendent Light of the World. As the of, or accord with, its luminous form. To be sure, Aquinas' considerations were Trinity. It was the Beauty of the Son of God he intended to define. Thus Jesus Second Person of the Trinity, he possesses the "perfection" of the Father's Divine Nature; and as the Image of that Perfection, He realizes a "perfect proportion" between Himself and the Divine Nature He reflects.

What characterized Transcendent Beauty, however, defined the goodness

5. For the aesthetics of light, see de Bruyne, *Etudes d'esthétique médiévale,* especially vol. 3, chap. 1.

6. *Ibid.,* pp. 263–77.

7. *Summa Theologiae*, 1: 39, 8c. For an analysis of Aquinas' theory of beauty, see de Bruyne, 3: 280–315.

45. *Hans Memling,* Portrait of an Old Man. *In the Metropolitan Museum of Art, New York, bequest of Benjamin Altman,* 1913.

and beauty of the created world as well. The *claritas* of created things was thought to manifest the degree to which they actualize their form, their ideal. But here, in the corporeal world, because of the resistance of matter to form, a scale of perfection emerges. A hierarchy of "natural lights" (as Dionysius called it in his *Celestial Hierarchy*)[8] stretches between the *Pater Luminum* and the lowliest object of His creation. The Divine Ideas which matter passively receives, and by which the corporeal objects of the world are formed, emanate from the Pure Light in grades of diminishing force. From the highest transparency of the Empyrean Heaven to the dense globe of the earth, they create a scale of luminous beings, and the beings so formed tend upward, in turn, by means of the inner, radiating force of love. In successive stages, they strive toward the ideal which will perfect them, hence they strive toward God in whom the Ideal is fully present. The One Pure Light, in the Neoplatonic metaphysics, thus pours itself out and down, through various levels of being, into a manifold of "visible lights," and all these natural lights aspire to rise again through love to their single Source.

This creative emanation and return of the Spirit left its traces upon the form of the medieval cosmos, giving it its gradated structure. Each luminous sphere of the heavens was held to produce the next lower sphere as the reflection of its radiance. Down to the sphere of the moon, according to the Neoplatonic *Liber de intelligertiis,* the higher spheres are the source of the beauty and perfection of the lower ones. They are "superior" in both a spiritual and a spatial sense.

The same hierarchical principle prevails in the sublunar realm. The moon engenders, as its reflection, the zone of fire. Fire produces air and air produces water. The globe of earth, surrounded by water, air, and fire, is thus the least irradiated body of the cosmos. It is the farthest from the super-sensible Light which pours down through the heavens in these diminishing intensities of radiation and reflection. But here, the ascent of beings commences toward the Pure Light. The four elements of the sublunar realm extend themselves in varying degrees by means of their inner, radiating force. The expansive force of water exceeds that of the dense earth; the more subtle and volatile air rises above water; and fire, the rarest element of the four, moves directly upward. Fire is also that bright force that glows in the visage and eyes of man, for as an earthly creature, man is composed of all four elements. In man, the head holds the element of fire which is the source of that *blanc et vermeil* beauty which the medieval poets praised, a beauty which still shines forth in the minutely worked faces of Flemish art.[9]

8. On Dionysius and the hierarchical world order, see Pierre Duhem, *Le système du monde,* 4: 329–64, and Ernst Cassirer, *Individuum und Kosmos in der Philosophie der Renaissance,* chap. 1. The description of the mid-thirteenth century *Liber de intelligentiis* that follows below is from de Bruyne, 3: 239–43.

9. de Bruyne, *Etudes,* 3: 239–43.

The cosmological ideas which were discursively worked out by medieval philosophical speculation were presented directly to the imagination by medieval art, and this is why the introduction of classical forms in the Renaissance effected such a general cultural disruption. The successive heavens of Dante's Paradise, which stunned the poet by their increasing radiance, gave imaginative embodiment to the mystical, metaphysical theory of light and to the hierarchical pattern which that theory imparted to the medieval world picture. The Gothic cathedral presented another powerful image of this simple cosmological scheme.[10] Here the yearning for Light seemed to melt away the solidity of the walls, and the builder's design urged all lines upward, like the thrusting, vital forces of some cosmic forest straining toward the sun.

The spatial images of medieval art contain distinctive, heterogeneous places, as the medieval cosmos did. The circles of Hell, the grades of Purgatory, and the several Heavens of the *Divine Comedy* made perceptible the religious and metaphysical distinctions by which medieval thought set off different "spaces" from each other. The orientation of the Gothic cathedral, pointing toward the east, toward Jerusalem and the source of Light, did so, too. As Emile Mâle has shown, the north side of the cathedral was reserved for statues of Old Testament figures, the warm and light south side harbored figures of the New, and the portals of the west, "lit up by the fiery rays of evening," impressed scenes of the Last Judgment upon the mind's eye.[11] Even the statues around the portals of the cathedrals displayed not simply the host of heaven but the everlasting arrangement of the blessed and of the heavens themselves. They stand in tiers, each statue with its own canopy and footrest marking off its particular "place";[12] and they articulate, row above row, the same gradated, vertical plan which the entire building repeats on a grand scale. Inside and out, the Gothic cathedral is one great movement upward through a mounting series of grades, one ascent through horizontal levels marked by arches, galleries, niches, and

10. "Verticalism" has long been recognized as a characteristically Gothic objective. In *Form in Gothic,* Wilhelm Worringer has given what is perhaps the classic description of the progressive dematerialization of the cathedral by means of vaulting as the Gothic "will to form" was realized. The relation of this verticalism to the aesthetics of light was brilliantly demonstrated by de Bruyne, to whom I am greatly indebted. Otto von Simson has called attention to the role of Pythagorean musical theory in medieval architecture, and hence to a continuity in this respect between Gothic and Renaissance art in *The Gothic Cathedral.* Proportionality was always subordinated to the hierarchical spatial schema in Gothic art, however, and in fact contributed to it. In Renaissance architecture, proportionality was detached from the aesthetics of light and brought about a homogeneous spatial schema. See also Dagobert Frey, *Gotik und Renaissance als Grundlagen der modernen Weltanschauung* and Erwin Panofsky, *Gothic Architecture and Scholasticism,* on the relations between medieval cosmological thought and Gothic architecture.

11. Emile Mâle, *Religious Art in France, XIII Century,* pp. 5–14.

12. Panofsky has noted that each Gothic statue has its baldachin which attaches it to the building and also assigns to it its own "piece" of space. "Die Perspektive als 'Symbolische Form,' " *Vorträge der Bibliothek Warburg,* (1924–25): 258–330.

towers. So multiplicity aspires to unity, the material ascends to the spiritual, the natural is assumed into the supernatural,—all in a graduated rise.

Flemish art, which achieved a merely external exactness to Renaissance eyes, was really the final phase in the representation of this aesthetic intuition. Strong empirical tendencies were directing it toward a new mode of spatial organization and expression, but a dominant interest in the luster of things still held these three-dimensional, recessional motifs in check. A preference for luminous values, and hence for light-absorbing and light-reflecting robes, kept the body in a relatively insignificant place. And the surface patterns created by these robes, as by the tapestries, tiled floors, crystals, and other glowing objects of the picture, interfered with and obstructed the new illusion of depth. The surface of the Flemish picture never became a completely neutral "glass"; it remained part of the total artistic image. Far distant areas, although proportionally smaller, have distinctive luminous values, as if each "space" carried with it a fixed character; and the objects in those spaces, the clarity and intensity of their colors, bring even the most remote places to the fore to contribute to a planar pattern of "lights." Indeed, the illuminated surface of the Flemish picture is so striking at times that the flesh and blood faces depicted on it seem to be looking out at us as if through holes cut in a two-dimensional, painted panel.

Not until mathematics began to serve as the primary instrument for representing nature did a fully homogeneous, three-dimensional space emerge in European art.[13] Renaissance art knows no heterogeneity of places that rise through determinate levels to the Ideal, because all places manifest for it the ideality of proportion. All spatial "parts" are united by the generality of number; all are governed by the universality of law. This homogeneity of spatial parts so impressed Alberti that he had great difficulty even in understanding the earlier notion of spatial differences. In a passage in *De re aedificatoria* on the placing of statues, he observed that the common people attach emotionally felt "powers" to particular places. He yielded to this belief insofar as he prescribed fixed places for religious statues, but he marveled at it, for after the revolution in spatial conception which he himself had effected, the traditional notion of heterogeneous "spaces" seemed a baseless superstition:

> And here I cannot help enquiring what should be the reason of a very whimsical, though very old persuasion, which is firmly rooted in the minds

13. Cassirer's *Individuum und Kosmos,* pp. 183–201, is the standard work on the transformation of the notion of space during the Renaissance and on the shift that took place in the various categorial relations as the new relational logic of mathematics was introduced. See also *Das Erkenntnisproblem,* 1: 231–372. The systematic work which rests upon these historical studies is his *Philosophie der Symbolischen Formen.* Panofsky incorporated some of Cassirer's ideas and demonstrated their relation to painting in "Die Perspektive als 'Symbolische Form'" and Rudolf Wittkower did somewhat the same for architecture in *Architectural Principles in the Age of Humanism.* It was Wölfflin who first saw in the Kantian idea of a "spatial schema" the primary and characteristic creation of the visual art of a period.

of the vulgar, that a picture of God or of some saint in one place shall hear the prayers of the votaries, when in another place the statue of the very same God or saint shall be utterly deaf to them. Nay, and what is still more nonsensical, if you do but remove the very same statue, for which the people used to have the highest veneration, to some other station, they seem to look upon it as bankrupt, and will neither trust it with their prayers, nor take the least notice of it. Such statues should therefore have seats that are fixed, eminent, and peculiar to themselves."[14]

In Alberti's mind, an abstract, quantitative notion of space had superseded the mythic notion of space as a qualitative aggregate of places to which different emotional values adhere. He accordingly ignored the east-west orientation when discussing the ground plan of churches and the placing of portals, altars, and statues, even though Vitruvius required the altars of temples to face east.[15] In fact, the church form which Alberti and his age came to prefer is the circular one which obliterates all such differences in spatial values.[16] In the centralized plan, the outer points of the church are all equidistant from the center; they are all bound by the same rule, so that none can be "superior" or "inferior" to any other. What plan could better suit the unity and lawfulness of the spatial conception of the Renaissance?

The basic features of European art were shaped by this Euclidean spatial conception down through the nineteenth century. In perspective, in the ideal of organic form, and in the classical orders, the spatial logic of proportionality persisted long after the aesthetic theory of *concinnitas* was abandoned. After the rise of empiricism in philosophy, regular proportions could no longer be looked upon as "objective" per se, as the harmonious relations by which Nature binds the elements of the phenomenal world. Yet artistic space continued to remain geometrically lawful and uniform. It remained rational, governed by "rule" through all the modifications of the Renaissance style, from Mannerism through Impressionism, and this was so because the spatial intuition which ordered the new artistic image of the world gave rise to a theoretical world picture as well. A new cosmology came to support the artistic image, taking the place of its earlier, aesthetic-metaphysical basis. What ultimately justified modern Europe's artistic faith in the homogeneity of the universe and its systematic, rational order was the scientific cosmology that had its inception in the Copernican system of the world.

As long as the Ptolemaic astronomy held sway, the hierarchical conception

14. *De re aedificatoria,* bk. 7, chap. 17.

15. Cf. *De arch.,* bk. 4, chaps. 5, 9 and *De re aedif.,* bk. 7, chaps. 4, 5, 10, 13, 17. Traces of the earlier ideas of beauty as light, and of the metaphysical and ethical connotations of these ideas, can be found in some of Alberti's earlier works. Giovanni Santinello points these out in *Leon Battista Alberti: una visione estetica del mondo e della vita,* pp. 203–24, although I think he exaggerated the significance of some innocuous passages in doing so.

16. *De re aedif.,* bk. 7, chap. 4. See the first part of Wittkower's *Architectural Principles* on the Renaissance circular church.

of space and being could continue to dominate cosmological thought, despite artistic changes. Ptolemy's system of the world lent considerable support to the gradated ontological structure of medieval metaphysical speculation.[17] With the earth at the center of the world (or of the solar system which, along with the distant "fixed" stars, was all of the world that was presumed to exist until the latter half of the sixteenth century), the Ptolemaic system allowed for a neat division of the cosmos into two metaphysically disparate realms: the sublunar realm, to which the dark, base, and immovable earth was consigned, and the realm of the heavens which held the concentric spheres that perpetually turn about the earth, illuminating it with the pure light of their orbs—the spheres of the moon, Mercury, Venus, the sun, Mars, Jupiter, Saturn, and the firmament of the fixed stars.

To the Ptolemaic picture of the world, the Middle Ages merely added the spheres of the Crystalline Heaven, the *Primum Mobile,* and the Empyrean, literally placing the Empyrean beyond the limits of the finite world (fig. 46). The Empyrean Heaven was the boundless "place" of the Unmoved Mover who transmitted the light and motion of Being through the *Primum Mobile* to the spheres. Aristotelian physics accounted for some of the general features of motion in the geocentric universe. The motion of the spheres was held to follow from the "nature" of the heavenly bodies and their fixed "natural places." In the *De caelo et mundo* of Albertus Magnus, the motion and velocity of the concentric spheres that revolve about the earth is explained by their proximity to the *Primum Mobile:*

> They have no other mover; and since a single and simple mover can produce only one movement, each one of these spheres can have but one movement; but this movement is stronger in the spheres immediately contiguous to the mover, and weaker in the most distant sphere. . . . When the first sphere has finished its revolution, the second one has not yet completed its revolution . . . and so as one descends from sphere to sphere, the movement becomes slower in each inferior sphere because of the greater distance which separates it from the *Primum Mobile.*[18]

Perfect, circular motion belongs to the "superior," incorruptible bodies of the heavens, and the velocity of this motion decreases as the descent is made from "superior" to "inferior" spheres. In the sublunar realm, the most "inferior" sphere

17. "Or si le système de Ptolémée avait pu accorder que les astres fussent des êtres sans analogie de nature avec ceux du Monde sublunaire, il n'en pouvait aller de même du système de Copernic. Celui-ci devait essentiellement consister en cette affirmation que la terre et l'ensemble des éléments forment une masse analogue de tous points à l'un quelconque des astres errants. Si donc la Terre n'est mue ni par un dieu ni par un ange, si, sans cesse, tout y nait, change et meurt, il faut qu'il en soit de même de Mars, de Jupiter ou de Saturne." Duhem, *Le système du monde,* 4: 317. See also Alexandre Koyré, *Etudes Galiléennes.*

18. *De caelo et mundo,* 1. 3. 5.; in Duhem, 3: 330.

46. *Pre-Copernican world picture. From the* Cosmographia *of Peter Apian, 1584.*

of being, the earth forms the immobile center of the universe. There can be no perfect circular motion in this realm of corruptible, changeable objects composed of the four elements. Terrestrial objects experience rectilinear motion only, as the dominant element of their nature seeks to return to its natural place once the object has been moved, the "earthiest" of the four elements tending toward the center of the earth, the subtlest rising toward the zone of fire, and air and water finding their places in between. Clearly, the metaphysical world picture of the hierarchy of beings could not only assimilate but could, in fact, rest upon this combined system of Aristotelian physics and Ptolemaic astronomy.

While the assignment of earth to the lowest rung of the cosmic ladder may have humbled man, it also assured him of the religious significance of his fate. All other beings were spatially and spiritually "fixed," but Man, a creature of body and spirit, seemed born to work out his destiny upon the stage of earth. His material being could draw him down toward brutishness and Hell; his quest for the Good could draw him toward Heaven, initiating a gradual ascent into the realm of perfection where he would find his ultimate resting place in the "next world." The task of life on earth was to strive against the baseness of the body, to seek salvation by rising "above" the prison of this death.

What could the Copernican picture of the world offer to match the completeness, the moral and metaphysical assurance of this outlook? Not empirical evidence, for astronomical systems were then thought of as mathematical rather than physical systems. The Ptolemaic and Copernican world

153

pictures were both plausible geometric descriptions of the scheme of things. Moreover, when Copernicus (1473-1543) revived and reformulated the heliocentric theory, there was not enough evidence to make his plan of the heavens seem any more acceptable than the other.[19] Due to the crudeness of the instruments then available, the relative positions and paths of the heavenly bodies could be determined with equal accuracy (or inaccuracy) in both systems.

The Ptolemaic system of the world contained a number of geometric constructions, however, which were designed to "save" appearances that could not be accounted for in terms of the geocentrically arranged scheme of concentric circles alone. The revolving crystalline spheres presumably bore the planets in perfect circles about the earth, but the planets were observed to pursue unmistakably irregular paths. Equants, deferents, and epicycles were therefore introduced to describe them. By means of these constructions, motions which were apparently irregular and retrograde could be depicted as uniform circular motions after all. But the reliance upon epicycles and eccentric circles and the like proved to be very disturbing, for these constructions destroyed the systematic coherence of the Ptolemaic world picture. They described the paths of the planets taken singly, but they could not be derived from any general principles of the geocentric theory and they defied physical explanation as well. There was no explanation, no necessity for them, and by the sixteenth century, this constituted a major cause of dissatisfaction.

Historically, when Ptolemy and the Alexandrian astronomers first resorted to equants, deferents, and epicycles to bind their observations to the geocentric framework, astronomy and physics began to part ways. The Aristotelian physicists sought explanations for the motions of the heavenly bodies. Some of their medieval heirs elaborated a hierarchy of intelligences, or spiritual "powers," which were said to dominate the planets and determine their movements. Others, like Albertus Magnus, attributed the motion and velocity of the spheres to the *Primum Mobile.* But in no case, except for the most general features of the geocentric plan, did the "causal" ideas of the physicists have any relation to the complicated system of circles that made up the astronomical world picture. The astronomers, for their part, remained faithful to appearances, but they had to give up causal explanation and content themselves with mere description. Their geometric models could make no pretence to physical truth.

It was with a single stroke, then, that Copernicus brought systematic order into the plan of the heavens and suggested a connection between descriptive,

19. It is often pointed out that the empirical objections to the Copernican theory were considerable. The chief problem was the annual parallax, an apparent displacement of the fixed stars which should have been observable—but was not—as the earth changed its position in relation to them by revolving about the sun. This difficulty was not resolved until Bessel was able to observe that parallax in 1838.

There are a number of good books on the Copernican revolution. See especially Angus Armitage, *The World of Copernicus;* T.S. Kuhn, *The Copernican Revolution;* Stephen Toulmin and June Goodfield, *The Fabric of the Heavens.*

astronomical data and physical explanation. The heliocentric theory provided a unified world picture, and it accounted for some of the major irregularities of planetary motion in terms of a new and simple "cause": the rotation and revolution of the earth and the other planets around the sun. A possibility of reunifying physics and astronomy was thereby opened, a prospect which was to fire the scientific imagination of Kepler. For Copernicus' time, however, and for Galileo who followed Copernicus in this respect, the heliocentric theory represented the final step in freeing the world system from the claims of Aristotelian physics.[20] By raising the earth into the heavens and permitting it to pursue a perfect, circular course, Copernicus renounced the Aristotelian doctrine of the essential heterogeneity of beings, places, and motions. He effaced the impassable boundary between the base, immobile earth, the realm of generation and corruption, and the heavenly realm of perpetually circling bodies.

The repercussions of this act literally shook the world. The Copernican Revolution overturned much more than the authority of Ptolemy and Aristotle; it unhinged the entire structure of a heterogeneous, hierarchically ordered cosmos. But if Copernicus shattered the world picture of medieval cosmology, he affirmed the renascent conception of a harmonious, mathematical world order. A uniform world with essentially commensurable parts emerged in the Copernican astronomy. Relating the orbits of all the planets to the "module" of the earth's annual orbit around the sun, the Copernican system exemplified the Pythagorean-Platonic intuition of the world which had already appeared in the context of Renaissance art and aesthetics.[21]

In the 1490's, Domenico Maria Novara, Copernicus' teacher of astronomy at Bologna, had been highly critical of the Ptolemaic system. Its inconsistencies and complexities obscured rather than disclosed what Novara believed to be a grand, systematic world order, and his outstanding student took his criticism to heart. What led Copernicus to seek a simpler, more systematic description of the heavenly bodies and their motions was a firm belief in the principle of universal harmony. Even though he meant his world system to be numerically accurate, he himself made very few observations. By and large, he accepted Ptolemy's positions and those handed down in the planetary tables of his day; for what Copernicus was really after was "a more reasonable arrangement of circles" by which to describe those positions.[22] The heliocentric theory provided such an

20. On the relation of the Copernican theory to Aristotelian physics, see Cassirer, *Das Erkenntnisproblem,* 1: 253–75, 340–72, and Edward Rosen's introduction to *Three Copernican Treatises* (New York, 1959), pp. 25ff.

21. It is the Pythagorean-Platonic current of thought that Edwin Arthur Burtt was referring to when he inquired after that "alternative background besides Aristotelianism, in terms of which . . . metaphysical thinking might go on, and which was more favorable to this astonishing mathematical movement." *The Metaphysical Foundations of Modern Science,* pp. 52, 36–63.

22. Copernicus, "Commentariolus," *Three Copernican Treatises,* translated by Edward

arrangement. It would require, he hoped, "fewer and much simpler constructions" than the geocentric scheme, and this was warrant enough for the daring innovations of his *De revolutionibus orbium caelestium*. The justification of this work which he gave in the preface echoes the Renaissance conception of Nature, God, and Beauty in its assertion that here, at last, is a plan of the world worthy of the Divine artistry:

> It began to weary me that no more definite explanation of the movement of the world-machine established in our behalf by *the best and most systematic builder of all,* existed among the philosophers. . . . Wherefore I took upon myself the task of re-reading the books of all the philosophers which I could obtain, to seek out whether any one had ever conjectured that the motions of the spheres of the universe were other than they supposed who taught mathematics in the schools. And I found first, that, according to Cicero, Nicetas had thought the earth moved. Then later I discovered, according to Plutarch, that certain others had held the same opinion. . . .
>
> Thus, supposing these motions which I attribute to the earth later on in this book, I found at length by much and long observation, that if the motions of the other planets were added to the rotation of the earth and calculated as for the revolution of that planet, not only the phenomena of the others followed from this, but also *it so bound together both the order and magnitude of all the planets and the spheres and the heaven itself, that in no single part could one thing be altered without confusion among the other parts and in all the universe.* Hence for this reason in the course of this work I have followed this system.[23]

The reasons why the newly emerging theoretical and artistic constructions of the world should reflect each other in this way are precise and determinate and far more interesting than an "explanation" couched in terms of an amorphous spirit of the age. Indeed, one of the enduring attractions of the Renaissance, as of the Hellenic age which, in this respect, it closely resembles, is the complete visibility of the relations among its various activities and interests. It is as if its rich and complex culture were intended, like its works of art, to show forth its coherent rational form. And this form is truly rational, for many of the characteristic developments of Renaissance culture can be seen to spring from a new logical orientation and method: from an application of geometric ideas and procedures to problems of an artistic, physical and technical nature. Innovations in diverse fields of interest are brought about by a single current of thought, and

---

Rosen, pp. 57–58. Copernicus made use of approximately twenty-seven observations of his own in his *De revolutionibus* and he made a few other observations which he jotted down on the margins and fly leaves of various books that have been preserved. Armitage, *Copernicus,* p. 85.

23. Dedicatory Letter to Pope Paul III, translated by Burtt, *Metaphysical Foundations,* pp. 49–50. Italics mine.

often by the same group of people who used the methodic key of applied mathematics to open up new possibilities in a number of different cultural areas. So it is with the innovations of Renaissance art and the Copernican astronomy. Both express the spatial intuition of a homogeneous and lawful world order, and they do so because in art and astronomy alike, the logical basis of this world view was being revived and developed.

The systematic origins of Renaissance art and of the Copernican astronomy can be found in a movement of thought which may be properly called a "Ptolemaic renaissance" even though Ptolemy was to be deprived of his authority because of it. We have seen how Alberti established the rules of artistic representation by modifying Ptolemy's principles of projection. When scientific "pictures" of the world came to be constructed according to these same principles, modern astronomy and geography began their rise. The period of modern scientific cosmography dates from the middle of the sixteenth century, when Ptolemy's *Almagest* and *Geography* were superseded by the Copernican system of the heavens and the geographical works of Mercator and Ortelius. But before the Alexandrian master could be surpassed, Europeans had first to relearn from antiquity, and particularly from Ptolemy, the relational ordering of space. This was one of the major accomplishments of the fifteenth century, and it unites the theoretical and artistic revolutions that ushered in the modern conception of the world. The conquest of the principle of proportional mapping in the quattrocento made possible a transformation in science as well as a transformation in art.

Alberti's works bear witness to this methodic unity. He played a leading role in the Ptolemaic renaissance, in almost all its many aspects, and insofar as he did, his writings helped lay the foundation for the view of nature which Renaissance art and science came to share.

The Measure of the Earth

Until the revival of Ptolemy in the fifteenth century, the development of geography was obstructed as much by the nature of its maps as by factual ignorance.[24] Empirical knowledge about the various lands of the world expanded steadily from the twelfth century on as more and more information was gathered, first from Arabic sources, and then from Western mariners and travelers; but

24. On the general development of cartography, see G. R. Crone, *Maps and Their Makers;* Max Eckert, *Die Kartenwissenschaft;* A. E. Nordenskiöld, *Facsimile-Atlas to the Early History of Cartography.* On medieval geography and cartography, C. R. Beazley, *The Dawn of Modern Geography,* vol. 1; G. H. T. Kimble, *Geography in the Middle Ages;* Charles Singer, E. J. Holmyard, A. R. Hall, and Trevor I. Williams, *A History of Technology,* vol. 3; and the works listed below which treat the special areas of medieval cartography.

despite the accumulation of geographical data, the picture of the earth fell far short of ancient standards.

The world maps[25] of the Middle Ages were almost entirely devoid of scientific value. Indeed at first glance, they seem completely fanciful. Their arrangement of the countries and continents of the world is grossly incorrect, as on the Hereford World Map of the late thirteenth century (fig. 47), where Europe (in the south-west quadrant, at right bottom) is shown south of Africa (in the north-west, at left bottom). Even within the European section, one looks in vain for the contours of identifiable pieces of land, such as the Iberian peninsula or the boot of Italy; but all the creatures of the medieval bestiary can be located without difficulty. Empirical accuracy was evidently no concern of the makers of the *mappaemundi;* but if they were indifferent to objective relations among the earth's known points, they were very much concerned with man's affective experience of the world, and this they represented by certain conventional spatial relations.

47. *The Hereford world map, 1276–83. East is at the top of the picture.*

They placed the east at the top of these generally circular world maps, for the east oriented the geographical picture of the Middle Ages much as it oriented the Gothic cathedral. The east held the Garden of Eden, shown at the top of the Hereford World Map as a small detached circle within the great circle of the earth, holding the figures of Adam and Eve. Although part of the earth, Eden was a sacred "space" which man could never again encounter, let alone re-enter in his mortal life. Jerusalem lay at the center of the *mappaemundi,* a circle surmounted by a Crucifix on the Hereford map, because Scripture set Jerusalem "in the midst of nations and countries." And surrounding the earth, a ring of Ocean was bound to its "natural place" on the surface of the earth's sphere. On the map, as on the cosmological drawings of the pre-Copernican world (fig. 46), the zone of Ocean formed an impassable, watery boundary by its elemental difference from the earth. Near the end of its career, in the fifteenth century, the medieval map of the world began to reflect actual geographical knowledge, but until it was replaced by classical models, it continued to depict an aggregate of heterogeneous places which were essentially incommensurable with each other. Special values, rooted in religious doctrine and other mythically held notions about the world, adhered to special places, even in cartography.

The world maps were not the only ones that failed to achieve a unified representation of space. Even maps of areas that had been actually traversed and carefully observed did not exhibit a uniform scheme of geographical space. This is the case with the Portolan charts,[26] the most accurate maps of the Middle

25. For medieval *mappaemundi,* see Roberto Almagià and Marcello Destombes, *Monumenta cartographica vetustioris aevi, A.D. 1200–1500,* vol. 1, *Mappaemundi.* For the Hereford World Map, see Konrad Miller, *Die ältesten Weltkarten,* pt. 4, *Die Herefordkarte.*

26. For the Portolan charts, see Roberto Almagià, *Monumenta cartographica vaticana,* vol. 1; and Konrad Kretschmer, "Die italienische Portolane des Mittelalters,"

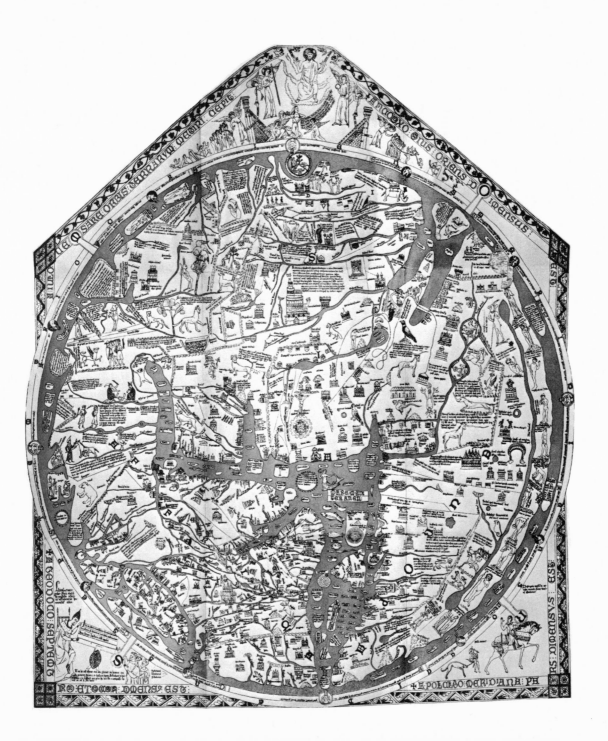

Ages, depictions of the coasts of the Mediterranean and Black Seas, and later of the Atlantic. Unlike the *mappaemundi,* the Portolan charts served a practical purpose, showing the positions of ports of call, islands, shallows—information necessary for navigation. And unlike the *mappaemundi,* they were logical pictures, isomorphic with what they represented. Relative positions were determined on the Portolan charts, not by means of a graduated, rectangular grid of geographical coordinates, however, but by the estimated distances and azimuths of course lines.

This technique worked well enough for small areas. Wind roses, groups of straight lines which radiate from one point in eight, sixteen, or thirty-two directions, corresponding to the principal and secondary winds, were scattered over the chart (fig. 48). Generally, one such wind rose had a roughly central position, the others being distributed around the periphery of the circle covered by the chart (although this circle was seldom delineated). The lines of the rose represented loxodromes or course lines (later, compass directions); and when these lines came to be scaled, they also showed the distances along the course lines. The contours of the coasts were filled in from observations.

The only thing wanting on these precise and beautiful mariners' charts was a network of parallels and meridians to support the course lines and define the relative distances among depicted points. A uniform scheme of this sort was essential if special charts were to be combined to form an exact image of large areas, and ultimately of the entire globe. The Portolan charts were not constructed by means of any such scheme, however. As the Pisan Chart (shown in figure 48) indicates, they did not contain the principles for generalizing and unifying their knowledge of particular areas. Several charts of parts of the Mediterranean basin were combined to form this late thirteenth-century map of Italy, but those charts differed from each other in scale. There was, as yet, no common principle for scaling maps such as Ptolemy's grid of coordinates would provide, and the distortions of the Pisan Chart can almost all be traced to this fact.

The special maps of land areas drawn during the Middle Ages failed to achieve even the partial isomorphism of the mariners' charts. They were not graduated in any way and did not exhibit a method of schematization comparable to course lines until the Renaissance. The makers of regional maps sometimes began with the coastlines given in the Portolan charts and tried to fit in towns, mountains, rivers, and other details, but they made no attempt to measure the relative positions of the points of their ground. Only from the 1380's and on is there an occasional land map which can be classified with the Portolan charts as belonging to the early history of scientific cartography.[27]

Veröffentlichung des Instituts für Meereskunde und des geographischen Institut an der Universität Berlin, pt. 13.

27. See, for example, the map of the region around the Lake of Garda in Roberto Almagià, *Monumenta Italiae cartographica dal secolo XIV al XVII,* pl. 7, no. 2 described on pp. 5f

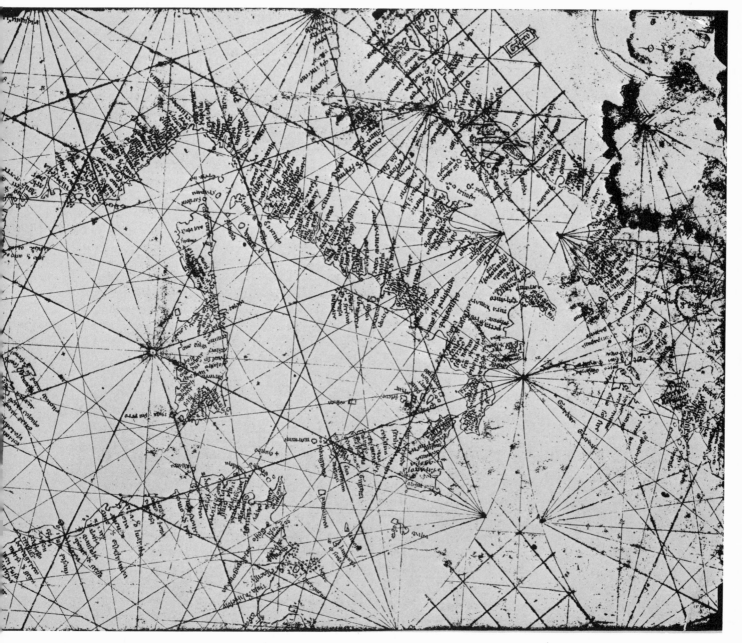

48. *Italy in the Pisan chart of the late*
thirteenth century.
(Bibliothèque nationale.)

These are maps of very small areas, apparently drawn for military purposes, and although they contain no measures, they reflect careful empirical observations. Before their appearance, however, and for some time thereafter, medieval land maps, most of which were itinerary maps, cannot even be called rough approximations. Proportionally untrue to their originals, they commonly magnified "interesting" landmarks and regions as well, much as medieval paintings magnified worthy or sacred personages. "Significant" objects and places cried out for depiction, not the spatial relations among them.

This characteristic accentuation marks the town views and plans of the late Middle Ages, too. The views copy the features of the buildings and walls of cities, but they present them in a naive, impossible space. Any number of viewpoints may vie with one another, as in the picture of Florence that appears in a fresco of 1352 (fig. 49); and the buildings huddle so closely together that they squeeze out all the space—and all the relations of distance and direction that obtained among them. This exclusive concern with the physical appearances of the buildings, rather than with the spatial relations among them, cannot be blamed solely on the fact that such views were carried out by painters and hence express pictorial rather than scientific considerations. The idea of a view (or a map) as a logical copy of the arrangement of things would be common enough among painters in the Renaissance, whereas before the fifteenth century it is absent, or not fully grasped, even in plans of cities. And plans, like the itinerary maps of the Middle Ages, served a scientific, or at least a practical purpose, rather than an artistic one.

The plan of Rome attached to the fourteenth-century *Compendium o Chronologia Magna* of Fra Paolino of Venice[28] was drawn to illustrate the major features of the city, probably for the use of pilgrims (fig. 50). Its elevations are crude; there are hardly any architectural details; yet even here, where the spatial relations among the hills, monuments, and churches of the city would seem to be of primary interest, they are not consistently bound to any one orientation. It is not simply that the elevations of the buildings were drawn differently; some, such as the Colosseum (the large building, roughly in the center) holding to the general orientation of the picture which has east at the top, while other buildings were obviously drawn while the south (right) side of plan was held to the top, and so forth. The *relative positions* of the buildings were depicted this way, too. Take, for example, the arrangement of the Colosseum, the Capitol (the shaded "mountain" area just below the Colosseum), and the Pantheon (Santa Maria Rotonda) which lies just to the left of the Capitol. The Pantheon actually does appear to the left (north) of an observer who stands at the Capitol and faces east (toward the top of the map). And

28. On Fra Paolino, see Almagià, *Mon. Italiae cart.,* pp. 3–11; Amato Pietro Frutaz, *Le piante di Roma,* 1: pp. 18–19, 115–9, 120–22; Walter Holtzmann, "Der älteste mittelalteriche Stadtplan von Rom," *Archäologisches Institut des Deutschen Reiches, Jahrbuch,* 41 (1926): 56–66.

CIVITAS · FLORENTIE

49. *View of Florence in a fresco of 1352.*
In the Loggia del Bigallo, Florence.
(Alinari-Art Reference Bureau.)

the Colosseum will appear directly across from him—but only if he changes his position and faces not east but south (cf. fig 59, showing south at the top of the page).

If the fourteenth-century "view" of Florence is really no view at all but a composite picture of several views, the fourteenth-century "plan" of Rome shows not the spatial plan of the city but relations among some of its buildings as they appear from several different vantage points.

To my knowledge, there are no more sophisticated views and plans of cities than these before the fifteenth century, and certainly none that reflect actual measurements taken in a land survey. This is the case with Florence and Rome, at least, and the mapping of these cities was particularly advanced. Florence was to become the center of the new Ptolemaic tradition of geographical and cartographical work which began in the first decade of the fifteenth century. But before then, and for several decades thereafter, there are no known planimetric views of the city or geometrically inspired plans.[29] Rome boasts the greatest number of plans and views, and the most highly developed ones, because of the never ending stream of visitors and pilgrims who needed descriptions of the city. But again, not until the second decade of the fifteenth century do "plan-views" appear which may be said to be moving toward, and perhaps to be even reflecting, the Ptolemaic conception of a geographical picture. There are about half a dozen of these first plan-views of Rome[30] (fig. 51). They are all drawn on the north-south (Ptolemaic) axis, with south, however, at the top of the picture, and they are based upon a common prototype. They are not in any sense of the word measured, but they do mark the beginnings of an empirical effort to show the "positions" of the chief buildings of a city; "how they are situated," as Ptolemy said, "in regard to one another, how situated as regards the whole."

There was still a long way to go before the genuinely scientific idea which Ptolemy had of geography could be attained, even in such plan-views. The idea of geography as "a survey of the earth in its just proportions," the geometric idea of the map as a scaled picture, proportionally reflecting actual measurements—

---

29. Giuseppe Boffito and Attilio Mori, *Piante e vedute di Firenze; studio storico, topografico, cartografico*, p. xx. Florence may have had a more accurate fourteenth-century view than those known today, however. The trecento painter, Ambrogio Benincasa, did a picture of Florence which was described by a contemporary as showing "tutta la città di Firenze, cioè tutte le mure e la loro misura, tutte le porte e loro nomi, tutte le vie e piazze e loro nomi, tutte le case che orto avessero, sicchè chiaramente si conosceano et ancora scritto era di sua mano in su ogni via e luogo il nome." *Ibid.*, pp. xix–xx. Although the walls of the city were measured, it sounds from the description as though the measurements were written on the view, as were the names of the gates plazas, etc., rather than being proportionally reproduced.

30. See plates 76–90 in Frutaz, *Le piante di Roma*, vol. 2, and the descriptions in vol. 1, pp. 19–20, 137–44.

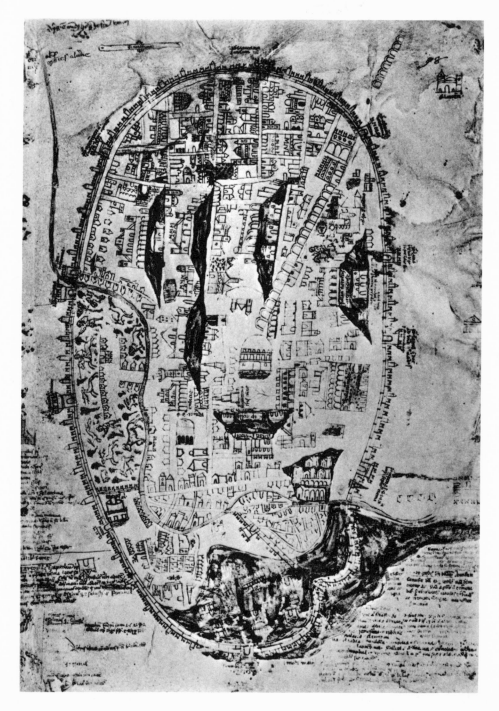

50. *Plan of Rome in a fourteenth-century codex of the* Compendium o Chronologia magna *of Fra Paolino the Minorite (Marc. Zan. lat. 399).*
East is at the top of the picture.
(Deutsches Archäologisches Institut.)

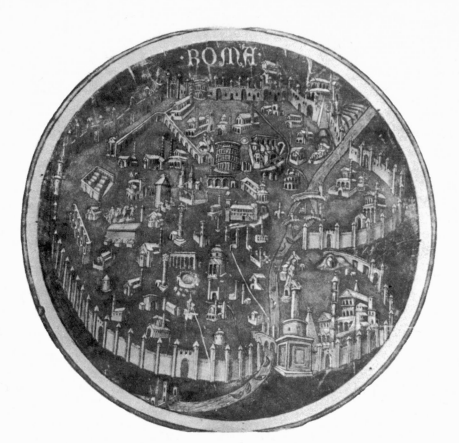

51. *Plan-view of Rome in a fresco by Taddeo di Bartolo, 1414. South is at the top of the picture. From* Le piante di Roma, *ed. A. Pietro Frutaz (Rome: Istituto di Studi Romani, 1962).*

this was either not understood until the works of Alberti and others like him appeared in the fifteenth and sixteenth centuries, or if understood, was not put into practice. Well into the fifteenth century, diagrams of land plots drawn by surveyors were not drawn to scale, although numerical dimensions were sometimes given down to half an inch.[31] And conversely, medieval surveyors seem not to have known how to supplement their direct measurements with indirect calculations based upon sightings and the ratios provided by geometric pictures. The geometry of *Geometria Culmensis*,[32] a fourteenth-century

31. See the diagrams reproduced in John H. Harvey, "Four Fifteenth-Century London Plans," *London Topographical Record,* 20, no. 85 (1952): 1–8.

32. Conrad von Jungingen, *Geometria Culmensis.* The only surveyor of the late fourteenth century mentioned by George Sarton, *Introduction to the History of Science,* 3, pt. 2: 1498–99 is one Bertran Boysset. Boysset (c. 1345–c. 1414) was a sworn surveyor and the author of a Provençal treatise on land measuring, but according to Sarton his treatise "is without order, and as far as I could see (for only parts of the text were available to me) without mathematics." For a general description of medieval surveying, see Singer *et al., Hist. of Technology,* 3: 515.

surveying manual by Conrad von Jungingen (1393–1407), belongs to Egypt rather than Greece, teaching the age-old, primitive method of surveying by dividing an area into squares, equilateral triangles, and/or right-angled triangles so as to allow for some indirect measurements.

Alberti also described this method in one of the problems of *Ludi matematici,* but in certain other problems he explained—and was evidently one of the first to do so[33]—how to take sightings for surveying a land area, and how to depict the relative measures among the points of a ground by means of a scaled picture. He first set forth these ideas in *Descriptio urbis Romae,* the brief Latin treatise of the 1440's which probably reflects the understanding of surveying and mapping which he had reached in his early years in Rome, between 1432 and 1434. This was in part a humanistically motivated work, constituting one of many archeological efforts made by the humanists of the time to identify and describe the characteristic features of the Eternal City. Flavio Biondo's description of the topography and monuments of Rome in *Roma instaurata,* and Poggio Bracciolini's *Ruinarum urbis descriptio* belong to the same genre. Since all three humanists were papal secretaries, Poggio and Biondo may well have been the *amici literati* who, Alberti claimed, urged him to set down his method for noting the course of the walls, the Tiber, and the aqueducts of Rome, and the position of its gates, temples, and monuments *by means of mathematical instruments* and for depicting them proportionally, in a drawing of any size.[34] Later, Alberti improved upon and generalized the techniques of surveying and mapping which he had worked out for his geography of Rome, and he incorporated these developments in *De re aedificatoria* and *Ludi matematici,* the book of mathematical "games" which he sent to Meliaduso d'Este in the 1450's.

Although Ptolemy's ideas helped him in the conception of his first geographical project, Alberti's geographical work as a whole represents a synthesis of a number of ideas and practices, ancient and contemporary. He drew from many sources, much as he did for his work on perspective; and as in painter's perspective, it was the governing idea of *analogia* which brought a new, systematic unity to elements which stemmed from many different

33. As far as I have been able to ascertain, Albert's *Descriptio urbis Romae* and *Ludi matematici* are among the earliest works on surveying land areas by sightings and mapping by scaled pictures. There was a work written in Austria about the time Alberti began his cartographical studies (c. 1434) which sets forth a method almost identical with the one in *Descriptio urbis Romae.* See Dana Bennett Durand, *The Vienna-Klosterneuburg Map Corpus of the 15th Century,* pp. 164–68 and below, n. 46.

Before Alberti's time, Roger Bacon had advocated the use of parallels and meridians on terrestrial maps as early as the thirteenth century, and about the same time, Robertus Anglicus wrote a work on the astrolabe in which he explained the principles of measuring by triangulation. But neither procedure seems to have affected the mapping of land areas until the Ptolemaic revival of the fifteenth century.

34. "Descriptio urbis Romae," *Opera inedita,* p. 36.

traditions. One such aspect of his geographical work is his application of the Greek principles of surveying. The rules for finding heights and distances by sightings, although not used in actual land mensuration, were, of course, known in the Middle Ages.[35] They were taught as part of the "liberal" discipline of geometry, to illustrate the principles of similar triangles. Like the optical principles of natural perspective, they were the object of theoretical study only. It was in their practical, applied form, however, that Alberti set down the rules of triangulation in the book which he sent to Meliaduso d'Este to entertain him in his monastic quietude. And he was careful to point out that Meliaduso should both "contemplate and put into practice" the "games" he had devised to exemplify them:[36] the surveying exercises of the book, most of which consist in constructing geometric pictures so as to determine magnitudes indirectly (as in figure 8).

When the rules of triangulation are applied to problems of actual measurement in this way, even if only in "games," measuring devices are needed. The "mathematical instruments" which Alberti describes represent another of the traditions that entered into his geographical work. Among them are the astrolabe and quadrant (or square) which had been known for centuries. Western mariners, and the map makers who constructed the Portolan charts, had learned from the Arabs how to determine altitudes and azimuths with them. Alberti could have become familiar with their use in Genoa or Venice, for these were two of the leading centers of Portolan cartography in the fifteenth century, and both cities were centers of the Alberti family's mercantile enterprise. As mentioned before, Alberti was born in Genoa and spent most of his youth in Venice where his father managed a branch of the family business. He could also have heard lectures on the astrolabe given at the University of Padua by Prosdocimo de Beldomandi (d. 1428), mathematician and professor of astrology,

---

35. Singer *et al.*, *Hist. of Technology*, 3: 528, 537.

36. *Op. volg.*, 4: 405. In this work, Alberti mentions his indebtedness to the "ancients," Columella (first century A.D.) and Savosarda (eleventh century), and to Leonardo of Pisa "among the moderns." Leonardo of Pisa stands outside the academic tradition of the schools. The thirteenth-century author of a *Practica geometriae*, he is noted for his concern with practical mathematics, particularly with the application of arithmetic to problems that arise in mercantile practice. Alberti's mathematical writings developed this current of applied mathematics and broadened it considerably. See Moritz Cantor, *Vorlesungen über Geschichte der Mathematik*, vol. 2, and Guillaume Libri, *Histoire des sciences mathématiques en Italie*.

The historical significance of Alberti's mathematical writings has been appreciatively discussed by Leonardo Olschki, *Geschichte der Neusprachlichen Wissenschaftlichen Literatur*, 1: 45–87; Dr. Winterberg, "Leon Baptist Albertis technische Schriften," *Repertorium für Kunstwissenschaft*, Bd. VI (1883), 326–56; Georg Wolff, "Leon Battista Alberti als Mathematiker," *Scientia*, 60 (1936): 353–59. These works do not do full justice to his originality, however, particularly in surveying and cartography, and they fail to indicate the astonishingly wide range of problems which he handled by means of relatively few principles of elementary geometry.

while he was attending Barzizza's Gymnasium in that city. But again, familiar as these instruments may have been on shipboard or in lectures on astronomy at the University, their application in geodetic surveys seems to have been unknown before the fifteenth century.

Alberti's detailed directions for using these and other devices to measure land areas and make scaled drawings of the surveyed ground betray the novelty of his procedure, and indeed, modern studies usually attribute the geographical use of such instruments to the sixteenth, not the fifteenth, century.[37] A book of 1518 on "theoretical and practical" arithmetic and geometry, for example, has been cited as the first original work on surveying because its author, Francesco da Lazisio, employed the square for taking indirect measurements.[38] Alberti used an arrow or a plumb line in *Ludi matematici* for problems like the ones da Lazisio treated with the square. In this respect, da Lazisio's work is certainly an advance, but it is a technical advance only. His methodic ideas, and those of sixteenth-century surveying manuals in general—the way they use the square, say to measure a distant tower—are the same as Alberti's procedures. Furthermore, the square was not unknown to Alberti. When he wrote, not for the liberally educated Meliaduso d'Este, but for architects and engineeers in *De re aedificatoria,* he explicitly advocated its use. In a passage on the digging of sluices, he remarks that "ignorant workmen try their slope by laying a ball in the trench, and if the ball rolls forward, they think their slope is right for water. But the instruments of dexterous artisans are the square, the level,

37. For example, Singer *et al., Hist. of Technology,* 3: 537: it is "not until the opening of the sixteenth century that any direct evidence of cartographical surveying or discussion of the appropriate instruments can be found." The author does take note of two exceptions, though: in 1478, a printed edition appeared of the thirteenth-century *Astrolabii canones* by Robertus Anglicus, and c.1455 a manuscript written by a gun founder applied the principle of sightings to range finding. These are works on surveying principles, however, not on cartographical surveying. See also p. 528.

Also, Gustavo Uzielli wrote: "Per immaginare quale fosse la condizione della geometria pratica nel secolo XV, basta ricordare che questa consisteva nella misurazione numerica delle distanze el delle aree, ma non in una rappresentazione grafica." *La vita e i tempi di Paolo dal Pozzo Toscanelli,* in *Raccolta di documenti e studi, R. Commissione Colombiana,* 5, vol. 1, 429. This may seem strange coming from the biographer of Toscanelli, one of the first modern cartographers, but Uzielli holds even greater wonders in store. As proof that there were no new surveying devices beyond the rod, the quadrant, and the plumb line in the fifteenth century, Uzielli cites Alberti's *Ludi matematici* (p. 430). He dismisses Alberti's "town plan" instrument (which is an adaptation of the astrolabe and a forerunner of the surveyor's "circle"), claiming that it bore little or no relation either to navigation or to terrestrial mapping! (p. 434).

38. Uzielli, 429–32. De Lazisio's book was entitled *Libro de arithmetica et geometria speculativa et praticale &c. intitulato Scala grimaldelli.* First published in 1518, it went through fifteen editions by 1692. To be sure, Uzielli is not to be regarded as a modern authority on these matters, but his erroneous belief that the practices described by da Lazisio and other sixteenth-century authors originated in the sixteenth century is commonly held.

plumb-line, and, in a word, all such as are terminated with a right angle.[39]

Instruments for taking some kind of indirect measurements on land were known and used in the fifteenth century, then, if not in surveys, at least in canal digging by "dexterous artisans." From them, the new practices must have spread to the "ignorant workmen"; but at the same time, educated men like Alberti took up these instruments and practices and applied them to related problems of practical mathematics, making them part of the "liberal" study of geometry. This is really what Alberti was doing in *Ludi matematici,* and this is why the work contains such thorough descriptions of instruments which are more primitive than those referred to offhand in his work on architecture.[40] In his mathematical games, he was not merely applying the geometry of the schools to surveying problems; he was also treating technical procedures, familiar to him from ancient sources and current practice, as knowledge worthy of a disinterested, intellectual pursuit.

In this respect, *Ludi matematici* and *Descriptio urbis Romae* fall into the same category as Alberti's writings on the arts. All of these works bespeak a distinctive turn of thought, an intellectual attitude which sought the exemplification of abstract principles in practical problems and which thereby raised manual and mechanical practice to a higher level, the level of scientific study. This had made *Della pittura* the first work of its kind, a theory of the manual art of painting; and this same intellectual intention made *Ludi matematici* one of the earliest representatives of another new genre. Alberti's book of exercises heads the list of a number of works on "practical mathematics" which became increasingly popular in the course of the sixteenth century, works which almost all describe, with a characteristic sense of novelty, the instruments and methods of surveying.[41]

39. *De re aedif,* bk. 10, chap. 7.

40. When Alberti explains the use of the level in *Ludi matematici,* he does not merely describe the instrument; he gives in elementary terms the rules for its construction: "Take an arrow or anything straight and tie a string of four *braccia* to each end. Then tie together the ends of these strings, thus forming a triangle. From the knot of the two strings, tie a third also four *braccia* in length, and from this let a weight hang." Only after this preliminary step does he describe how his friend may use the level, to determine, for example, the height and hence the course of waters. *Op. volg.,* 4: 424–27.

In many passages, Alberti alludes to the fact that *Ludi matematici* is a popular book which avoids really difficult problems. "Ma sono cose molto intrigate e non atte a questi *Ludi* quali io proposi, e quanto attaglia e' vostri piacere," p. 423. See also pp. 424, 439–40.

41. A few such works are Cosimo Bartoli, *Del modo di misurare* (Venice, 1564); Silvio (Vincentino) Belli, *Quattro libri geometrici: il primo di misurare con la vista, nel quale s'insegna, senza travagliar con numeri, a misurar facilissimamente le distantie, l'altezze, e le profondità con il quadrato geometrico, e con altri stromenti* (Venice, 1595); M. Girolamo Cataneo (Novarese), *Dell'arte del misurare, libri due* (Brescia, 1583); Jacques Chauvet, *Instruction et usage du Cosmometre* (Paris, 1585); Philippe Danfrie, *Déclaration de l'usage du Graphomètre* (Paris, 1597); Orontius Finaeus, *De re et praxi geometrica, libri tres, figuris et demonstrationibus illustrati. Ubi de quadrato geometrico* (Paris, 1556); Abel

The seemingly sudden appearance of so many books of this kind during the sixteenth century probably accounts for the belief that this was the period of "rebirth" for geodetic surveying and mapping. But actually, the sixteenth-century manuals (made more numerous by printing) only indicate that the educated classes had by now developed an abiding interest in these practical pursuits.[42] The methods they describe go back a hundred years, and possibly more. *Ludi matematici* contains all the principles of mensuration and mapping to be found in them, including a description of the most sophisticated measuring device of all, the instrument that came to be called the Dutch circle. This, of course, is Alberti's surveying disk. It reappears in *Ludi matematici* in what Alberti took to be the most "delightful" exercise of all, the one in which he presented, in somewhat different form, the surveying and mapping procedures first set forth in *Descriptio urbis Romae.*

In this part of *Ludi matematici,* Alberti gives us another glimpse of the practices he was relying upon. He mentions that the surveying disk was being used in gunnery for range finding,[43] and he indirectly reveals that he was applying to land surveys the principles, as well as the chief instrument, of nautical surveying. The disk Alberti took his measures with was originally an astrolabe[44] (fig. 52). Like the astrolabe, his Horizon was divided into four quadrants and its perimeter was graduated. Its radius, like the rule, or alidade, of the astrolabe, was a radial arm that pivoted from the center of the instrument. The navigator (or astronomer) used the radius as a sighting rod for taking

---

Foullon, *Descrittione et uso dell'Holometro* (Venice, 1564); Gemma Frisius, *Libellus locorum describendorum* (Antwerp, 1533).

42. For example, Fine's book (see above, n. 41) is dedicated to the King of France. Cosimo Bartoli was the editor and translator of a number of Alberti's works, including *Ludi matematici* which he relied heavily upon in his own *Modo di misurare.* It is interesting to note that Alberti is the earliest of the "modern" authors whom Bartoli acknowledges as his predecessors in this subject. He lists Orontius Finaeus, Albrecht Dürer, Archimedes, Euclid, Gemma Frisius, Giovan Roia, Giovanni Stoflerino, Leon Battista Alberti, Georg Peurbach, Peter Appianus, treatises on perspective, Ptolemy, Vitullion, Vitruvius. Bartoli himself was a gentleman scholar, not an engineer or surveyor, yet evidently felt that surveying was to be included in a gentleman's learning.

43. "Voglio alle cose dette di là aggiugnere certo instrumento atto (come voi penserete) molto a questi bisogni, massime a chi adoperassi il trabocco e simile macchine belliche. Ma io lo adopero a cose molto dilettevole come a commensurare il sito d'un paese, o la pittura d'una terra, come feci quando ritrassi Roma." *Op. volg.,* 4: 429–30.

44. On the astrolable, see Robert T. Gunther, *The Astrolabes of the World.* Also, Singer *et al., Hist. of Technology,* 3: 627: "The first surveying-instruments were ... modifications of older astronomical measuring-devices; in particular the maker adopted the alidade and circular angle-scale found on the *dorsum* of astrolabes, adding to the instrument a socket by which the surveyor could mount it upon a tripod stand or a staff to hold the instrument steady in the field. With the addition of a magnetic compass for taking bearings, this became the circumferentor or 'Dutch circle.' ... Perhaps by combining circumferentors in vertical and horizontal planes, perhaps as a direct adaptation of the torquetum, the theodolite was evolved as a universal surveying instrument."

52. *An Italian astrolabe, c. 1400 From Gunther,* The Astrolabes of the World *(Oxford, 1932).*

vertical angles, or elevation, of the sun or stars. When the instrument was rotated 90° around the horizontal axis, the radius could also be used to mark off horizontal angles, or bearings, on the units of the disk's perimeter. This is the way Alberti (and artillery men) used the disk; and this very instrument, employed in this fashion, appears in the hands of the surveyors and cartographers of the sixteenth century (fig. 53).

Alberti's Horizon bears different names in the course of the sixteenth century and undergoes various modifications and refinements, but it is the unmistakeable prototype of the *polimetrum* of the German cartographer, Waldseemüller (1470–c.1521), of the *circumferentor* (the Dutch circle), of Tartaglia's (1506–57) *torquetum,* and so forth, many of which added the compass needle

Diſegniſi dipoi con le ſeſte ſopra un foglio, un cerchio grande a
modo noſtro, ſcompartendolo in 360. parti, o gradi; (&) il ſuo centro
ſia G, che rappreſenti il punto della poſitura, doue ſtette nell'operare
lo Aſtrolabio, quando ſi preſono le diſtantie delli alberi. Da queſto
punto G, che haremo fatto ſul foglio, tiriſi una linea diritta, lunga
a beneplacito noſtro, che ſia G A; et queſta diuidaſi in tante parti fra
loro uguali, quante furono le braccia, che ſi trouaron eſſere fra G, et
A, quali preſupponemmo che erano 60. Preſa dipoi la diſtantia
de gradi, che noi trouammo eſſere nello Aſtrolabio infra A, (&) B,

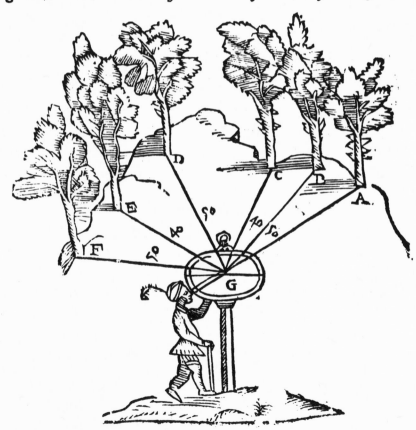

53. *Surveying by means of the Horizon.
From Cosimo Bartoli,* Del modo di
misurare, *1564.*

G   tiriſi

to the circular disk. The Horizon, in short, is one of the earliest forms of the *theodolite,* the rather complex instrument which Thomas Digges was to describe in 1571 and which is still the fundamental tool of the surveyor today.[45]

Alberti did not use the disk to take altitudes or latitudes as the sixteenth-century geographers did, because his map of Rome covered too small an area. However, in *Descriptio urbis Romae,* he gave one of the earliest descriptions of how the instrument could be used to determine "longitudes" which were really bearings measured on land.[46] He oriented himself by the north-south axis as

45. The simplest form of the circle or Horizon is in *De re aedificatoria,* bk. 10, chap. 7. Here it is a circle some ten feet in diameter drawn in the dirt on the summit of a hill. A large pike is set erect in its center. Alberti used the circle and pike to sight the proper line for a sluice to convey water.

46. One of Ptolemy's projections for a world map was a modified conic projection with curved parallels and straight meridians. (His other world map had curved parallels and meridians; all twenty-six of his special maps were drawn according to a rectangular projection.) Alberti's special map of Rome would seem to be like Ptolemy's modified conic projection because of its circular form and central point at which all lines (meridians) drawn from the points of the ground converge. His map could be rolled around so as to form a cone. However, closer examination shows that it bears almost no relation to Ptolemy's world map and was probably not derived from it. There are no curved parallels, and the imaginary straight lines radiating from the center to the circumference are lines of bearing from the Capitol to points of the ground. They resemble the rhumb lines of navigational charts or the azimuths of star maps far more than they do Ptolemy's meridians.

Around the same time as Alberti was working out his geography of Rome, an azimuthal projection (or mapping of bearings) was recommended for terrestrial maps by one of the map makers of the Vienna-Klosterneuburg school of cartography. Maps carrying out this suggestion were actually constructed by this school as early as 1434. According to the description of a modern historian who did not know of Alberti's work, these maps seem to differ from Alberti's only in minor details:

A point of origin was selected on the surface to be plotted. . . . One leg of a compass was then placed on the map, preferably at a slight distance from the central town in order not to obliterate it. A light circle was then drawn, enclosing the area to be reproduced. . . .

This outer circle was then marked off in degrees, which were grouped in *signa* [units]. . . . These divisions were called 'longitudes' although they corresponded roughly . . . to azimuths. The 'latitudes' were really equi-distances measured along a radius from the point of origin to the outer circle. . . .

The co-ordinates were probably measured by a strip of parchment graduated into 'latitudes' pivoting about the center. (Durand, *Vienna-Klosterneuburg Map Corpus,* pp. 178–79, 164–68.)

Alberti did not use *signa* units and his radius was divided into fifty rather than the ninety units used by this school. But otherwise the same principles are operative here as in *Descriptio urbis Romae:* coordinate tables were used as Ptolemy advised, to express each measurement in terms of *gradus* and *minuta* (and *signa* for the Vienna-Klosterneuburg school); and the astrolabe and its alidade were used to measure and draw the bearings of objects from a single point of origin, as well as their distances from it.

Here, then, are two contemporary but apparently independent techniques of mapping in which the inspiration of Ptolemy and the practices of medieval surveying

(astronomical and nautical) are patent.

Ptolemy did, and took measures which he set down in coordinate tables, but his method of schematization was that of a Portolan chart. He located the points of his ground by marking their distance from zero on the disk (fixed at due north) when sighted from the Capitol. The Capitol, that is, functioned as the center of a wind rose, and all the points of the map were plotted along "course lines" that radiated from it (fig. 54).

Rejecting Ptolemy's system of rectangular coordinates, which would have required two sets of cumbersome measurements for a small city map, Alberti proceeded to find the relative positions of the points of his ground much as a navigator would. He found their *bearings* from his vantage point by means of an astrolabe-Horizon; and in this first geographical work on Rome, he found the *distances* between the points on his "course lines" as mariners did who measured their distances by the rough method of the log: he counted off the actual steps between them.

By the time he wrote *Ludi matematici,* Alberti discovered a way to eliminate all but a few direct measurements in mapping a small area (e.g., the one that determines the scale of the map). The Horizon he describes here has no radial arm because there are no radius units of "latitudes" (distances) as before; and here the surveyor no longer takes bearings from a single central position. He arrives at almost all of his measures by sightings; and resembling the navigator more than ever, he takes these sightings from more than one vantage point.[47] For his first vantage point, he chooses any place where the Horizon can rest on a high flat base. Here, standing two *braccia* away from the instrument, he takes sightings through a plumb line which he holds over its center. He keeps the disk stationary but walks around it, sighting as many objects as he wishes and noting on a sheet of paper the units in degrees and minutes *at which* the sightings are made and *through which* his line of sight passes as it strikes its object. These are the values that replace the horizon and radius coordinates of *Descriptio urbis Romae.*

As he moves from one vantage point to the next, the surveyor keeps his "bearings" by means of a principle long familiar to navigation and nautical surveying, though unknown in medieval plans like that of Fra Paolino. All the vantage points after the first one are places which have already been sighted from some other point; and as the surveyor adopts a new vantage point, he matches up his instrument with a prior reading (fig. 55).

The nautical model Alberti had in mind is expressed in the example he uses to illustrate this rule. "Go to a place which has been seen from the first one," he directs, "and place your instrument flat and in such a position that it lies on the line of that same number through which you first saw it on your instrument. That is, place it so that a ship which had to navigate from the first to the second place could go along the same wind-line."[48]

47. *Op. volg.* 4: 430–34.
48. *Ibid.,* p. 432.

LIBRO

tirisi una linea dal centro G, la quale sarà G B, & verrà all'albero B, & la diuideremo in 50.paati uguali, che sono comprese infra
G B. Preso d'poi nello Astrolabio il numero de gradi, che era com-
preso infra B C, tirisi un'altra linea dal centro G, che sia G C, la qua
le diuidasi nella distantia delle sue braccia, che furno 40. Questo
medesimo si faccia de gli altri alberi con la medesima regola, & ti-
rinsi le lor linee dal centro G, a ciascuno di essi, & diuidinsi nelle distantie delle braccia. Ultimamente congiunghinsi insieme le teste
di queste linee, cioè A B, B C, C D, D E, E F, con linee rette, & aperte
le seste piglinsi le distantie infra l'uno albero, & l'altro, & traspor-
tinsi nella distantia, che è fra il G, & lo A, & veggasi quanto le seste
abbracciano di quelle parti, che rappresentano le braccia, & si saprà
per questa via quante braccia sieno fra l'uno, & l'altro di ciascun
di essi alberi, che è quello, che si cercaua.

54. *Mapping by means of the Horizon.
From Cosimo Bartoli,* Del modo di
misurare, *1564.*

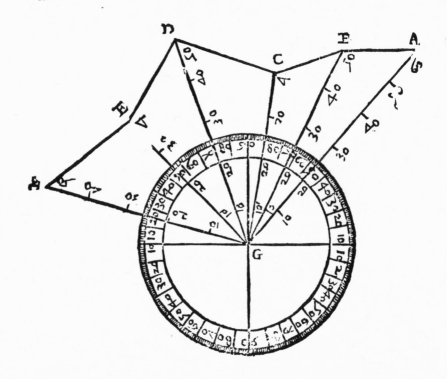

55. *How to take sightings from several vantage points (with the "Graphomètre" of Phillipe Danfrie). From Danfrie's* Déclaration de l'usage du Graphomètre, *1597.*

Maps drawn according to these new coordinates do not have a unique central point of orientation such as the Capitol on Alberti's map of Rome. Any point may be taken as the first vantage point. On this point, Alberti directed his reader to lay a miniature of his surveying instrument and to plot the points of his map much as the modern surveyor does with scale and protractor. Following his tables, he is to draw lines through the units of the miniature disk, lines which represent the sight lines from the stations he took at the first vantage point to the objects he viewed from them. The second vantage point is found along one of these lines, although it requires "a little adjustment," as Alberti put it, to determine its proper distance from the first. The lines drawn from the second vantage point to the points sighted from there will intersect lines drawn to these same points from the first position, but for accuracy Alberti recommended that two vantage points be used in conjunction with the first in order to arrive at the exact position of the second, and so forth. Plotting the several vantage points one by one, and drawing the lines that correspond to sightings taken from them, the reader will find the points of the measured ground where the sight lines radiating from the many centers of observation meet on his map.

In this way Alberti succeeded in eliminating all direct measurements of distance except those required for scaling (and perhaps for establishing a few of the vantage points)—an achievement usually attributed to the surveying and mapping procedures of the sixteenth century. And in a related problem, he taught Meliaduso d'Este to find distances by the very method which Gemma Frisius is said to have introduced into surveying almost a hundred years later.[49] Here he used the rule of triangulation, taking angles of position of a distant tower from either end of a corridor; and he found the unknown distance to the tower by constructing a geometric picture, again with a miniature of his surveying disk (fig. 56).

Even if we did not know of geographical writings like Alberti's, the cartographical advances of the Renaissance should compel us to suppose that someone had worked out some such rules by this time. For it was just about in the middle of the fifteenth century that loxodromes or wind roses began to appear on the interior land areas shown on Portolan based maps.[50] On a map of

49. For example, Singer *et al., Hist. of Technology*, 3: 539: "In 1533 a notable technical advance was made in survey when Gemma Frisius (1508–55), professor of mathematics at Louvain, explained the principle of triangulation, which eliminated all distance-measurement save that of the base-line. The method involved taking angles of position, that is, bearings, of the same feature from either end of a chosen base-line. The line is then plotted to scale on paper, and rays to the object are ruled in at the correct angle from each end. The point at which the rays meet is the position of the object, and its distance can thus be measured on the scale of the base-line."

Obviously, this is the same method Alberti recommended. Gemma Frisius also used the back of an astrolabe, laid upon a parapet, as his surveying instrument.

50. Almagià, *Mon. cart. vat.,* 1: 31–40.

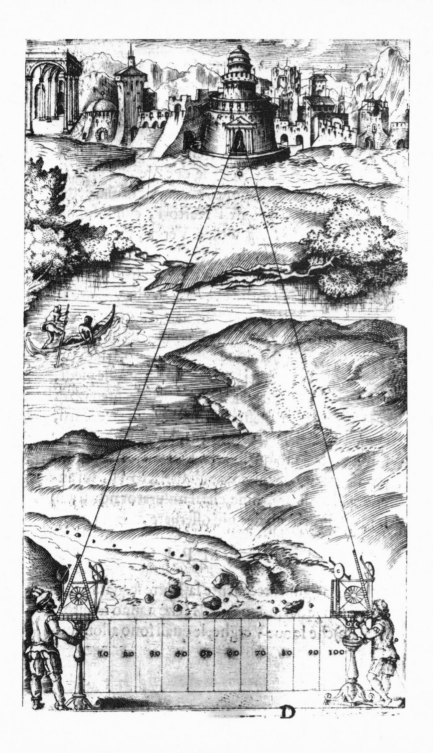

56. *How to find the distance to a tower by means of a geometric picture (with the "Holometro" of Abel Foullon). From Foullon's* Descrittione et uso dell'Holometro, *1564.*

Alberti's instructions were to place the depicted tower at the intersection of the lines drawn through the proper units of a miniature of the surveying disk from either end of a base line which represents the corridor. As many times as the base line in the picture goes into a line drawn from its center to the tower, so many times does the known length of the corridor go into the unknown actual distance from the corridor to the tower.

the Eastern Mediterranean and Black Sea (fig. 57), shown with north (the Black Sea, Constantinople, the Sea of Marmora) at the bottom of the page, the cities and ports along the coasts are named, as they are on earlier Portolan charts. But now inland centers also appear—Damascus, Jerusalem, Cairo; and their positions are determined (not too accurately as yet) by the lines of wind roses. This map is part of a large nautical chart in three sections which was prepared around 1450 in the Venetian *laboratorio* of Fra Mauro, maker of the last great *mappamundi*. Alberti's geographical work paralleled this development in the surveying and mapping of land areas, except that he improved upon it by insisting upon exact measurements and true scaling. The changes brought about in the plans and views of cities by procedures such as he describes are noticeable by the last quarter of the century, and they are dramatic ones.

To appreciate the transformation that took place in city plans, we need only compare Fra Paolino's fourteenth-century "plan" of Rome, totally lacking in measurements and helter-skelter in its placing of buildings, with Leonardo's completely mathematicized, bird's-eye view of Imola (figs. 50 and 58). The plan of Imola is one of several survey maps which Leonardo did for Cesare Borgia after the Duke's conquest of the Romagna in 1502, and it beautifully reveals the kind of development which the Renaissance brought about in the depiction of towns and small land areas, as well as the methods that made this development possible. It is a true logical copy, a geometric picture of the spatial arrangement of the town and its surrounding fields; and the traces of the techniques of nautical surveying and mapping which Alberti brought to land are still visible upon its face (cf. Alberti's plan, fig. 23). It is drawn within a circle and oriented by a wind rose of sixty-four radii; and the streets and buldings of Imola, and the roads, waterways, and fields outside, have been plotted on the map by means of compass readings (bearings) and measured distances.

The historical role played by Alberti in this development is obscure, although his systematic or logical role is quite clear. His principles of mapping, and some of the very procedures he described are present in the new plans and survey maps of the Renaissance, and as in Leonardo's plan of Imola, they account for the scientific character of these works. There is no evidence to suggest which, if any of them, were directly putting into practice his formulations of the rules of surveying and mapping, but Alberti's writings demonstrate that he was the systematizer, the rule giver of the mathematical methods employed in their construction—perhaps even their inventor. His own plan of Rome, whether or not it was actually drawn, is the first known scaled map in what had been a purely empirical tradition of city maps, a tradition which seems to have begun with the Roman plan-views that appeared a few years after Jacopo Angeli della Scarperia translated Ptolemy's *Geography*

57. Detail from a Venetian nautical chart with chorographic elements, c. 1450. South is at the top of the picture. From Roberto Almagià, Monumenta cartographica Vaticana, *vol. 1.* (Biblioteca apostolica Vaticana.)

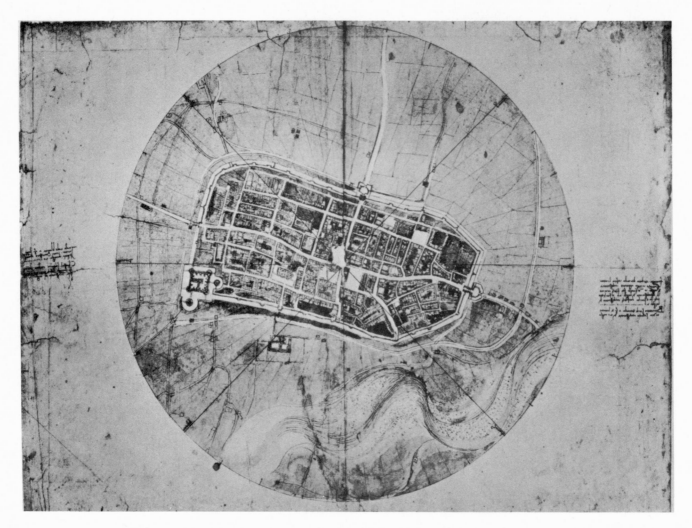

58. *Plan of Imola by Leonardo da Vinci (Windsor, 12284). From Ludwig H. Heydenreich,* Leonardo da Vinci, *vol 1 (New York: The Macmillan Company, 1954).*

from Greek into Latin in 1406.[51]

Ten such plan-views were appended to the codices of the *Geography* which were executed between c.1456 and 1472 by the copyist, Hugo de Cominellis,

51. Before Jacopo Angeli's translation of the *Geography,* there were three Greek mss. of the work (and copies of them made during the thirteenth and fourteenth centuries) which circulated with maps. The maps were based entirely upon the text, but a few observations were added to the maps of the two fourteenth-century copies. For the history of the Ptolemaic texts and maps, see J. Fischer, *Claudii Ptolemaei Geographiae,* 1: 365–75; and Johannes Keuning, "The history of geographical map projections until 1600," *Imago Mundi,* 12 (1955): 1–24. Nordenskiöld gives a critical catalogue of the printed editions of the *Geography* in *Facsimile-Atlas,* pp. 12–31.

and the Florentine painter, Pietro del Massaio.[52] They show the cities of Milan, Venice, Florence, Rome, Adrianople, Constantinople, Damascus, Jerusalem, Cairo, and Alexandria; and all of them stand at that first stage of the Ptolemic revival which introduced into the depiction of cities the geographical idea of a map—roughly understood. That is, they all present a consistent (almost a bird's-eye) view of the spatial plan of a city, but this was apparently done without direct measurements of any kind. Pietro del Massaio collected and copied these city maps, but he did not design them. The one of Rome, for example, belongs to the same tradition as that of the fresco of 1414 (cf. figs. 51 and 59). And the one of Constantinople is a copy of a work designed around 1420 by the Florentine geographer, Cristoforo Buondelmonti (fig. 60).

Buondelmonti, a cleric who wrote two geographical works describing Crete and the islands of the Greek archipelago, belonged to the Florentine group surrounding Nicolò Niccoli, the circle in which Ptolemy's *Geography* began its modern career.[53] Since the first manuscript of the Latin *Geography* had no maps, and since the first maps to be added to it were merely copies of those in the medieval Greek manuscripts (copies drawn again by Florentines, the humanists Francesco di Lapacino and Domenico di Lionardo Buoninsegni), Buondelmonti's failure to graduate and schematize his drawing of Constantinople in some geometric way is not surprising. It took a while before the principles of Ptolemaic science could be mastered and applied anew. The maps appended to the Ptolemaic text do not show corrections until the 1427 copy of the *Geography* owned by Cardinal Fillastre, but then additions appear which were gleaned from mariners' charts and entirely new regional maps also came to be added to the classical atlas. Claudius Clavus' 1427 map of Scandinavia was the first of these new maps to be plotted by Ptolemy's rectilinear coordinate system, and the famous map of central Europe of c. 1450 owned by Nicholas of Cusa was another such work, constructed from newly compiled tables of latitude and longitude.

For the city maps, however, a coordinate system had yet to be devised,

---

52. There are three of these codices: Bibl. Nat. Fond. lat. 4802, not dated but believed to have been executed before 1458; Cod. Vat. lat. 5699, dated 1469 and executed in Florence; and Cod. Vat. Urb. lat. 277, dated 1472. A facsimile of the Paris codex has been published. H. Omont, editor, *Géographie de Ptolémée. Traduction Latine de Jacopo d'Angiolo de Florence. Reproduction réduite des cartes et plans du manuscrit Latin 4802 de la Bibliothèque Nationale.* A new plan-view of Volterra was added to the Urb. lat. 277 codex.

53. For Buondelmonti, see Emil Jacobs, "Cristoforo Buondelmonti, Ein Beitrag zur Kenntnis seines Lebens und seiner Schriften," *Beiträge zur Bücherkunde und Philologie August Wilmanns*, pp. 313–40; same, "Neues von Cristoforo Buondelmonti," *Archäologisches Institut des Deutschen Reiches, Jahrbuch*, 20 (1905): 39–45; Almagià, *Mon. cart. vat.*, 1: 105–17; A. Campana, "Da Codici del Buondelmonti," *Studi Bizantini e neoellenici*, Vol. 9 (1957): 32–52. Thomas Goldstein has an interesting article on "Geography in Fifteenth-Century Florence" in *Merchants and Scholars*, pp. 11–32.

59. *Plan-view of Rome in a fifteenth-century codex of Ptolemy's* Geography *(Vat. Urb. lat. 277). South is at the top of the picture. From G.B. de Rossi,* Piante iconografiche e prospettiche di Roma *(Rome, 1879).*

60. *Plan view of Constantinople, c. 1420, by Cristoforo Buondelmonti.*
From a fifteenth-century codex of Ptolemy's Geography *(Paris Cod. lat. 4802). (Bibliothèque nationale.)*

and until it was, the plan-views inspired by Ptolemy were drawn without measures or any kind of scaling. The only developments possible within this tradition were those resulting from closer empirical observations. The plan of Rome copied by Pietro del Massaio shows improvements of this kind over the fresco of 1414: it depicts more buildings (particularly outside the walls), the spatial relations among them have been somewhat clarified, and a greater effort has been made to place them in proportion to each other and to the city as a whole.[54] Yet the Ptolemaic plan, although considerably later than Alberti's work, has none of the proportional accuracy which his tabulated measurements introduced into the depiction of the city.

Alberti's plan was probably conceived within the tradition of the early fifteenth-century plan-views of Rome. It shares the orientation of the fresco of 1414 and of Pietro del Massaio's plan; and although the tables in *Descriptio urbis Romae* give the coordinates of a few buildings which do not appear in the Ptolemaic plan, most of the buildings and monuments Alberti tabulated are the ones named on the Ptolemaic picture.[55] But Alberti's methods produce a conspicuous graphic change (cf. figs. 23, 51, 59). Based upon a survey which gave to each point of the ground a set of numerical values, and constructed as a scaled picture, his plan exhibits a new kind of exactitude, particularly noticeable in the course of the walls and of the Tiber. This exactitude is due not to sharper observations but to the mathematicizing of observation and representation alike.

This development, namely, the transformation of the procedures of observation and depiction into those of surveying and mapping, marks the beginning of the scientific tradition of city plans. It brought about a totally new kind of city map, and it took some time before it was understood and assimilated. The purely empirical tradition of plan-views persisted without measures well into the 1470's, in the Ptolemaic atlases and elsewhere; and sometimes the new geometric ideas threatened to overwhelm the empirical

54. This development is probably not due to Pietro del Massaio but to the author of the (unknown) plan-view of Rome which he copied. There is no such improvement in the plan-view of Constantinople, for example. In the Paris codex, which is the only one I have been able to examine throughout, the plan-views of Rome and Florence are the most highly developed in this respect.

The finest and most finished of these plan-views of Rome is a pen drawing of 1474 done in Venice by Alessandro Strozzi (Laur. Red. 77). It is reproduced in Frutaz, *Le Piante,* 2: pl. 90; and in Giovanni Battista de Rossi, *Piante iconografiche e prospettiche di Roma anteriori al secolo XVI,* 2: pl. 4. Rossi believed that Alberti's procedures were responsible for the noticeable improvements in this sketch, but all of them are of an empirical rather than a mathematical nature and would seem to owe little or nothing to Alberti.

55. Alberti gives co-ordinates for seven "templa et publica Urbis aedifica" which I cannot find on Pietro del Massaio's plan-view or on the Strozzi drawing: Fastigium Constantini, Sabae, Balbinae, Jo. apostoli, Stephani rotundi, Jo. et Pauli, and Vitalis. On another ms., he lists Honofrii in Monte and Brancatii which I also cannot find. All the other named buildings and monuments, about twenty-five in number, are on the Ptolemaic plan.

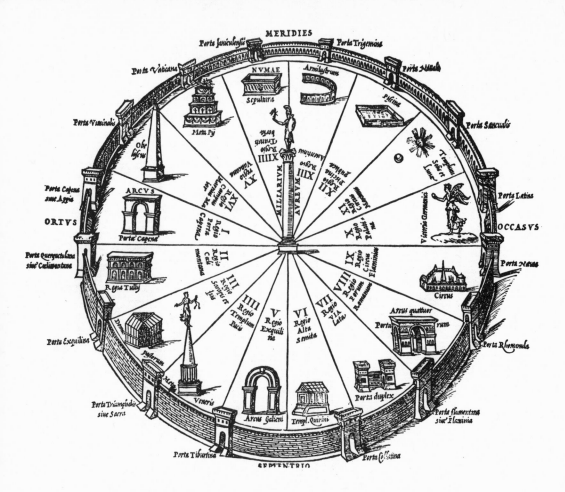

content in mapping rather than to order it and give it precise definition. This tendency can be found in the crude use made of Alberti's surveying disk in certain diagrammatic plans of ancient Rome which were drawn in the sixteenth century. Marco Fabio Calvo designed and published two such circular "plans" in 1527 which were then copied by Sebastian Münster and published in his *Polyhistor* of 1538.[56] Calvo was one of Raphael's collaborators in a papal-sponsored project to prepare an archeological plan of ancient Rome, but Raphael, who certainly would have done a more sophisticated work than what we now have from Calvo's hand, died before it could be completed. Calvo's drawings, which are all that remain of the project, show the city divided like a pie into sixteen regions, with a major monument in each of the "slices" (fig. 61).

61. *Plan of ancient Rome by Marco Fabio Calvo, 1527.*
From Le piante di Roma, *ed. A. Pietro Frutaz*
(Rome: Istituto di Studi Romani, 1962)

56. Plates 9, 10, 11 of vol. 2, Frutaz, *Le Piante*. Described on pp. 53–55 of vol. I. Frutaz does not relate these drawings to Alberti or his procedures.

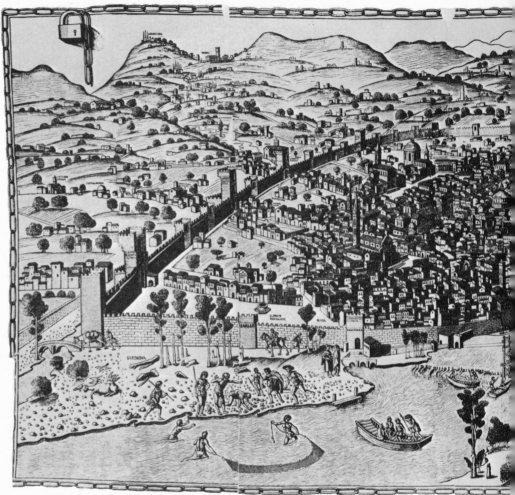

62. *Planimetric view of Florence, c.*
1470–82. East is at the top of the picture.
From G. Boffito and A. Mori, Piante e
vedute di Firenze: Studio storico,
topografico, cartografico *(Florence:*
L. Franceschini, 1926).

The radii of Calvo's circular plans are far fewer than the forty-eight
measures on Alberti's disk or the sixty-four radii on Leonardo's plan of Imola;
but Calvo had adopted their method of locating and representing the points of a
ground by bearings. His diagrammatic plans give a geometrically consistent
picture of the arrangement of the monuments of Rome, although in its way it is
as unscientific a picture as that of the empirical plan-views. The positions of the
gates and monuments with respect to the compass points are not at all accurate,
and the monuments stand symmetrically at the same distance from the center
of the circle they are drawn in, their actual distances from it being neither
measured nor guessed at.

Plans such as Alberti envisioned and Leonardo carried out did not become

common until about the middle of the sixteenth century.[57] City views rather than plans were the more immediate and popular beneficiaries of the new methods of surveying and depicting. The principles of mapping a small area tended to combine with the dominant perspectival, pictorial outlook of the fifteenth and early sixteenth centuries, giving rise to pictures of the urban centers of Renaissance Italy which were at once works of science and of art. The view, of course, can show only one aspect of a city, as the first of these new views of Florence of c.1470–82 presents the city as seen from a height outside it, facing east[58] (fig. 62). Large buildings, such as the Duomo, blot out

57. Genuine plans of Rome, for example, do not appear until about 1550. See Frutaz, *Le Piante*.

58. Described in Boffito and Mori, *Piante e vedute di Firenze,* pp. xx–xxi; 12–21,

what lies "behind" them, and dimensions decrease as they "recede" from the viewer. The plan, on the other hand, if drawn in accordance with Alberti's rules, shows all the bearings and relations of distance among the points of the ground, and these relations remain constant or "true" whether we look at the picture from north, south, east, or west. Yet Alberti's cartographical principles are present in the planimetric views of the Renaissance just as his perspectival principles are. Vasari's description of the construction of a view of Florence in the second decade of the sixteenth century makes this plain:

> The Pope [Clement VII] commissioned Benvenuto di Lorenzo della Volpaia, a good *maestro* of clocks and quadrants and an excellent astronomer . . . to do a plan [*pianta*] of that city, that is, the countryside for a mile outside with its hills, mountains, rivers, cliffs, houses, churches, and other things; the plazas and streets inside, and the walls, bastions, and other fortifications around the city. He did this by intersections with a compass in all directions and by going outside to compare the Duomo, which he had marked as the center, with the mountains.[59]

The compass (*bussola*) is, of course, the surveying disk, to which the compass needle came to be added in the sixteenth century; and since Vasari speaks of "intersections" with it, making no mention of actual measurements of distances, the method he describes was probably closer to one of those given in *Ludi matematici* than to that of *Descriptio urbis Romae*. That is, the Duomo may have been one but not the only vantage point for sightings, so that its "central position" here refers merely to the place it was to have in the picture. The mountains "outside" obviously provided another vantage point for the sightings, perhaps the only other vantage point; or perhaps the Duomo was no vantage point at all and the height outside the city provided two vantage points, like the two ends of the corridor in the sighting problem Alberti gave to Meliaduso d'Este. In either case, the mountain could serve as a perspectival vantage point, too, and it sounds from Vasari's words as though it did. If this were a plan he was describing, such as Leonardo's plan of Imola, there would be no need to "compare" (*riscontrar*) the Duomo with the mountains; but from the mountains, one could get a "view" and rough elevation of the Duomo.

The author of the fifteenth-century planimetric view we do have of Florence apparently did something like this. A handful of buildings (most of them named) stands out from the others in his picture: the Duomo, Baptistery, and Campanile at the center of the city; to the left, the Innocenti, Annunziata, and Santa Maria Novella; to the right, Or San Michele, the Palazzo della

---

139–46. The authors tend to see the "influence" of Alberti in this view. The view itself was first mentioned in a sixteenth-century inventory of the *bottega* of Alessandro di Francesco Rosselli, *merciaio stampatore*.

59. Vasari, *Vita di Niccolo il scultorre, detto il Tribolo*, quoted in Boffito and Mori, *Piante e vedute di Firenze*, pp. xxi–xxii.

Signoria and the Loggia; and over the Arno, the Pitti Palace and the Carmine. Whereas almost all the other buildings are indistinguishable from each other in appearance, these are carefully rendered so as to show their architectural features. And whereas almost all the other buildings barely differ from each other in size, the dimensions of these major ones seem to reflect "measures," probably rough relative elevations as sighted from the perspectival vantage point. The positions of these buildings relative to each other and to the surrounding walls seem to have been "measured" also, perhaps by means of the *velo,* or perhaps—as Vasari's description suggests—by a few sightings made with the surveyor's disk. In either case, a rough plan would result, an arrangement of points upon which the entire view of the houses, churches, and walls of the city, together with the surrounding fields and landmarks, could rise.

There is again no evidence of a direct relation between Alberti's cartographical work and this first planimetric view of Florence, or the view Vasari describes, although Alberti appears to have been engaged in constructing plans and/or views other than his Roman one. Vasari attributes to him a picture of Venice showing San Marco "in prospettiva,"[60] and Alberti himself claims to have used his Horizon to survey and depict "cities and provinces."[61] What is certain, however, is that the new views of the Renaissance, insofar as they were based upon some kind of ground plan, embody some of the concepts and procedures that Alberti set down. Ideas of sighting and scaling, even if roughly applied, entered into their construction, making them part of the general cartographic movement of the period. The quattrocento view of Florence, unlike its compressed, fourteenth-century predecessor, belongs to geography as well as painting (cf. figs. 49 and 62). It represents a good number of the spatial relations that really obtained among the major features and buildings of the city, for its author had learned to focus upon measurable relations—ratios. Depicting the relative dimensions and positions of things as seen from a particular vantage point, his objective was to portray the city "in its just proportions."

A comparable development marks the new set of Roman views which supplanted the earlier type belonging to the first quarter of the fifteenth century.[62]

60. Vasari, *Vite cinque Annotate,* p. 40. Mancini conjectured that this may be the Panorama of Venice owned by the Museum of Dresden because of its close resemblance to one of the first planimetric views of Rome (to be discussed below) which, he believed, reflected Alberti's rules and perhaps his actual measures. *Vita di Leon Battista Alberti,* p. 40, n. 3.

61. *De re aedif.,* bk. 10, chap. 7.

62. Described in Frutaz, *Piante e vedute di Firenze,* 1: 20ff. G. B. de Rossi, *Piante iconografiche ... di Roma,* pp. 100–1, 109–10, and Mancini were tempted to attribute the development of the Roman planimetric views to Alberti or a "school" of Alberti. O. Lehmann-Brockhaus in "Albertis 'Descriptio urbis Romae,' " *Kunstchronik,* 13 (1960): 345–48, and Frutaz reject this claim, and they are right to do so insofar as Alberti's surveying and mapping procedures give rise to a plan, not a view. But the authors of the

Many of these views were executed in the sixteenth century, but they all show the city as it was around 1490 and they are believed to reflect a lost prototype drawn shortly before that time by Francesco Rosselli. When not directly based upon some kind of ground plan, that is, they are copied from a prototype which most probably was. As far as our knowledge goes, Alberti was the only fifteenth-century author of a measured plan of Rome, or at least of a method for drawing such a plan, complete with tables, before Francesco Rosselli. The planimetric views of Rome need not trace their descent directly from his plan or tables, of course, to be indebted to him; and in point of fact, they are far less accurate than they would have been had his methods of mapping been strictly followed. But once Alberti's general procedure of taking sightings and reproducing them proportionally (by a miniature surveying disk or by the *velo*) was known, the author of the prototype of these views, and the authors of the views themselves, could find and represent "measures" of their own.

One possible link between these views and Alberti's *Descriptio urbis Romae* ought to be pointed out, however. Within this new tradition there is a view by Sebastian Münster, from his *Cosmographia universalis* of 1550 (fig. 63). Like the others in this tradition, it shows the city as it was around 1490, but this picture, and the ones copied from it, do not depict the Colosseum. It is an odd omission, but Alberti also gave no measures for the Colosseum; and a marginal note on Münster's view (note 6) explains that there was no room on the picture to fit it in, as if the Colosseum were to be placed in position only after all the other buildings had been drawn.

The new techniques of surveying and mapping to which the views and plans of the Renaissance are indebted brought to the depiction of land areas the same isomorphism that characterizes the Portolan charts. The principles of Portolan cartography alone were not sufficient, however, to construct accurate maps of large areas. As we have seen, the piecing together of many small special maps required an ideational grid such as Ptolemy's network of parallels and meridians, a geographer's *velo* which could be used to transpose relative measures from the face of the earth to its pictures, and from smaller pictures to larger ones. Thus the revival of Ptolemaic methods of mapping, which also began in the fifteenth century, was vital to the development of modern geography.

The liberating effect of Ptolemaic geography and its well-known shortcomings are both aptly symbolized by Columbus. With a rational picture of a unified world in mind, Columbus dared treat the once impassable ocean as a medium connecting the land masses of the earth. But the route across the

---

planimetric views did take some sightings and tried to reproduce them, if not in a scaled plan, at least by using some kind of "reducing and enlarging" device; and in this, I would say, they were carrying out ideas which Alberti, more than any one else in the fifteenth century, was responsible for developing.

Quorundam locorum huius Romanæ picturæ explicatio.

A Moles Adriani, hodie Castellum S. Angeli.	D Columna Antoniana, & è regione eius, Maria rotunda.	G Templü pacis, ubi quoq; stare debuerat Collossus ingēs ædificiü, sed loci angustia excludit.
B Palatium papæ.	E Columna Adriani.	H Thermæ Diocletianæ.
C Ecclesia S. Petri.	F Arcus Septimij.	

I Pons Sixti.	K Capitoliü.	N Aquæductus.	R S. Laurentius.
L S. Bartholomei insula, iuxta pontem Sixti.	O Arcus Titi & Vespasiani.	S S. Sebastianus.
M S. Iohannes Lateranus.	P S. Susanna.	T S. Vitalis.
	Q S. Maria de populo.	V Caput bouis.

Western Ocean to Cathay and India, even when cut short by America, was far longer than he had supposed. Paolo Toscanelli, who was a friend of both Alberti and Nicholas of Cusa, drew the chart of 1474 that guided Columbus on his first voyage, and he evidently incorporated in it some typically Ptolemaic mistakes and miscalculations. There were many gaps in Ptolemy's tables, such as his ignorance of the Scandinavian peninsula, America, and so forth, and elsewhere his coordinates were wanting in observational accuracy, yet Toscanelli, and the fifteenth century in general, had to rely upon his tables, particularly for areas of the world unknown to the Portolan chart makers. Moreover, certain errors of calculation were built into Ptolemy's system of graduation. He gave too great a longitudinal extension to the known world, partly because his

63. *View of Rome in Sebastian Munster's* Cosmographia universalis, *1550.*
West is at the top of the picture.
From Le piante di Roma, *ed. A. Pietro Frutaz (Rome: Istituto di Studi Romani, 1962).*

193

methods for determining longitude were defective, and he seemed to know of no technique by which to check or supplement them. The Portolan charts, on the other hand, could depict small areas with great accuracy. Maps drawn from the Ptolemaic tables could be corrected in part by such data; and of even greater importance, the Portolan charts yielded the principles for ascertaining exact bearings.

The geographers of the fifteenth and early sixteenth centuries not only revived the Ptolemaic tradition, therefore, and they not only extended Portolan principles and instruments to land surveys: they fused the technique of surveying by bearings with the Ptolemaic system of graduation, and they did so in three distinguishable kinds of maps. In all three categories, this unification marks the characteristic geographical work of the Renaissance, and it led to maps which became the true precursors of the works of modern scientific geography. Mariners' charts, stemming from the medieval Portolan tradition, began to be graduated around 1500. Regional survey maps, growing out of the plans and planimetric city views of the quattrocento, began to encompass larger areas and took on measures of latitude in the first decades of the sixteenth century. And the Ptolemaic atlas, appended to the successive copies of the *Geography,* was both corrected by nautical and land surveys and augmented by the addition of entirely new survey maps. Renaissance geography thus secured the means by which to overcome the limitations of the past. Drawing upon ancient and medieval sources, and combining the principles and techniques of both in its maps, it learned how to acquire new empirical contents and to order them systematically.

The methodic foundations were thereby laid for the two epoch making works that ushered in the age of modern scientific geography: Mercator's coherent and accurate map of the entire known world, and Ortelius' atlas of its special parts.[63] By 1570, Ortelius' atlas of modern maps superseded the various Ptolemaic collections. Mercator's map of the world was completed just the year before, a map which systematically incorporated the many mariners' charts of small areas. All the geographical information which they contained was at last accurately and proportionally ordered, so that "the positions of all points," as Mercator declared, "not only according to the latitude and longitude, but also in regard to their mutual direction and distance, precisely agree with the reality."[64] With Ortelius and Mercator, the magnificent world picture of

63. Nordenskiöld describes the period of geography ushered in by Mercator and Ortelius as "characterized by the effort to found the knowledge of the lands and seas of the earth, not on commentaries of the writings of more or less classical authors, but on new and careful investigations, based if possible on topographical surveys and astronomical observations." *Facsimile-Atlas,* p. 124.

64. Mercator, quoted by Keuning, *Hist. of geog. map projections.* Gerard Mercator (1512–94) was taught the mathematical principles of cartography by Gemma Frisius. He became a manufacturer of instruments and a surveyor, draftsman, and engraver of maps.

modern geography had begun to take form, but underlying it, and still ordering the depiction of the earth and its parts, are the uniform spatial schema of Ptolemy and the methods of surveying and mapping derived from the Portolan charts: the principles of medieval and ancient cartography which Alberti and the Renaissance fused to satisfy their new quest for a proportional picture of the world.

The Measure of the Heavens

The intellectual movement that revived the science of geography brought about similar changes in the representations of the celestial world, and often the same people were engaged in both tasks. For example, Conrad of Dyffenbach[65] in 1426 made the first known attempt to project the astronomical knowledge of the Middle Ages onto a celestial map. Western mariners had made use of astronomical tables of latitude and longitude since at least 1252, when the Alfonsine Tables were drawn up in Spain. Such tables listed the coordinate values of the heavenly bodies as given in Ptolemy's *Almagest,* enriched by a few Arabian and Western additions. Until Conrad's map of 1426, however, no one drew a picture of these points. Conrad was obviously inspired to do so by Ptolemy: he plotted the points of his star map by means of Ptolemy's rectilinear coordinate system; and like the master, he applied this principle to the earth as well as the heavens. He constructed two terrestrial maps along exactly the same lines. There are no land masses drawn on these strange "maps." Conrad simply located his geographical points on a grid of meridians and parallels, plotting them the way he plotted the positions of the stars. But although these are hardly maps in the full sense of the word, they are skeletal plans for genuine maps, for they were based upon the geographical coordinate tables and lists of (longitudinal) distances between cities.

If the celestial and terrestrial maps of Conrad of Dyffenbach are but two expressions of a single aim, it should occasion no surprise to learn that Alberti, too, aside from being a geographer, also played a part in the early development of scientific astronomy. No less an astronomer than Regiomontanus (1436–76) attributes this role to him. Criticizing his contemporaries as "credulous little women" who accepted as "admissible and divine" whatever they found in the planetary tables; who preferred to "believe in writers" rather than seek the truth, Regiomontanus singled out Toscanelli and Alberti, along with his teacher, Peurbach, as "learned men" concerned with empirical verification of what they held to be true. Most astronomers, he went on to say, claim that the "maximum

Ortelius (1527–98) was neither a surveyor nor a map maker himself, but he formed the first systematic collection of modern maps in his *Theatrum orbis terrarum.*

65. Durand, *Vienna-Klosterneuburg Map Corpus,* pp. 107–09, 114–19.

declination of the sun in our days is twenty-four degrees and two minutes"; but "my teacher [Peurbach] and I have ascertained with instruments that it is twenty-three degrees and twenty-eight minutes, and I have often heard Magister Paolo, the Florentine, and Battista Alberti say, that by diligent observation they found that it did not exceed twenty-three degrees and thirty minutes, the figure I have decided to register in our table."[66]

Evidently Alberti, who was a close friend of Toscanelli (1397–1482)[67] and shared his enthusiasm for Ptolemy's *Geography,* also joined him in making fresh surveys of the heavens. Alberti probably did little more than assist Toscanelli in this project, however. There is little evidence of any astronomical activity on his part beyond that referred to in Regiomontanus' letter. Toscanelli, on the other hand, was a professional "physicist" and mathematician. He was at work throughout his lifetime correcting the astronomical tables of the period by exactly formulated observations of the positions of the heavenly bodies. Alberti's participation in this effort could hardly have been persistent; but the fact that he participated at all testifies to his general interest in the principles of geometric representation. He may have drawn some of his geographical ideas and practices from this work of celestial observation, but it was probably an active concern with the techniques of measurement and proportional depiction per se that formed the intellectual bond between him and Toscanelli, as it bound Toscanelli and Nicholas of Cusa (1401–64).[68] All three were involved in the construction

66. "Letter of February, 1464," in Mancini, *Vita di L. B. Alberti,* p. 376.

67. Alberti's friendship with Toscanelli, who was seven years his senior, goes back at least to his first stay in Florence from 1434–36. Uzielli, *Vita e i Tempi di Toscanelli,* pp. 200–7. Mancini pointed out that they could have met earlier, while Toscanelli was a student of medicine and natural philosophy at Padua and Alberti was at Barzizza's Gymnasium. During the years 1439–43, while Eugenius IV and his court were residing in Florence, Alberti collected a number of his brief *Intercoenales* and dedicated them to Toscanelli. His letter of dedication is written in a familiar tone and ends on a note of affection: "Tu igitur, mi Paule, Leonem Baptistam tuum amabis ut facis, nostrumque libellum cum a ceteris tuis majoribus studiis vacabis perleges, proque nostra vetere amicitia dabis operam, ut per te quam emendatior sit." *Op. ined.,* pp. 122–23.

68. There is no direct evidence that Alberti ever knew Cusa personally, although both were close friends of Toscanelli. Cusa studied at the University of Padua from 1417 to 1423, when he received his doctorate in law, and Toscanelli was at the University as a student during these years. There the two became friends and remained so throughout their lives. Alberti left Padua in 1421. He may have known Cusa and Toscanelli there, but there is no evidence that he actually did. There were several occasions at which Alberti and Cusa could have met after that. During the Council of Florence-Ferrara, Alberti was at Ferrara with Eugenius IV, as was Cusa who received his appointment there as apostolic visitor to Germany. In 1450, Alberti was residing in Rome when Cusa was made a cardinal by Nicholas V, another mutual friend. In the late 1450's, Cusa's home in Rome was a gathering place for men of science like Peurbach, Regiomontanus, and Toscanelli; Alberti must have been a member of this group.

Santinello draws a number of parallels between Cusa's ideas and Alberti's writings on beauty, art, and perspective in *Leon Battista Alberti,* pp. 265–96. As he admits, this

of proportionally accurate pictures of the observable world, a project which readily took root and prospered in fifteenth-century Italy.

The humanistic study of the languages and literature of antiquity, together with new practical problems arising from commerce and the early voyages of exploration, tended to stimulate a renewed interest in both of Ptolemy's sciences. It was not only the *Geography* that received a new translation and wide circulation in the fifteenth century. The medieval text of the *Almagest,* which had been translated from the Arabic into Latin in the twelfth century, was now supplemented by a fresh Latin translation from the Greek made by another of Alberti's friends, George of Trebizond. Manuscript copies of the original Greek also circulated in Italy and were studied by Toscanelli and Regiomontanus. What the Renaissance students of the *Almagest* sought in the work, however, was not the Ptolemaic plan of the heavens. Rather, as Regiomontanus' attitude indicates, they took Ptolemy's *rules* for "measuring" appearances as their authority, and they applied these rules anew in both of the Ptolemaic domains. The first terrestrial maps that transcended the limitations of medieval cartography originated with men who were consciously reviving not the Ptolemaic picture of the earth but the forgotten science that gave rise to it, and this kind of "renaissance" animated Renaissance astronomy, too. Peurbach (1423–61), who planned an epitome of the *Almagest* which Regiomontanus completed, made the same kind of astronomical observations as Toscanelli and Alberti; and Regiomontanus, who in turn planned an edition of the *Geography,* constructed new almanacs for navigators.

Even Copernicus, despite the fact that he rejected the Ptolemaic geocentric theory, was hailed as a revivor and imitator of Ptolemaic science by his disciple, Rheticus—a "science" which embraced geography for the great Copernicus, too. For Copernicus was not only an astronomer; he also did a preliminary work on the geography of Prussia which Rheticus completed and issued in a map. Astronomers were geographers, in short, and geographers astronomers, because the Ptolemaic renaissance which they were bringing about

---

constitutes no evidence of a personal or even an intellectual relation between them. They both had access to the same sources and, I would add, were both so oriented by the new mathematical outlook as to select the same ideas from these sources and develop them in the same direction. However, scholars familiar with both Cusa's writings and Alberti's tend to think that they must have known each other's ideas. This is my belief, and Professor Raymond Klibansky of McGill University has recently told me that he has held this opinion for many years. He has also pointed out to me that Toscanelli was not the only friend Cusa and Alberti had in common. Giovanni Andrea de Bussi, to whom Alberti sent the Latin manuscript of *De statua,* was one of Cusa's closest friends, and after Cusa's death, it was Bussi who sought to make Cusa's achievements known to his Italian contemporaries. See Raymond Klibansky, *Ein Proklos-Fund* (Heidelberg, 1929); "Plato's Parmenides in the Middle Ages and the Renaissance," *Medieval and Renaissance Studies,* vol. 1, no. 2 (1943): 281–331. *Plato Latinus,* vol. 3 *Parmenides* (London, 1953), pp. x, xiii ff., and Index s.v. Ioannes Andreas de Bussis.

constituted a general scientific effort to measure the world and re-order its picture in exact mathematical terms. This powerful stream of thought, swelling the twin channels of geography and astronomy, even caught up Renaissance artists and directed them toward its goal. Not only did their own properly artistic works assimilate the objectives and methods of proportional depiction, but painters such as Gentile Bellini and Raphael worked directly at the new plans and planimetric city views as well.[69] Others, Leonardo and Albrecht Dürer among them, followed the lead of Alberti and became surveying cartographers. In a variety of ways, all of them, artists, geographers, astronomers, were engaged in the many-sided task of applying to the visible world the mathematically inspired outlook of proportionality, that "science" which the age had discovered in Ptolemy and called *Prospettiva.*

In the fifteenth and sixteenth centuries, all spatial constructions fell under the sway of *Prospettiva,* and in every domain she entered, she effected the same transformation. She banished the substantival conception of space, forcing the medieval "container" of ontologically real and qualitatively disparate places to yield to a uniform and relational spatial conception.[70] The personification of *Prospettiva* on Pollaiuolo's Tomb of Sixtus IV holds an astrolabe in her hand (fig. 39), the instrument Alberti used in astronomy, geography, and sculpture. For in each of these fields, her gaze was fixed upon "the position rather than the quality," as Ptolemy said of *geography,* noting with her instrument "the *relation* of distances everywhere."[71] Hence all Renaissance images of the world, whether artistic or scientific, exhibit the same homogeneous and relational spatial form, for all of them spring from the geometric intuition and methodological ideas of *Prospettiva.*

Like all the other developments of Renaissance culture which issued in a

69. There is a fine article by Eugen Oberhummer on the artists who worked at the new planimetric views and maps of the Renaissance. "Leonardo da Vinci and the Art of the Renaissance in its Relations to Geography," *The Geographical Journal,* 33 (1909): 540–69. Even before Oberhummer's article, the cartographical interests of Alberti, Leonardo, and Dürer were known, although they were not fully explored. It is therefore surprising that Durand, a specialist in Renaissance cartography, should state that "there is no direct evidence of a reciprocal influence between painting and cartography.... And yet the resemblance between the trapezoidal 'Donis' projection, and the pattern of checkered squares receding toward the background, which is so common a motif in interiors of the fifteenth century, is sufficiently close to suggest that it may have been more than fortuitous." *Vienna-Klosterneuburg Map Corpus,* p. 287.

70. This is the way modern philosophical thought would later characterize this kind of spatial order. Leibnitz, for example, said of space: "In order to have an idea of place, and consequently of space, it is sufficient to consider these relations [of position] and the rules of their changes. It is not necessary to imagine any absolute reality outside the things whose situation we consider." *Oevres philosophiques de Leibnitz,* 3: 776.

71. "Geography looks at the position rather than the quality, noting the relation of distances everywhere." *Geography,* bk. 1, chap. 1.

picture of a universal, rational world order, the new Copernican astronomy also rests upon the fundamental notion of a relational order of space, and in this it reveals its indebtedness to the Ptolemaic astronomy it supplanted. The Ptolemaic renaissance was well under way when Copernicus crossed the Alps in 1496 to study canon law at Bologna and to pursue in Italy his studies of Greek, mathematics, and astronomy. The geographical and astronomical pictures of the world were being mapped; and because of the successful transposition of the principle of *analogia* to art, art works were also aspiring to represent the proportional order of nature. The rational, harmonious pattern of the world was becoming evident everywhere. In this cultural milieu, the unsystematic character of Ptolemy's astronomy would have been reason enough to reject it, if, as Copernicus said, "a more rational system of circles" could be found. But the lever that actually unhinged the geocentric theory, and with it the entire hierarchical world order, was the principle of the relativity of place and motion: a principle which became compelling once the relational conception of space was assumed.[72]

To bring systematic order into the positions and movements of the planets, Copernicus had to replace the ontologically fixed center of the universe by a neutral mathematical point. He had to wrench the observer's standpoint free of the metaphysical, hierarchical chain of being and impart to it the perpetual, circular motion of heavenly bodies. Only then could he explain the apparent retrograde and irregular movements of the planets as a combination of their motion with the motion of a rotating and revolving earth. But this meant that no "part" of space was privileged any longer. Every position had to be regarded as relative to every other, and all had to be placed on the same logical level. Space was "neutralized"—as in a perspectival painting or a scientific map; and the leveling of what had hitherto seemed to be fixed, qualitative spatial differences affected the different kinds of motion, too. Up and down, movement and rest, all became purely relative determinations. Motion and position alike came to be bound to the observer's standpoint by the heliocentric system: to its relative place and state of motion.

The Copernican Revolution thus involved a prodigious amount of a priori reasoning. Looking ahead to Galileo, Kepler, and Newton, we tend to see it as giving rise to the scientific idea of nature as a uniform system of lawful relations. We see it signal the approaching dominion of the quantitative over the

72. Cassirer has demonstrated the dependence of the new cosmology upon the principle of the relativity of place and motion and he has accomplished this by a critical analysis, not only of Copernicus' thought, but of Cusa's speculative cosmology as well. The intellectual basis of Cusa's conception of a homogeneous cosmos was a metaphysically inspired epistemology, whereas the basis of the Copernican system was formed by the principles of scientific astronomy and the assumption of a rational universe which these principles seemed to support. Nevertheless, both thinkers employed the relational conception of space in forming their ideas, a conception to which both were led by the methods of mathematics. See *Individuum und Kosmos,* pp. 7–48 and *Das Erkenntnisproblem,* 1: 52–77.

qualitative mode of thought, and of science over myth. But in its own historical moment, looked at in and for itself, the Copernican system of the world represents the single greatest achievement of the geometric intuition of the Renaissance. Displacing for all time the geocentric hierarchical cosmology, it was the most stunning triumph of that methodic outlook which sought not the quality of things but their relative positions.

The Scientific Mode of Thought

To the extent to which Renaissance thought prepared the methodological attitudes and aims which a Copernicus, a Kepler, and a Galileo could assume, it played a necessary part in the development of exact science, even though it did not always distinguish itself by scientific procedures and ideas. Religion, myth, and metaphysics continued to dominate much of the thinking of the fifteenth and sixteenth centuries, for even as the Renaissance outgrew the context of medieval culture, it remained bound to it by a thousand vital fibers. Its ideas about the supernatural and the occult were not at all the mere "survivals" that Burckhardt took them to be. They were an integral part of the total outlook of the age, so much so that magic and astrology, which Christianity and the Church had hitherto kept in check, acquired new significance and force as many thinkers explored and revived ancient occult themes. Despite the fact that some of them opened up new and distinctively "modern" directions of thought, the age taken as a whole persisted in older, more familiar ways.

But if the Renaissance could not, and did not, effect any sudden and complete transition from religious and metaphysical modes of thought to rationalistic and scientific ones, this is not to say that it was a scientifically "fallow period," as certain medievalists, notably Lynn Thorndike and Pierre Duhem, have made it out to be.[73] Its interest in the occult was lively and

73. This is the view of historians who see in science only the empirical, experimental attitude and not the mathematical theory that shaped this attitude so as to form the systematic structure of modern physics. Lynn Thorndike is the dean of this school. For him, the fifteenth century was "a fallow period, when men's minds were recovering their fertility. . . . Then presently seeds that had lain dormant since the fourteenth century were, as Duhem has shown, to sprout and fructify in modern philosophy and science" *A History of Magic and Experimental Science,* 4: 615.

Thorndike began to develop this anti-Renaissance view in his earlier *Science and Thought in the 15th Century* and he repeated it in all his later works (unlike Sarton, who began with this view but later amended it). Ignoring mathematics, and hence the entire current of artistic-technical thought which applied mathematics to physical problems, he omitted Alberti from his histories of thought and science in the fifteenth century, and cited Leonardo only twice, and then *en passant,* in the fifteenth-century volume of *Magic and Science.* In the subsequent fifth volume, he depreciated Leonardo's scientific achievements to the point of absurdity, describing him as "interested in and puzzled by the stock questions and problems of centuries past, rather than fertile in formulating new lines of investigation"

pervasive, to be sure; and its characteristic intellectual work took place outside the traditional Scholastic domain of Aristotelian natural philosophy, the "physical" discipline in which Galileo was to accomplish his scientific revolution. Yet the prevalence of speculative theories about the empirical world did not hinder the development of sound methodological ideas. It may even have provided a stimulus, by helping to liberate empirical thought from the confines of Aristotelian categories. And as for the abandonment, or disregard, of philosophy by the humanists and artist-technicians of the Renaissance, this was an unmistakable gain for science. It was only by avoiding the traditional corpus of philosophical ideas that humanistic and technical thinkers could bring about their new unification of experience and thought, a union in which the twin seed of the cultural and natural sciences found its start.

The fruitfulness of this development for natural scientific thought can be gauged by its results in astronomy and geography. Geometry and visual experience combined in the geography and astronomy of the fifteenth and sixteenth centuries to form the first coherent, and rationally cumulative pictures of the world since antiquity. And this was not the only scientific consequence of the new methodological ideas which the artist-technicians of the Renaissance had seized upon. Alberti's technical writings indicate how wide the range of applied mathematical thought was in the Renaissance; and just as important for a proper evaluation of the significance of this mode of thought, his writings reveal the scientific intention it embodied, even at this early stage in its formation.

If we judge Alberti by our present standards of scientific and logical rigor, he will, of course, disappoint us. He made no effort to combat or eschew commonly held religious and astrological ideas, and he uncritically espoused, and even helped formulate, the metaphysics of universal Harmony and "objective" proportions. In these particulars, he would seem to fit the picture of those who see little but naïvete and superstition in the representative figures of the fifteenth and sixteenth centuries. But if Alberti did not apply our criteria

---

(p. 18). Finally Thorndike urged that the very term "renaissance" be proscribed. "Renaissance or Prenaissance?" *Journal of the History of Ideas,* 4 (1943): 65–74.

By this time, however, Olschki, Cassirer, and, a little later, Koyré had made known their more objective and penetrating assessments of the mathematical, technical thought of the Renaissance. As Cassirer pointed out in the same volume of *Journal of the History of Ideas* in which Thorndike's essay appeared, the question of the "originality" of the Renaissance should no longer have been a matter of dispute. By the 1940's, it was a pseudo-problem, a reflection of logical confusions rather than a disagreement over historical "facts" "Some Remarks on the Originality of the Renaissance," pp. 49–56. This historiographical dispute still has to be borne in mind, however, for by now the latest textbooks have almost all reached the Thorndike stage of the argument.

The best critical discussion of the matter, at once bibliographical and substantive, is by Edward Rosen in *The Renaissance,* edited by Tinsley Helton, pp. 77–103. Panofsky's essay on Leonardo is full of penetrating insights into the scientific importance of the work of the Renaissance artist-technicians. "Artist, Scientist, Genius: Notes on the 'Renaissance-Dämmerung'" *The Renaissance: Six Essays,* pp. 77–93.

of truth to the speculative notions of his time, this is because those criteria were just then in the process of forming. Alberti's contemporaries were noticeably impressed by his accomplishments in "the study of nature," and their appreciation is a sensitive index of his position in the history of scientific thought. The fifteenth century could not demand of him a kind of thought which did not reach self-conscious awareness and expression until Galileo. If Alberti's technical knowledge seemed at the time novel and full of promise, this is because it really was so: it did represent the new empirical-mathematical mode of scientific thinking, but at the moment of its inception as it was beginning to find its proper form and direction.[74]

Alberti had not yet reached the reflective awareness of Leonardo, who recognized that experience sets the bounds of genuine knowledge. But his intention in physical questions was already moving toward that recognition: he clearly meant to shun "philosophical" speculation and to concentrate upon the kind of knowledge that arises from, and is bound to, practice. Even in *De re aedificatoria,* which contains his most dogmatic, metaphysical ideas on nature and beauty, he consistently set aside questions of origin, final cause, and essence to take up problems of function and method instead. Only with respect to the problem of beauty did he succumb to a metaphysical "solution," and then unavoidably. Elsewhere he scrupulously dismissed metaphysical ideas and the teachings of natural philosophy alike, refusing with an almost positivistic firmness to conjecture about such matters. "We shall not spend any time here in philosophical inquiries about the principle and origin of stones," a typical passage runs,

> whether their first particles, made viscous by a mixture of earth and water, harden first into slime, and afterwards into stone; or what is said of gems, that they are collected and concreted by the heat and power of the rays of

74. To Alberti's younger friend, Cristoforo Landino, Alberti "seemed born only to investigate the secrets of nature." *Apologia de' Fiorentini premessa al commento sopra Dante,* in Bartoli, *Modo di misurare,* p. x. Uzielli held that Alberti had no scientific ideas at all, primarily because he was a disciple of Aristotle in the mathematical and physical sciences (!), and because he believed in astrology: *Vita e i Tempi di Toscanelli;* 202–7, 221. On both counts, Uzielli's judgment has reappeared in Saitta to mar his otherwise faithful sketch of Alberti's thought. Saitta characterizes Alberti as "un volgarizzatore della scienza antica. . . . Non ricorre ad esperienza e cita gli antichi": *Il pensiero italiano nell'umanesimo e nel rinascimento,* 1: 686–87. And on p. 688 he writes, "questa fede nell'astrologia era fede anche d'un Alberti."

Actually, Alberti tolerated rather than advocated astrological ideas. "Following their instructions may be of great service if true," he wrote, rather pragmatically, "and can do little harm if false." *De re aedif,.* bk. 2, chap. 8. The experiential character of his thought should be apparent to the reader by now. His "empiricism" has recently been hailed by Santinello, *L. B. Alberti,* pp. 81–85; but Santinello, like most of Alberti's biographers (except Mancini), does not give due emphasis to the systematic side of Alberti's thought. See p. 24 *et passim.*

the sun, or that there is in the bosom of the earth certain natural seeds, as of other things, so of stones. Though these disquisitions might serve to adorn our work, I shall omit them and proceed to treat of the method of building, addressing myself to artificers approved for skill and experience, with more freedom than would be allowed, perhaps, by those who are for more exact philosophising.[75]

So marked was his reliance upon practical experience, that Alberti's fifteenth-century biographer portrayed him as a sort of Socrates who seeks his learning in the marketplace.[76] He converses with smiths, architects, sailors, even bootmakers, inquiring, like the Socratic figure of Cusa's *Idiota,* into their "skill and experience" as craftsmen. Alberti's writings do contain, in point of fact, the most advanced technical knowledge of his day on an astonishing variety of topics. For example, the earliest account we have of a canal lock with gates at both ends comes from Book 10 of his treatise on architecture.[77] What he was describing here was an intermediate stage between a single barrier canal (of the kind that was first installed on the Naviglio Grande of Milan around 1395), and a canal consisting of multiple sluices. To build a canal of this latter type, Bertola da Novate, a ducal engineer of Milan, had to construct eighteen locks of the kind Alberti described, that is, locks consisting of pairs of gates separated by a distance about equal to the length of a ship. While it is possible that Novate carried out Alberti's design, it is more likely that Alberti was describing Novate's lock in *De re aedificatoria,* yet even if this is the case, we must be impressed by the contemporaneousness of his technical knowledge. This part of *De re aedificatoria* was written around 1452, and Novate built his locks between 1452 and 1458 to control the eighty-foot slope of the canal he was cutting on the Naviglio Grande.

All the manual tasks and practical knowledge pertaining to the art of building were treated with this same thoroughness and grasp of contemporary developments. Much of Alberti's technical knowledge came from classical sources, to be sure; he cites Theophrastus and Cato on the cutting and preserving of wood, Columella on the materials used by architects, Varro on pressures and fortifications. But phrases such as "the learned tell us . . ." are balanced and often outweighed by statements like "workmen proceed in this way . . ." and "the practice is. . . ." Alberti consistently fused practice and literary learning, whether in painting, surveying, cartography, or in architecture and engineering; and this meant, not only that as a scholar and man of letters he wrote about the manual arts, but that he himself mastered and practiced with considerable skill the arts he described. To miss this point is to miss the most distinctive feature of his

75. *De re aedif.,* bk. 2, chap. 8.
76. *Op. volg.,* 1 : c.
77. William Barclay Parsons, *Engineers and Engineering in the Renaissance,* pp. 373–77. Singer *et al., Hist. of Technology,* 3 : 445–46.

personality, for theory and practice were completely integrated in his life as in his thought. Hence developments in the one aspect of his work almost invariably gave rise to developments in the other. His study of Vitruvius, for example, and his ambition to produce a comparable literary work, led him to become a practicing architect and engineer, and books issued from this engineering experience in turn. His efforts to raise the Roman galley from the Lake of Nemi inspired two treatises: *Navis,* a lost treatise on ships which Leonardo mentions, and *De motibus ponderis,* another lost work on the lifting of weights.[78]

The nature of Alberti's technical knowledge was necessarily experimental, then, for it was born of and checked by practice. This does not mean that his treatment of physical problems was "empirical," however, in the sensistic meaning of the word. Alberti turned from "philosophical" issues to "experience," but not for the sake of observing and collecting the raw data of perception. This line of inquiry was to be pursued during the Renaissance by the natural philosophers who held that nature could be known directly, "through her own principles," as Telesius put it, without the mediation of categories of thought.[79] Alberti was opening a different path of natural inquiry, the path that was to be taken by Leonardo, Tartaglia, and all those who held that mathematics, and only mathematics, could grasp the "reasons" of the phenomenal world. "Nothing satisfies me so much," says a figure in one of Alberti's dialogues, "as mathematical investigations and demonstrations, especially when I can turn them to some useful practice as Battista here did, who drew the principles of painting from mathematics, and also drew from mathematics those incredible propositions *de motibus ponderis*."[80]

The new intellectual task as Nicholas of Cusa saw it in "De staticis

78. *Navis* has not yet been found. Leonardo wrote in a memo, "Vedi de navi messer Battista e Frontino de' aquidotti." Richter, 2 : 445, no. 1472. See Mancini, *Vita di L. B. Alberti,* p. 281 on *Navis,* and pp. 286–88 on *De motibus ponderis*. Mancini thought that this latter work might be the one that Leonardo refers to several times as *De ponderibus,* but Duhem has shown that the work used by Leonardo was a thirteenth-century treatise: *Études sur Leonard de Vinci* (Paris, 1906–13), 3 vols. Mancini also believed that the *Trattato dei pondi lieve e tirari* in the Laurentian ms. of the Ashburnham series, n. °361 was by Alberti, and he published it in the Appendix of his edition of Vasari, *Vite cinque.* Following Mancini, Michel listed this *Trattato* among Alberti's works, *Un idéal humain au XVe siècle: La pensée de L. B. Alberti,* p. 33. Parsons (see above, n. 77) doubted that the *Trattato* was Alberti's because of its style and because it contains a description of a canal lock inferior to the one in *De re aedificatoria,* although the treatise was written after 1459: *Engineers and Engineering,* p. 376. I find Parson's argument convincing. Moreover, the *Trattato* is entirely empirical in character; it describes the functioning of machines in great detail but with none of the mathematical considerations which Alberti would have brought to the subject.

79. Cassirer describes these two intellectual directions in *Individuum und Kosmos.* In ch. 4, he shows how the empirical-sensist line of inquiry led to animism and the occult because it lacked an objective criterion of "experience" such as mathematics would furnish.

80. *Op. volg.,* 1: 128.

experimentis," the fourth book of his *Idiota* (1450), was to take the measure of the empirical world: to weigh, to clock, to determine sizes, distances, weights, durations, and speeds.[81] This aim, at once practical and abstract, was the objective of all Alberti's technical writings. All of them represent experience mathematically, for he extended to almost every technical problem that engaged him the same kind of geometric "seeing" that characterizes his aesthetic outlook. In art, Alberti had fused perception and abstract mathematical ideas to produce the kind of artistic form which he could regard as truly representative of nature. In the domain of physical problems, his mathematical imagination saw machines as similar instantiations of ideal, proportional rules.

Most of the machines and measuring devices Alberti described in *De re aedificatoria* and *Ludi matematici* he recovered from ancient sources, chiefly Vitruvius. He did not invent them; but in his reconstruction of them, and in the measuring "games" he set up for them, we can virtually feel the quickening of the mechanical mode of thought.[82] Machines occupied his imagination when he was sleepless; and he was so excited by the geometric principles they embodied that he felt constrained, as he explained them to Meliaduso d'Este, to urge once again that he actually put them into practice. In Exercise 18, for instance, he taught Meliaduso to construct an odometer, and he advised him to use it the next time he traveled anywhere by land. Fill a box with pebbles, he wrote, and attach it to the hub of the wagon wheel, so that every time the wheel turns one pebble will fall out of a little aperture in the box into a receptacle. The number of pebbles collected in the receptacle stand for the number of revolutions made by the wheel. The rest is a matter of simple arithmetic or "proportion": as one revolution of the wheel is to the known number of *braccia* covered by it, so the number of pebbles is to the unknown number of *braccia* that will be covered during the journey.

In this, and in most of the remaining problems of *Ludi matematici,* Alberti used the same elementary "method of solving by proportions" with which he unlocked the secrets of accurate painting and cartography. He merely extended the range of the method from problems of depiction to problems involving motion; and although he used simple machines instead of geometric

81. Heidelberg, 1938.

82. In an autobiographical passage, Alberti has a figure in one of his dialogues say that when he is upset or cannot sleep, he learns a piece of literature by heart, designs a building, or "soglio da me investigare e costruire in mente qualche inaudita macchina da muovere e portare, da fermare e statuire cose grandissime e inestimabile." *Op. volg.,* 1: 127.

The experimental character of the "exercises" in *Ludi matematici* is vouched for by Leonardo who commented upon Alberti's solution for measuring the velocity of a ship. This method, he says, has been tried by experiment: "Ecco un altro modo fatto colla sperientia d'uno spatio noto da una isola a un altra, e questo si fa con un asse o lieva percossa dal vento, che la percuote o più or men velocie, e questo è in Battista Alberti." Richter, 2: 273, no. 1113. (Leonardo then points out the limitations of Alberti's method and puts forth his own more general method, one which can be used in all situations.)

pictures to supply the terms of his proportions, he conceived the machines on the model of a logical picture. Like the odometer, they are all instruments through which he could apply a set of abstract, geometric relations to a physical situation.

This "geometric" conception of machines marks the mechanical writings of Nicholas of Cusa and Leonardo too (although Leonardo's mechanical understanding exceeds Cusa's and Alberti's by far, in refinement as well as scope). All three were fascinated, for example, by the barometer of Savosarda (Ibrahim ben Jahiah), the twelfth-century Spanish-Jewish mathematician. All three left descriptions of it, Alberti in *De re aedificatoria,* Cusa in "De staticis experimentis," and Leonardo in the *Codice Atlantico.*[83] Yet this simple device was nothing more than a wad of dry wool balanced on a scale. What the "barometer" actually measures is the weight of the wool; but because the weight varies as the wool absorbs moisture, the varying measure of weight can stand for a change in the weather which is a function of the varying amount of humidity in the air.

Alberti's mechanical ideas, and the machines and measuring devices he describes, did not advance much beyond this stage of thought. But if we look not so much for sophistication and originality as for a consistent intention to subject empirical phenomena to mathematical analysis, we find that his technical writings have a decided bearing upon the history of scientific thought. They stand at the beginning of a successful renewal of what Koyré has called "the Archimedean attitude" of modern physical science (the final "game" of *Ludi matematici* is, appropriately enough, the Archimedean problem of the crown). That is, they point toward Leonardo and, ultimately, to Galileo's new science in the geometric formulation of their physical problems, in the intention to solve such problems in terms of proportions and their rules.

This is not to say that Galilean mechanics does not owe a tremendous debt to the Aristotelian tradition whence it emerged. The fourteenth-century Scholastics and the Paduan Aristotelians of the fifteenth and sixteenth centuries sharply criticized a number of Aristotle's ideas and advanced more refined physical and methodological notions which Galileo incorporated and built upon. The empirical spirit of modern inquiry was fostered largely by the late Scholastics. But it was the Renaissance which ensured that empirical inquiry would be directed along mathematical lines, and that, after all, was the chief issue, as Galileo saw it, between him and the philosophers. Only when the natural philosopher became a *filosofo geometra,* only when, in the person of Galileo, he systematically sought to explain problems of motion in geometric terms, was scientific physics born. Hence in this sense, in its "geometric interrogation of Nature," the new physics was to develop a mode of thinking

83. Pierre Duhem, *Études sur Leonard de Vinci: Ceux qu'il a lus et ceux qui l'ont lu,* 2: 239–40.

which had first been consistently employed by Alberti and the artist-technicians of the Renaissance.[84]

So productive had the new mathematical method proved for Alberti, and so universal in its application, that he brought its principles to bear upon yet another practical art which was innocent of quantitative procedures down to his time. The practice of coding was becoming increasingly important during the fifteenth century, particularly in Italy where the institution of permanent ambassadors was taking form. Around 1466, Leonardo Dati, a papal secretary and an old friend of Alberti's, asked Alberti for his ideas on the subject for the benefit of the papal chancery. Alberti's response came in the form of a little Latin treatise which today stands as the first modern work on cryptography. *De compondendis cifris*[85] established the theory and transformed the practice of ciphering and deciphering.

Alberti set forth an "extremely secret and convenient method of writing" in this work, one which he explicitly claims to have devised, by correlating the Latin alphabet with a scrambled alphabet by means of a cipher wheel. The idea may have occurred to him as he thought about the moveable type of the printing press, for he praises the new invention in an introductory passage which seems

84. In his *Etudes Galiléennes,* Alexandre Koyré wrote that classical physics "nous paraît avoir été le fruit d'une mutation décisive: c'est ce qui explique pourquoi la découverte de choses qui nous paraissent aujourd'hui enfantines avait coûté de longs efforts —pas toujours couronnés de succès—aux plus grand génies de l'humanité, à un Galilée, à un Descartes. C'est qu'il s'agissait non pas de combattre des théories erronées, ou insuffisantes, mais de transformer les cadres de l'intelligence elle-même; de bouleverser une attitude intellectuelle fort naturelle en somme, en lui substituant une autre, que ne l'était aucunement. Et c'est cela qui explique pourquoi—malgré les apparences contraires, apparences de continuité historique sur lesquelles Caverni et Duhem ont surtout insisté—la physique classique sortie de la pensée de Bruno, de Galilée, de Descartes ne continue pas, en fait, la physique médiévale . . . : elle se place d'emblée sur un plan différent, sur un plan que nous aimerions qualifier d'archimédien." 1–9, 1–10. This is the context to which Alberti's simple machines belong, and his exercises in applied mathematics.

On the relation between Aristotelian natural philosophy of the fifteenth and sixteenth centuries and Galilean science, see John Hermann Randall, Jr.'s *The School of Padua and the Emergence of Modern Science.*

85. Edited by Aloys Meister, *Die Geheimschrift im Dienste der Päpstlichen Kurie,* pp. 125–41. Also in Bartoli's *Opuscoli morali* in the vernacular, *La cifra.* On Alberti's place in the history of cryptography, see Meister, *Die Geheimschrift;* Charles J. Mendelsohn, "Cardan on Cryptography," *Scripta Mathematica,* 6 (1939): 157–68, and "Bibliographical Note on 'De Cifris' of Leon Battista Alberti," *Isis,* 32 (1940): 48–51; Luigi Sacco, *Un primato italiano: La Crittografiia nei secoli XV e XVI;* David Kahn, *The Codebreakers,* pp. 125–30.

Although Alberti's *De compenendis cifris* heads the list of many treatises on ciphering which came to be written in the late fifteenth and sixteenth centuries, it is interesting to note that once again Roger Bacon anticipated his interests in an *Epistola de secretis operibus et naturae et de nullitate magiae:* see Mendelsohn's list in "Cardan on Cryptography," *Scripta Mathematica,* 6 (1939): 157–68.

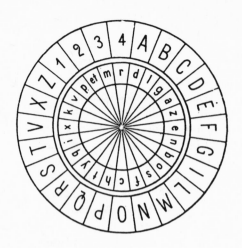

64. *Alberti's cipher wheel: the Formula*

irrelevant unless we make this sort of connection. The cipher wheel itself, however, which sets up the relation between the two alphabets, is unmistakably, if unexpectedly, another adaptation of his Horizon. This time Alberti called the instrument a Formula, the Latin word for "pattern" or "form of words"; and he made it out of two copper disks, one slightly larger than the other, with a pin driven through the center of both to serve as an axis. The smaller disk, which is placed on top of the larger one, is movable (fig. 64).

The perimeter of each disk of the Formula is divided into twenty-four units or "cells." In the cells of the larger disk, Alberti printed twenty letters of the Latin alphabet (omitting *H* and *K*) in upper case and in their proper order, from *A* to *Z*. In the four spaces between *Z* and *A*, he put the numbers 1 through 4. In the cells of the smaller disk, he printed twenty-four letters (including *h, k, et,* and *y*) in lower case, and these letters he put down in random order.

A child can code and decode messages with this simple instrument, yet the ingenious cipher wheel was still useful enough at the time of the American Civil War to be employed by the U.S. Navy essentially as Alberti had directed.[86] The first step in coding a message is to establish the key (Alberti calls it the "index") that correlates the two alphabets. Any capital letter of the larger disk may be chosen, say *B. B* is put down as the first letter of the written message, and the next lower-case letter in the message, say *d,* becomes its "substitute." The smaller of the two disks of the Formula is then rotated until *d* lines up under *B,* and the message is written in the substitute letters of the scrambled alphabet which appear under the letters of the standard one. After three or four words, the key ought to be changed. Alberti indicated this by writing one of the lower-case

86. John H. Haswell, "Secret Writing; The Ciphers of the Ancients, and Some of Those in Modern Use," *The Century Magazine,* 85 (1912–13) : 83–92. When I was a child, we exchanged the tops of Ovaltine cans for tin cipher wheels like Alberti's to decipher the "extremely secret" messages broadcast by the Little Orphan Annie Radio Show.

letters which appear under the numerals of the larger disk (while *d* and *B* are still lined up with each other). This letter, say *y*, replaces *d* as the key letter of the scrambled alphabet; it is moved into place under *B* on the Formula, and the message continues in this key for the next few words.

The coding is complicated by further refinements, such as spelling changes and sprinkling the message with capital letters which have no meaning. Alberti also drew up a fixed code in which the four numerals of the Formula were made to stand for certain agreed upon words; and he worked out tables of permutations of the digits 1, 2, 3, and 4 taken in groups of two, three, and four, so that altogether, three hundred and thirty-six proper names, words, and phrases could be represented by them. This code was then to be enciphered by the Formula. When the numbers (always two or more) were used in this way, they would refer to the fixed code. But they appear in the message as lower-case letters; and because of the continuous change of key as the message is enciphered, the words and phrases coded by the numbers are represented by different sets of letters throughout the message.

All this was very advanced for the fifteenth century, and later treatises on the subject did not bring the practice of coding beyond the stage which Alberti described for about a century, until just about the time, in fact, that Bartoli published *De compondenis cifris* in his 1568 collection of Alberti's writings.[87] Until then, cryptographers who knew the work in manuscript did not even exploit all of its ideas, to say nothing of furthering them. The principle of polyalphabetic substitution which Alberti founded with his cipher wheel was unknown before his time and its advantages were not immediately apparent. Jacopo Silvestri, a Florentine, repeated entire sections of Alberti's work in his own treatise of 1526 on coding, yet he used the cipher wheel in far simpler fashion than Alberti had some sixty years earlier.[88] Alberti created a new substitute alphabet each time he changed the key in the course of a message, and the substitute alphabet(s) had a completely random arrangement of letters. On Silvestri's cipher wheel, the two alphabets correspond exactly in their characters and their arrangement, and Silvestri used only one key throughout the message. The enciphered code, which was also Alberti's invention, was even further ahead of contemporary practice. As a historian of coding has recently pointed out, "the major powers of the earth did not begin to encipher their code messages until 400 years later, near the end of the 19th century, and even then their systems were much simpler than [his]."[89]

87. Cardanus, G. B. Bellasco, and Giovanni della Porta introduced certain practices which Alberti had not known. Still, as late as 1586, Blaise de Vigenère incorporated Alberti's ideas in his *Traicté des chiffres* and explicitly mentioned his indebtedness to Alberti.

88. *Opus Novum . . . principibus maxime utilissimum pro cipharis, lingua Latina, Greca, Italica* (Rome, 1526). Described in Sacco, *Un primato italiano.* Kahn credits Alberti with having founded polyalphabeticity in *Codebreakers*, pp. 125, 127.

89. Kahn, *Codebreakers*, p. 130.

The remarkable technical superiority of Alberti's work was due, as usual, to something more than mere practical ingenuity. Here as elsewhere, his practice was intimately bound up with and flowed from a theoretical analysis, an analysis this time of the principles of coding and decoding which appears in the first part of his treatise. Alberti understood a code to be a way of writing which represents, and hence must correspond in certain definite ways to, the language of those who employ it.[90] For purposes of deciphering, he accordingly sought those structural features of the original language (in this case, Latin) which must reappear in the substitute language of the code; and this brought him to construct a frequency table, the earliest one known.

With his customary meticulous regard for "measures," he noted the relative incidence of the letters of the Latin alphabet and the positions they normally assume with respect to each other. He set down, under the heading of *number,* the ratio of vowels to consonants in ordinary Latin usage (poetry as well as prose); the relative frequency of the vowels with respect to each other; the relative frequency of consonants with respect to other consonants. And under the heading of *order,* he analyzed the positions that letters assume within words. He noted which vowels generally follow which, and which do so with greater or lesser frequency; which consonants are regularly joined to vowels, which consonants are doubled, which never appear at the end of a word, or after a vowel, and so forth.

The frequency table, which became even more important to cryptography than the cipher wheel and is, in fact, presupposed by Alberti's construction and use of the cipher wheel, owes its conception to his characteristic logical procedure. Alberti's intellectual practice in his artistic and technical work was to construct logical copies—geometric pictures or simple machines—of the object under study, and to discover and exhibit in the copy the lawful relations among the elements of the object. Hence he was uniquely prepared to recognize that a code was but another logical copy, and to set about discovering the regularities in the ordinary use of Latin which necessarily reappear in the manifold of its possible coded expressions.[91] This time, the regularities

90. "Ista quidem ut commodius pervestigarem, coepi mecum ipse disquirere, quidnam pro se natura sui cyfram esse interpretarer. Atqui sic incidit in mentem ut ponerem *cyfram esse rationem quandam scribendi* notis ad arbitrium significantibus id quod inter se scribentes constituissent, ne ab aliis intelligerentur. Id si ita est, duo constituisse oportuit. Unum horum fuit, ut esset apud quosque inter se mutuo scribentes *constans et certum quidpiam,* quo fieret, ut alterum alter ex ea scriptione satis intelligeret, quid moneret, quid peteret, narraretve et eiusmodi." Meister, ed., p. 126. Italics mine.

91. The "maturity" of Alberti's conception of frequency analysis led Kahn to believe that Alberti must have been developing an already extant practice rather than originating it, as he implies. *Codebreakers,* p. 127. But it is impossible to conceive of frequency analysis unless one thinks as Alberti did, in terms of logical copies; and once one does understand coding and the principle of frequency analysis in this way, it is but a small (and again, typically Albertian) step to note the regular relations of number and order among letters.

he sought did not belong to the geometric domain, yet even here his procedure bears the mark of his mode of geometric "seeing." He grasped the formal relations of language under the mathematical categories of number and order. He expressed these relations among the letters of the (Latin) alphabet as ratios. And, as the scrambled alphabet of his Formula indicates, he took the letters of the alphabet to be the fixed elements of a serial order, an order or set of relations among the first, second . . . *n*th letters of a particular language which remains constant in all its coded substitutes. Detect a few of these patterns in a coded message, such as the relation between the fourteenth and eighteenth letters of the Latin alphabet, *q* and *u;* put the characters of the ordinary language in place of the ciphers; and the code will soon be broken as its substitution rule comes to light.

Remote, then, as cryptography may seem from the intellectual world which *Prospettiva* opened, the developments which Alberti brought about even here spring from the fundamental idea of *analogia* and his concern "for the position rather than the quality" of things. Indeed, his "extremely secret" method of coding embodies the principle of *analogia* as a kind of negative image of it. All of Alberti's rules for ciphering were designed to elude the very "science" of deciphering which he had been the first to grasp. The use of more than one substitute letter for the letters that appear most often in the original language; the breaking of spelling rules, particularly double consonants and *u*'s after *q's;* the use of a single character for double letters such as *st* and *sl;* and most inventive of all, the use of a cipher wheel with a scrambled alphabet and frequent changes of key—these practices were all intended to mask the orthographic pattern of the language so that the original message, of which the code is a logical copy, would not be discerned.

With this achievement, our study of Alberti's artistic and natural-scientific theories and practices comes to an end. We have seen how the same few intellectual steps led him to revise and revamp traditional methods in fields as diverse as painting, sculpture, architecture, cartography, surveying, and cryptography. The assumption of a rational order in all parts of the world, within themselves and with respect to each other, underlay his theoretical vision in each case; and in each case, it was this order which he strove to find. But Alberti's cosmos also held man. He was a humanist as well as an artist-technician, and we have now to see how he brought the same considerations of reason and measure to this aspect of his life and thought.

The one Alberti scholar who recognized the general importance of this logical procedure in Alberti's thought, even though he dealt only with Alberti's work in perspective, was Wm. M. Ivins, Jr., *On the Rationalization of Sight.*

5
Rational Man

The Humanistic Mode of Thought: Letters and Virtue

Alberti's humanistic writings constitute the most problematical part of his work and have given rise to radically diverging interpretations. Some commentators find them "idealistic" in the pejorative sense, utopian, remote from actual social and political problems, concerned with the cultivation of narrowly personal intellectual and spiritual values; others find an assertion of the early bourgeois spirit in them, practical, worldly, committed to the cares of the "active life." To Mario Petrini,[1] Alberti seems to aspire to *tranquillità,* raising himself above the storms of life and vicissitudes of Fortune to a plane of serene contemplation. He is too self-sufficient to invoke even the traditional support of religion: "one does not find a single passage in Alberti that makes one think of a sincerely religious mind," this author writes, confirming a judgment which Ruth Lang[2] had reached for precisely the opposite reason. Her Alberti is so caught up by the demands of a busy Florentine life that his religion has become wholly secular, his ethics wholly materialistic. And still another author implicitly rejects both views, finding in Alberti's writings an "austerely Christian" tone.[3]

Differences as sharp as these generally result when only a few of Alberti's humanistic works are studied; at best, these are interpretations which reflect aspects of a whole which has not been seen. Yet even so, the conflicts among such views cannot be resolved by simply referring to the entire corpus of Alberti's humanistic writings. There is a genuine problem here, for his writings do incorporate what would seem to be several antagonistic, if not contradictory, positions. All of these positions can indeed be found in them: an advocacy of intellectual pursuits and of the active life; philosophical and ethical idealism

---

1. "L'uomo di Alberti," *Belfagor,* 6 (1951): 665–74. As we shall see, Cristoforo Landino's portrayal of Alberti in one of his dialogues is partly responsible for this view.
2. *Leon Battista Alberti und die Sancta Masseritia.*
3. Vittorio Cian, *La Satira,* 1: 450.

and involvement in the urban society of his time; traditional Catholic sentiment and an almost deistic rationalism. It is for this reason that biographers and historians familiar with Alberti's total output have occasionally taken him to be a troubled, even confused, figure. Appreciative of the breadth of his thought, they have seen in the presence of these apparently conflicting ideas the sign of a deep inner conflict. Thus Paul-Henri Michel saw Alberti vacillating between the "medieval" and "modern" poles of his own thought;[4] and Sir Kenneth Clark found an unresolved tension in Alberti between a realistic, and a formal or intellectualistic approach to problems, "a conflict between a scientific and a stylistic approach, a dilemma . . . which underlies the whole of *Della pittura* in the same way that a conflict between his realistic Tuscan business philosophy and the teachings of Plato underlies his moral writings."[5]

The parallel Sir Kenneth draws in this respect between Alberti's ethical and artistic thought is instructive. As I see it, it leads to an entirely different conclusion, but it does present the proper starting point by placing Alberti's moral philosophy within the context of his general theoretical outlook. Alberti's artistic writings do make two seemingly antithetical demands: the naturalistic one of imitation and the idealistic one of adherence to an a priori norm of beauty. But the essence, the intellectual and imaginative core of his aesthetic theory consists precisely in his reconciliation of these two principles. The leading ideas of his artistic thought, and of all his technical writings as well, stem from and express a new and fruitful categorial relation between the natural and the ideal, the empirical and the rational, the practical and the theoretical. Surely it would be helpful to approach Alberti's humanistic writings with these considerations in mind, asking whether they reflect this same orientation, whether they manifest in their own fashion the intellectual aim that inspired and characterizes his scientific and artistic works.

At this point, however, another difficulty confronts us. The coherence of Alberti's ethical thought is much more elusive than that of his technical and artistic thought, and its distinctive character is much more difficult to grasp. In humanistic matters, he was not at all systematic; nor did he have any particularly original ethical ideas. Like most humanists, Alberti borrowed his moral philosophy from the ancients. He likened the humanistic author to an architect described by Vitruvius who completed the unworked pavement of an old and splendid Asian temple by composing a design out of bits and pieces of the materials he gathered from the edifice. In "letters," Alberti thought, the writer is responsible only for the form of his work. His ethical ideas, the "dottrine dovute a virtù e atte a viver bene e beato," have already been discovered by the ancients and can be gathered from their books: *Nihil dictum quin prius*

4. *Un idéal humain au XVe siècle: La pensée de L. B. Alberti*, pp. 132, 138–39.
5. *Leon Battista Alberti on Painting*, p. 15.

dictum.[6] There is consequently not a single ethical concept of any significance in Alberti's work which cannot be traced to Cicero or Aristotle, the Stoics or Epicureans, Plato or Augustine. Yet all his humanistic writings strike a certain consistent tone. Despite the eclectic aggregate of ideas they contain, their composition (for which alone he would claim credit) bears an unmistakeable Albertian stamp; and it is this form, this tone, we must analyze if we hope to capture and characterize his unique and unified style of thought.

In *De Familia,*[7] for example, his first major vernacular dialogue, Alberti has certain idealized members of the Alberti family discourse upon family life, civic duties, friendship, and education. They express Plutarch's views on liberal education, Cicero's rhetorical ideal of "letters and virtue," Xenophon's notions on domestic economy; but the ancient ideas have undergone a startling metamorphosis. They have been completely assimilated to the problems and ways of life of the urban society of quattrocento Italy, and they are convincingly couched in its Tuscan tongue. The speech of the Tuscan vernacular is cultivated and measured when spoken by the learned Adovardo Alberti, making his presentation of the ancient rhetorical ideals of learning seem fresh and persuasive; and when the businessman Gianozzo teaches his wife the virtues of industry and of husbandry, of bourgeois *masserizia,* his speech (like Xenophon's Greek) is plain and direct. The style and content of *De Familia* seemed so contemporary, in fact, that the work circulated as a handbook among the bourgeois families of fifteenth-century Florence. Yet for all its flavor of daily life, for all its domestic details and advice on how to manage a household, *De Familia* is, in inspiration and in its dialogue form, a classical work. The urban life it portrays is infused with the ancient ethic of civic responsibility, and its mode of presentation and forms of speech adhere to classical literary norms.

This fusion of classical learning with the affairs and the very language of daily life links Alberti's humanistic writings to his technical work. He treated artistic and scientific problems mathematically, of course, whereas language became his instrument when he handled matters of humanistic concern. But "letters" were not merely a means of communication in these works, as they are in his technical writings; they were the very organon for objectifying and

6. *Opere volgari,* 1 : 93–94. Alberti concludes this comparison by praising a friend's "composition" of ideas which have been long familiar but "ne'er so well expressed": "E noi, Agnolo, che vediamo raccolto da voi ciò che presso tutti gli altri scrittori era disseminato e trito, a sentiamo tante cose tanto varie poste in uno, a coattate e insite e ammarginate insieme, tutte corrispondere ad un tuono, tutte aguagliarsi a un piano, tutte estendersi a una linea, tutte conformarsi a un disegno."

7. Although the first three books of *De Familia* were written between 1432 and 1434 while Alberti was in Rome, he corrected the work and added to it down to the early 1440's. My references are to the Pellegrini and Spongano edition, *I primi tre libri della famiglia.* Another critical edition, without commentary, is now available in Cecil Grayson's new *Opere volgari,* vol. 1, which includes the fourth book, "Amicizia," as well.

passing on the wisdom of human experience. For the art of life, literary learning was essential; and literature had therefore to assume as its primary function the task of expounding this moral art, *a bene e beato vivere*. Literature was as much an instrument for regulating practice as geometry was, only the practice that comes to the fore in "letters" is the practice of virtue.

Alberti shared this pragmatic view of literary learning with most humanists. The theoretical basis of the humanistic curriculum was constituted by such didactic notions of letters and learning, and they account for a good deal of the antipathy humanists felt for the "empty words and disputations" of Scholastic philosophy and logic.[8] The fundamental aim of the *studia humanitatis* was to mold character and provide practical, moral lessons: "What the Greeks call 'paideia' we call 'studia humanitatis,' " one humanist educator wrote; "for learning and training in virtue are peculiar to man, therefore our forefathers [the Romans] called them 'Humanitas.' "[9] The literature of the Graeco-Roman world, particularly its poetry, history, and moral philosophy, seemed eminently suited to this ideal; and Alberti, who was "tutto dedito alle lettere liberali" by the time he finished Barzizza's Gymnasium,[10] accepted this practical, moral aim of his literary studies without question. The same tendency of thought that made him avoid "philosophy" in his technical writings and favor the problems of the *artefici* is manifest in his attitude toward humanistic learning. "Man is born to be useful to man," he says in one of his dialogues; "and the many arts of man exist only to serve man."[11] The arts should issue in useful knowledge, and in the literary arts this meant knowledge about "virtue and matters concerning the good life."[12]

The words "letters and virtue" are therefore regularly joined in Alberti's

8. On humanism as a pedagogical movement, see Paul Oskar Kristeller, *Studies in Renaissance Thought and Letters; Renaissance Thought: The Classic, Scholastic, and Humanistic Strains; Renaissance Thought II: Papers on Humanism and the Arts;* and William Harrison Woodward, *Vittorino da Feltre and Other Humanist Educators; Studies in Education during the Age of the Renaissance, 1400–1600.* On humanism in general, see especially Eugenio Garin, *L'umanesimo italiano;* Vittorio Rossi, *Il Quattrocento;* Giuseppe Saitta, *Il pensiero italiano nell'umanesimo e nel rinascimento,* vol. 1.

9. Battista Guarino, *De ordine docendi et studendi* in Woodward, *Vittorino da Feltre,* p. 177.

10. Panormita used this phrase in a verse he wrote for Alberti: "Sei piacevole, bellissimo, faceto,/ tutto dedito alle lettere liberali,/ nato dal chiaro sangue degli Alberti . . ." In Mancini, *Vita di Leon Battista Alberti,* p. 55.

11. *Op. volg.,* 3: 92. In "Fatum et Fortuna," one of his *Intercoenales,* Alberti presents this conception of learning in the form of an allegory. In the "river of life," the philosophers cling to empty words and disputations whereas those who practice the useful arts are borne up by their *tabulae* and are sure of their direction. *Opera inedita,* pp. 136–43.

12. ". . . dottrine dovute a virtù e atte a viver bene e beato." *Op. volg.,* 1:91. The Ciceronian phrases "a bene e beato vivere" and "lettere e virtù" can be found any number of times in almost all of Alberti's writings. In *I primi tre libri della famiglia,* for example, see pp. 59, 79, 144, 228.

thought and writing; but the commonly held humanistic theory of classical studies which he accepted led Alberti to a somewhat uncommon, "unclassical" position with respect to the language of literature. His use of the vernacular in *De Familia* constitutes a significant feature of his humanistic work. Here he began his imitation of the spirit rather than the letter of the ancient authors (as he did in a technical sense in *Descriptio urbis Romae,* and in an aesthetic one in *De re aedificatoria*). "Who will be so rash as to blame me," he wrote in defense of his use of the vernacular,

> for not writing in the manner he would like me to write? Rather, the prudent will perhaps praise me if, writing so that everyone can understand me, I seek to help the many rather than please the few: for you know how few *literati* there are these days.[13]

The Romans, he believed, responded to the needs of their society in their writings, hence his commitment to his *non litteratissimi cittadini* was to serve the cause of Italian prose much as Dante had served that of poetry, by developing the Tuscan vernacular as a medium for Italian literature.[14] In fifteenth-century Italy, the authority of Latin was still unquestioned in prose writings. But Alberti believed this was so only because men of learning continued to write in it. "Our own tongue will become comparable if our learned wish to refine it,"[15] he maintained; and he therefore proceeded to do just that, in a number of ways.

When he moved to Florence in 1434 with Pope Eugenius' court, Alberti not only joined Brunelleschi and Donatello in their artistic efforts; he also did what he could to further the tradition of vernacular poetry which was well established in Florence. He became a regular member of the group of versifiers who met in the shop of the barber-poet, Burchiello, and he wrote some Burchiellolike, satirical verse.[16] He sighed in Petrarchan sonnets: "Amor che fai? Perché non mi consigli?"[17] But what put him "in the vanguard of the Florentine tradition" in poetic literature[18] was not so much these popular poems

---

13. *I primi tre libri della famiglia,* p 232.

14. On this topic, see Paul Oskar Kristeller's "The Origin and Development of the Language of Italian Prose," *Renaissance Thought II,* pp. 119–41.

15. *I primi tre libri della famiglia,* p. 233. Cecil Grayson has said about Alberti's use of the vernacular: "There is perhaps no single aspect of his thought that so clearly demonstrates his desire to benefit the widest possible audience of his fellow-men." "The Humanism of Alberti," *Italian Studies,* 12 (1957): 48.

16. Vittorio Cian, *La Satira,* pp. 338–40. Alberti's poems are in vol. 2 of Cecil Grayson's edition of *Opere volgari,* pp. 3–51.

17. Grayson *Op volg.,* 2: 5. See also Giovanni Ponte, "Il petrarchismo di Leon Battista Alberti," *La Rassegna della letteratura italiana,* 62 (1958): 216–22.

18. Cecil Grayson's assessment in "Alberti and the Vernacular Eclogue in the Quattrocento," *Italian Studies,* 11 (1956): 16–29.

as his attempt to infuse vernacular verse with the form and spirit of Latin poetry. As in *De Familia,* where he revived the classical dialogue on moral and civic matters in the vernacular, so in vernacular elegies and eclogues he "imitated Virgil in Tuscan poems."[19] Although Politian later claimed that he could not tell whether Alberti excelled more in prose or verse,[20] few modern readers will experience this difficulty after reading Alberti's seventeen extant poems. Their artistic value is slight; but his elegies and eclogues do form a link between the poets of Lorenzo de' Medici's circle and Boccaccio, whose *Ameto* was the first vernacular eclogue. In this historical sense, at least, they merit Politian's praise, for they contributed to the development of the vernacular bucolic tradition which was to flower in the pastoral poetry of the High Renaissance.[21]

Poets, of course, such as Politian and Landino, welcomed Alberti's attempts to broaden the range of vernacular literature by introducing classical poetic forms, but some of the Latinists of the time evidently did not. In 1441, when the Papal court had returned to Florence, Alberti organized a poetry contest on the theme of friendship.[22] At first the contest developed as a festive public event. Piero de' Medici assumed the expenses, and most of the high officials of Florence attended: the members of the Signoria, the Archbishop, the officials of the Studio, and the prelates of the Papal Curia. For the occasion, although not for the contest, Alberti wrote a prose dialogue, *Amicizia,* which he appended to *De Familia,* as its fourth book. Two poets declaimed in *terza rima,* the form hallowed by Dante; and then Alberti's close friend, Leonardo Dati, and Alberti himself, did something unexpected: they imitated ancient meters (hexameters and sapphics) in the vernacular and voiced "learned" ideas of classical origin which were usually reserved for Latin. The Papal secretaries who were supposed to award a silver garland to the author of the best work gave the prize to the church of Santa Maria del Fiore instead, claiming they were unable to agree upon any one of the contestants. Alberti subsequently accused the judges of envy in a *Protesta,* and because the affair continued to create bad feeling among the humanists involved, he gave up his plan to make the vernacular literary contest a regular feature of Florentine life.

He was rather surprised and hurt by the ill will that had been displayed, in fact, and he seems to have withdrawn from the affair in a state of depression. Shortly after the contest he sent the second of his moral dialogues in the vernacular to Leonello d'Este, claiming that he had composed the work

19. Alberti, *Op. volg.,* 1: 115; also pp. 232, 234. For the poems in question, see *Mirzia, Agiletta, Corimbus,* and *Tirsis* in Grayson *Op. volg.,* 2: 11–27.

20. In *Op. volg.,* 1: lxxx.

21 Grayson, "Alberti and the Vernacular Eclogue," pp. 16–29.

22. See Antonio Altamura, *Il certame coronario.* Bonucci collected the poems of the contestants in *Op. volg.,* 1: clxvii–ccxxxiv. Alberti's hexameter *De Amicitia* is in Grayson *Op. volg.,* 2: 45.

(*Theogenius*) to console himself, and that he had written it in the vernacular so that it might help others as well. "They say," he continued, apparently referring to the contest and its aftermath, "that I offend literary majesty by not writing eloquent material in Latin; but I shall respond to this elsewhere."[23] The form his response took was highly unusual, but characteristic: it was a grammar of the Tuscan vernacular, apparently the first one ever written.[24]

Alberti's objective here was to demonstrate that the vernacular was as "regular" a language as Latin. One theory about the various vernacular tongues, maintained by Leonardo Bruni among others, was that they descended from an ancient vulgar tongue which the Romans had used for daily speech, reserving the grammatical language for literature and learning—a practice which should continue to be respected. Alberti rejected this notion in *De Familia* where he correctly reasoned that the *volgare* resulted from a barbarization of classical Latin.[25] All known documents from ancient times were written in (classical) Latin, including letters to unschooled wives, children, and servants. Furthermore, and this was the most persuasive argument of all, the Roman authors would have failed in their social duty by writing in a scholarly language known only by a few. Convinced that the Tuscan vernacular was as grammatical as the language from which it had evolved, Alberti accordingly sought to exhibit its rules in a grammar book.

In methodic conception, his *Regule lingue florentine* was thus similar to the slightly later work on cryptography and may have helped him form some of his ideas about coding and decoding. Its aim was to make explicit the regularities of the vernacular and to show that they are governed by rule. Once these regularities are set forth, it becomes evident that the conventions of the vernacular either mirror those of Latin or depart from Latin usage in certain lawful ways. That is, the Tuscan tongue appears almost like a "code" of Latin, as orderly and rational as its "original."

Of all his efforts to regularize and refine the vernacular, perhaps the most

23. "Io scrissi questo libretto non ad altri che a me per consolare me stessi in mie avverse fortune. E parsemi da scrivere in modo ch'io fussi inteso da' miei non litteratissimi cittadini. Certo conobbi a me quest'opera giovò a sollevommi afflitto: e vedoli pur richiesti da molti più che se io gli avessi scritti latini. . . . Dicono che io offesi la maestà letteraria non scrivendo materia si eloquente in lingua piuttosto latina. A questa fia altrove da rispondere" *Op. volg.,* 3: 59–60.

24. *La prima grammatica della lingua volgare,* edited by Cecil Grayson. This book contains a critical edition of Alberti's grammar and a convincing demonstration of his authorship which has been confirmed by the discovery of a ms. of a part of the grammar written in Alberti's hand: see Carmela Colombo, "Leon Batista Alberti e la prima grammatica italiana," *Studi Linguistici Italiani,* 3 (1962): 176–87. For the controversy over the relation between Latin and the vernacular, the context in which Alberti's grammar was written, see Professor Grayson's Introduction.

25. Prologue, book 3.

effective were Alberti's own prose writings. If his technical works helped shape the clear, graphic language as well as the cultural tradition of lay science,[26] his humanistic writings, embodying the genres, stylistic devices, and moral philosophy of classical literature, imparted to the Tuscan tongue a measure, a charm, and urbanity which helped considerably in winning it acceptance as the literary prose language of Italy. "No one has striven to enrich this language more than Battista Alberti," Cristoforo Landino declared in the following generation: "Notice with what industry he has managed to transfer to our tongue the eloquence, composition, and nobility of Latin."[27] Thus even in a linguistic sense, Alberti's humanistic writings were intimately bound up with the vital interests and needs of his day. The Graeco-Roman authors gave him a theory of learning which encouraged him to embrace the affairs of daily life, and they provided a model of style which helped him clarify and standardize the common language.

His Latin writings also breathe this genuinely renewed classical spirit. There is no antiquarianism, no pedantic imitation in his mastery of ancient literary genres, but rather a quick aesthetic delight which spilled over in enthusiastic re-creations. At one time he wrote one hundred Latin fables in little over a week; these are his *Apologi*[28] which he appropriately dedicated to Aesop as well as to a friend in Ferrara. His Latin *Musca*[29] is a similar imaginative imitation of a classical work. The Greek scholar, Guarino da Verona, had dedicated a Latin translation of Lucian's *Encomium of the Fly* to Alberti, and Alberti responded by writing an encomium of his own which he sent, in turn, to the young poet, Cristoforo Landino. Although renewing the form and urbane manner of Lucian's work, Alberti's "eloquent" praise of the fly pokes fun at the stylistic foibles of contemporary humanists: it abounds in comparisons between the fly's rare qualities and those of the heroes of the classical age and is weighted down with citations of unimpeachable classical authorities. *Canis*[30] is a similar comical work inspired by Lucian but contemporary in its reference. Written in overblown Latin, it is a mock funeral oration for Alberti's dog in which he lauds the studious manner of his departed friend, his rectitude, and other sterling characteristics which would go into a typical humanistic eulogy for Alberti himself. The brief, "between-meal" satirical dialogues of his *Intercoenales*[31]

---

26. The classic work on this subject is Leonardo Olschki's *Geschichte der Neusprachlichen Wissenschaftlichen Literatur*. However, its denigration of Renaissance Latin needs to be corrected; Alberti (and many other heroes of the vernacular tradition) wrote limpid Latin prose, as his most outstanding technical work, *De re aedificatoria*, attests.

27. In Mancini, *Vita*, p. 441.

28. *Opera*, edited by H. Massainus. Cecil Grayson's projected collection of Alberti's Latin works will contain a new edition. A vernacular translation is available in Bartoli's *Opuscoli morali di Leon Battista Alberti, Gentil'huomo Firentino*.

29. *Opuscoli inediti: "Musca," "Vita S. Potiti,"* edited by Cecil Grayson.

30. *Opera*, H. Massainus and a vernacular translation in Bartoli's *Opuscoli morali*. *Canis* is one of the works that Burckhardt admired.

31. There is no complete critical edition as yet. Until Cecil Grayson's collection

which he gathered together around 1439, dedicating them to the busy Paolo Toscanelli, were also modeled upon Lucian and filled with quattrocento good sense—about learning, clerical abuses, human folly, and the like. All told, these are the kind of works that account for Alberti's reputation as one of the finest Latinists of his time. They bear the stamp not of imitation but of that live intuition of form, be it artistic or logical, which left a classical imprint on almost everything he produced.

Many of Alberti's technical works were also written in Latin and followed classical examples, but there is a marked stylistic difference between his technical and his purely literary writings, whether in Latin or the vernacular. The technical works are economical and to the point; the humanistic ones are often, though not always, repetitious, roundabout, and wordy. The technical works proceed systematically and deductively, progressing from principles to rules and techniques; the literary ones renounce system altogether. The lack of a coherent development of thought, which is often sorely felt in humanistic writings (as in Cicero), was deliberate with Alberti. The didactic theory of literature to which he subscribed seemed to demand the *modo d'istoria* of classical literature rather than a logical, "Scholastic" mode of reasoning. "Scholastic definitions and descriptions are agreeable enough in leisure and idleness among the learned," he maintained. "They are like a preparation, as fencing is to the use of arms; but in public we have to labor with the usages of men."[32] Since ethical convictions are generally formed in the midst of experience, works written on practical, moral issues ought to draw upon experience as histories do and convey the feel of it. That is, they ought to pursue not a scientific aim but an imaginative and practical one, following "the literary fashion of the ancients."

At their best, Alberti's humanistic writings do achieve this delicate balance between the respective claims of "letters and virtue"; but his humanistic conception of literature is responsible for the faults, as well as the felicities, of his style. There are tedious passages in *De Familia* which occur whenever he felt constrained to spell out its moral lessons and support them by a redundant host of classical maxims and exemplars; and *Momus,* the work that should have been and was intended to be his Latin masterpiece, is marred by an excess of didacticism (on the part of an allegedly "intellectualistic," "utopian" Alberti).

Momus is an allegorical satire modeled upon Lucian and built around the meddlesome son of Night after whom the work is named. This celestial trouble-maker is cast down to earth as punishment for disturbing the peace of heaven, but he is so successful among men as poet, philosopher, and demagogue that he becomes a menace to the gods, the heavens, and the very universe. Jove recalls him to heaven and finally binds him for eternity to a rock in the sea, and there a

---

appears, use Mancini's *Op. ined.,* pp. 122–235; Grayson, "Una intercenale inedita di
L. B. Alberti; Uxoria," *Italia Medievale e Umanistica,* 3 (1960): 291–307; Eugenio Garin,
"Leon Battista Alberti: Alcune intercenali inediti," *Rinascimento,* 4 (1964): 125–258.
  32. "Amicizia," *Op. volg.,* 2: 405–26.

vengeful Juno deprives him of his masculinity. The plot is enriched by some very irreverent satire directed against familiar targets. Philosophers, for example, a favorite object of humanistic criticism, are chided in one episode in which Jove tries to learn their ideas about the best possible world. Having decided to destroy the world which Momus has made intolerable, Jove wants to create a new one in accordance with the most perfect philosophical scheme. In disguise, he attends a philosophical congress, but unduly respectful of the wisdom of philosophers, he flees before learning, as the reader does, that these myopic verbalists would never have discovered the Deity in their midst. He sends Mercury on the same confidential mission, but Socrates draws from the clever, thievish god all his secrets: his identity, Jove's intention to create a new world, everything. And from the "ignorant" Socrates, Mercury learns nothing at all. Finally Apollo goes to earth to discover the "truth" of philosophy, but he, too, fails. The author of the Delphic oracles simply cannot understand the philosophers' impenetrable language. (This turns out to be no great loss, though, for Jove later learns that only architects know how to design a proper cosmos.)[33]

A number of comic sketches like this one are highly successful; but taken as a whole, *Momus* is a confused work and has given rise to confused interpretations. Some of its commentators have thought that Scholasticism was being symbolized (and ridiculed) in one of its major figures, the philosopher Gelastus; whereas others believe that Gelastus stands for Alberti himself.[34] Actually, the conflict lies in the book, for certain sections support the one view, and other sections the other. Near the end of the book, the figures of Gelastus, Momus, and Jove all undergo a metamorphosis which is entirely out of keeping with the import of the work thus far. Gelastus who has been pompous, petulant, pedantic, becomes a guileless scholar whose lack of malice has aroused the ire of others against him. Momus complements this strangely altered picture by appearing as a well-intentioned god after all, whose frank but impolitic lack of duplicity earns him eternal punishment. And Jove, repenting his folly and regretting the loss of dignity he has suffered because of his desire for adulation, deplores the obsequiousness of his courtiers and misses his only honest attendant, Momus. Thus the story which has been ironic and ribald all along draws to a solemn and improbable close. Jove, at the end, picks up and begins to read with profit a manuscript which Momus has bequeathed him: it is an edifying work on "The Prince" who rules, of course, according to justice rather than whim.

33. *Momus o del Principe,* edited by Giuseppe Martini, p. 150. In a similar vein, Alberti has Charon, guide of the Netherworld, say that knowledge is discovered not by means of the verbal subtleties of philosophy but by the painter's contemplation of form: "Referam quae non a philosopho (nam vestra omnis ratio nisi in argutiis et verborum captiunculis versatur) sed a pictore quodam memini audivisse. Is quidem lineamentis contemplandis plus vidit solus quam vos omnes philosophi caelo commensurando et disquirendo." P. 164.

34. See Martini's introduction where these conflicting interpretations are examined, pp. xviii–xix.

The respectable conclusion of *Momus* conforms to the Prologue where Alberti states that the work is an allegory on government, a diverting way to impart moral instruction. But how much more significant *Momus* would have been had the comic intent rather than the moralistic one been carried through. For a while Momus had become a black Prometheus in Alberti's hands. He, too, represents the force of genius, only man's evil genius; and instead of bringing the divine fire, he exploited the vanity and ignorance of gods and men. Rebellious, recognizing no law, he threatened to utterly destroy society by playing upon its weaknesses, and thus he ultimately lost both heaven and earth. He is bound like Prometheus to the rock of eternal punishment; but unlike the noble Titan, Momus lost his humanity as well as his divinity in the symbol of his castration. This is the underlying intuition of the work, but Alberti interrupted its unfolding by tacking on to *Momus* a prosaic conclusion. Instead of completing the imaginative portrayal of man's moral life which he had been developing, he spoiled what could have been his finest piece of prose by turning it into a homily. *Momus* suffers precisely because Alberti's outlook was so practical, so essentially social—a cast of thought which his artistic successes convey in a far more agreeable fashion.

Some of Alberti's *Apologues* and *Intercoenales,* and particularly the last two of his four major dialogues in the vernacular—*De Familia, Theogenius, Profugiorum ab aerumna,* and *De Iciarchia*—are genuinely moving as works of literature. Where the poetic aim was allowed to shape the expression of his moral and social ideas, Alberti formed striking, unforgettable images of the new mode of life he envisioned. In *Profugiorum ab aerumna*[35] (sometimes called *Della tranquillità dell'animo*), the setting of the dialogue and the bearing and manner of the persons who engage in it are all imaginative symbols of the social and ethical ideal which is under discussion:

> Niccola di messer Veri de' Medici, a man distinguished by his manner and virtues, was strolling with me in our great church [the Duomo]. We were discussing agreeable matters, as was our custom, about learning and the study of worthy subjects. Then Agnolo Pandolfini joined us, a mature, grave man in whom nothing was wanting and who, because of his age and practical wisdom, was always sought after and reputed to be one of our outstanding citizens. He greeted us. . . .

And so the work opens, as Alberti holds a conversation with these exponents of Florentine humanism under the cupola of Brunelleschi's great dome. The Duomo itself, like a continuously felt presence, sustains a mood of harmony and balance. "This church surely has both grace and majesty," Agnolo Pandolfini is made to remark:

35. In Grayson *Op. volg.,* 2: 107–83. My references are to Bonucci's *Op. volg.,* 1:7–130, where the work is called "Della tranquillità dell'animo." The two long quotations below are from pp. 7–9.

I often think it delights me so because I see in it a graceful charm joined with a full and robust solidity, so that on the one hand, each of its parts appears to be placed so as to please the eye, and on the other, I know that everything has been made so as to endure. Add to this the fact that it keeps a constant, spring-like atmosphere: outside there is wind, ice, frost; here, closed in from the wind, there is mild air and quiet. Outside, summer and autumnal heat; here within, a most temperate coolness. . . . And what I appreciate most, there is a wonderful sweetness to these voices heard at the mass and other rites. . . . [They] quiet every disturbance of the soul and move me to a certain indefinable, what I call *lentezza d'animo*.

Music, architecture, atmosphere—all contribute to the idea of composure that forms the subject of this dialogue on "tranquillity of mind." The dialogue, too, in its rhythms and expressions, is a model of the development and expression of thought among *uomini colti:* "I'll tell you what just occurred to me, and let us see, Niccola, if I hit the truth." Or again, "What I just recounted is what occurred to me as we were talking, so perhaps it was a little confused." The conversational manner which is maintained throughout creates an image of civil, reasonable discourse, giving the impression of sudden insights and thoughtful reflection, of disagreement and reconsideration.[36]

For all its decorous effects, however, and its Stoic and Epicurean counsels of resignation to Fortune, *Profugiorum ab aerumna* conveys, like the Duomo, a feeling of "full and robust solidity." In fact its utterly confident tone contrasts a bit strangely with the teachings on the sway of blind chance and the narrow bounds of moral freedom which Alberti here repeats. We must recognize that Fortune can do to us what she can do to all mortals, he points out, then hastens to add that we should not let this knowledge deter us from doing what we want and ought to do:

> With the forethought that we are mortal, and that every adversity can befall us, let us do what the wise have so highly praised: let us work (*diamo*

36. The "logic" of this unsystematic treatment of ethical ideas finds its explanation in the following passage on *poesis* in Susanne K. Langer's *Feeling and Form,* p. 219: "All poetry is a creation of illusory events [to build up the image of social life], even when it looks like a statement of opinions, philosophical or political or aesthetic. The occurrence of a thought is an event in a thinker's personal history, and has as distinct a qualitative character as an adventure, a sight, or a human contact; it is not a proposition, but the entertainment of one, which necessarily involves vital tensions, feelings, the imminence of other thoughts, and the echoes of past 'thinking.' Poetic reflections, therefore, are not essentially trains of logical reasoning, though they may incorporate fragments, at least, of discursive argument. Essentially they create the *semblance* of reasoning; of the seriousness, strain and progress, the sense of growing knowledge, growing clearness, conviction and acceptance—the whole experience of philosophical thinking.

"Of course a poet usually builds a philosophical poem around an idea that strikes him, at the time, as true and important; but not for the sake of debating it. He accepts it and exhibits its emotional value and imaginative possibilities."

opera) so that past and present will contribute to the times that have not yet come.[37]

Let us work, in short, as if we and not Fortune were responsible not only for shaping our character but even for shaping the future. The entire dialogue moves in this way, in a direction quite opposed to the tendency of ancient Stoic and Epicurean thought. Where Seneca and Epictetus cautioned man to delimit the scope of his powers, Alberti's purpose was to urge him toward ever greater efforts. All too many refuse to undertake great tasks simply for lack of confidence: "Do not judge what you are able to do until you have first tried; and if you did not do well trying, you will do better the next time."[38]

The overt theme of *Profugiorum ab aerumna* is the *ataraxia* of the ancient sage, but the spirit of the piece (and of the "peace" of the Renaissance sage) is one of energy and effort. The imagery of the work strains toward action and the accomplishment of great things.

> And we, brought into life like a ship which is not meant to rot in port but to furrow long paths in the sea,—we tend by our work to some praiseworthy and glorious end.[39]

A wholly new spirit stirs in similes like these. They bespeak a fresh and lively, a newly emerging "modern" appreciation of work in this world. No self-sufficing "intellectualism" here shifts the good life from the sphere of activity to that of thought. On the contrary, it is the "work" of virtue, the making of the good life, to which Alberti consistently returns, here and in all his ethical writings. They all ring with terms such as *adoperarsi* and *esercitarsi:* "To live a good life requires continuous hard work (*adoperarsi*)." "Let us determine to refuse no labor (*fatica*) by which to become something more than we are." "In human life, work (*lo esercitarsi*) at some one thing opens the way to praise and fame." The ancient ethical ideas which Alberti adopted are all animated by this spirit; they are indeed made congruent by it, for he made all the "bits and pieces" gathered from the temple of ancient moral philosophy contribute, sometimes in rather arbitrary ways, to a distinctive pattern of life centered in the idea of work.

The economic and social historians who have linked Alberti's ideas to the bourgeois sense of industry and the Calvinistic notion of the "calling" have been correct in their judgment of the tenor of his thought, although it is usually Book 3 of *De Familia* which is referred to in this regard, the one in which Alberti was "imitating" Xenophon in the person of the good bourgeois, Gianozzo, and his ideas on *masserizia*.[40] A far better indication of the secular spirit emerging in his

37. *Op. volg.,* 1: 34.
38. *Ibid.,* p. 19.
39. *Ibid.,* p. 49.
40. See Max Weber, *The Protestant Ethic and the Spirit of Capitalism,* pp. 194–98, n. 12. Weber is here criticizing Sombart's contention that Alberti and Benjamin Franklin share the same notions of economic individualism, but despite the differences between

thought is the emphasis upon work in general, embracing all kinds of occupations, which is to be found in all his humanistic writings. While the idea of the sanctity of work has medieval antecedents, they are chiefly found in the monastic context of "work and prayer" (*orare et laborare*). Alberti's "work" is work in this world, and in this sense his moral philosophy is another expression of the newly forming common ethos of early modern Europe. Alberti, too, was overturning the typically medieval scale of values to exalt a function which neither the contemplative nor the aristocrat found congenial and which was, after all, God's curse on Adam. At the same time, however, he imparted to the idea of work certain theoretical notions which the bourgeois attitude and the Protestant sanctification of work in the world did not share, and from this source arose the characteristically classical features of his ethics. Alberti's dynamic conception of man is shot through with the ethical conviction of philosophical idealism, that human activity must be ordered by law, and that this moral order represents the rule of reason in human life.

The metaphor of the ship, which occurs so frequently in his writings to convey the notion of effort, of continuous *adoperarsi,* fuses very often with Platonic figures of thought and speech, as in the following passage:

> The oars give impetus and movement to the entire body of the galley; but if this impetus should perpetuate itself, and the ship move without heading toward a determinate goal, it will crash upon the rocks. It is the pilot who guides that movement and directs it, and thus the ship avoids every danger and reaches its port. That part of the soul in us which is the seat of reason should thus govern the part in which the appetites move.[41]

What Alberti's *adoperarsi* aims at is that ideal which Plato called the "health" or "perfection" of human nature: the right order which the governance of reason establishes among the powers of the soul.[42]

Man's primary and fundamental "work" is thus the work of Virtue for Alberti; and Virtue he understood in Platonic fashion. Like the Idea of beauty,

---

Weber and Sombart (and both are wrong on some points), both acknowledge the "modern" character of Alberti's emphasis upon (if not his idea of) industry and work. Ruth Lang's *L.B.A. und die Sancta Masseritia* develops some of the exaggerated notions which Sombart held of Alberti's bourgeois attitudes.

41. "De Iciarchia," *Op volg.,* 3: 22. On p. 64, he describes Virtue as man's primary and fundamental aim: "preporrenci, quasi come legge destinata al viver nostro, al tutto posporre ogni altra cosa alla Virtù." The same idea runs through his first vernacular dialogue: "Né a voi sia più caro, né prima desiderata alcuna cosa che la virtù." *I primi tre libri della famiglia,* p. 37; also p. 39.

42. Again I quote from the first and last of his vernacular dialogues to show the continuity of these ideas. *I primi tre libri della famiglia,* p. 90: "Tutti e mortali sono da essa natura compiuti ad amare et mantenere qualunque lodatissima virtù; e non è virtù altro se non in sé perfecta et ben producta natura." "De Iciarchia," *Op. volg.,* 3: 95: "La virtù in te studioso e vero buono uomo sta in te conceputa e parata, non come cosa impostavi e collocata, ma come innata sanità."

Virtue is the "ideal" which opposes the actual, but in the sense of a dialectical opposition, one which is to be overcome in the individual. The individual brings about this rational Form, this "right proportion" in his life by his work; and Virtue unifies, in turn, all particular kinds of work or occupations. Virtue is the universal ideal that applies to and regulates all human conduct. Thus the good man need not be a poet or an astronomer (or, for that matter, a monk), but the poet, the astronomer, and all other men require this one "rule of life."[43] Virtue belongs to no particular social grade, to no one way of life; it raises all kinds of life and work to an equal dignity. "You cannot achieve dignity and reputation by your skill as a man of letters?" Alberti asks:

> Then do as others have done who were well advised. Go forth from your nest, try yourself at arms, take to the sea, seek elsewhere in any occupation whatsoever to live honorably. Who does not seek his own good cares not for it; who cares not for it, deserves it not.[44]

When Alberti turned from the bourgeois life of *De Familia* to the wisdom of the ancient sage, concerning himself in *Theogenius* and *Profugiorum ab aerumna* with "the soul at peace with itself," he held fast to these two fundamental ideas of work and virtue. What he had exhibited in the personae of the Alberti family was not the possession of wealth, reputation, or family, but the life that was self-possessed. This remained the theme of the two principal dialogues of his middle years, only here, the life he sought to define was that of the intellectual, the "lover of wisdom" who is alone and perhaps even despised by family, society, and Fortune (as the illegitimate Battista was in fact despised and mistreated by many of his relatives and some of his "friends"). The unification of the ideal and the actual is consequently different in these works as the "philosopher" of Stoic and Epicurean thought comes to the fore. But far from forming a "medieval" or "contemplative" moment in his thought, these two dialogues indicate even more clearly than *De Familia* that there was no cleavage for Alberti between the inner life and the life of the community, between Virtue and one's work in the world. Alberti's conception of the scholar-sage is stamped not with the features of the contemplative life which Petrarch still saw there but with those of the civic-minded humanism of quattrocento Florence.[45]

43. "De Iciarchia," *Op. volg.,* 3: 63. See also *Op. volg.,* 1: 53.

44. "De Iciarchia," *Op. volg.,* 3: 25.

45. The exact date of the composition of *Theogenius* is unknown, but it is earlier than 1441, for Alberti sent it to Leonello d'Este in that year. Mancini speculated that Alberti wrote it around 1438, *Vita,* p. 158. Giovanni Ponte argued for 1440 in "La datazione del 'Teogenio' di L. B. Alberti," *Convivium,* 23 (1955): 150–59. All that can be said with certitude was that Alberti wrote it between 1438 and 1441. The critical edition which should be used from now on is in Grayson *Op. volg.,* 2: 55–104. My references are to Bonucci's *Op. volg.* 3: 161–229. *Profugiorum ab aerumna* was written between 1441–42.

The hermitlike wise man of *Theogenius,* who is as "withdrawn" as the intellectual ever came to be portrayed in Alberti's humanistic writings, still teaches us Alberti's credo of useful work. Theogenius is almost Petrarchan in his rural surroundings and intellectual pursuits, and he argues (successfully, of course) for the moral superiority of both in his dialogue with a representative of the city and society. Yet Theogenius himself acknowledges that he is an integral member of the society from which he (Alberti) at this moment evidently felt estranged. "As Plato said," he quotes, "we are not born for ourselves alone." Even the sage, disillusioned by the envy and malice of society, and tempted by his medieval heritage to seek spiritual well-being in an undisturbed pursuit of knowledge, even he believes that he is bound to the world by an obligation to expound what he knows for the sake of the common good.[46] Alberti's subsequent choice of Agnolo Pandolfini, an "outstanding citizen" and former magistrate, as spokesman for his ideas in *Profugiorum ab aerumna,* and his choice of the Duomo as its setting, are signs of a deepening appreciation on his part of this classical conception of morality which is at once personal and public. It is my duty to cultivate myself, he has Agnolo Pandolfini say, to develop "reason and society"—as if these were the twin fruit of the single "work" of Virtue.

> Shall I not deem it my duty, by exercising myself in important and noble undertakings, to cultivate my 'self' and become worthy by my industry and virtue? . . . . These two things, which Seneca said were more valuable than all the things given by God, reason and society, shall I extinguish them by my sloth and inertia, and let them mean nothing to me?[47]

Probably Alberti's single most important contribution to the humanistic movement is to be found in these persuasive literary presentations of the renascent conception of the good life as the life of the citizen. The famous humanist-chancellors of Florence—Coluccio Salutati (d. 1406), Leonardo Bruni (1369–1444), and Poggio Bracciolini (1380–1459)—were largely responsible for re-establishing the bonds between learning and virtue, and virtue and one's role in society; but to give this synthesis of *lettere e virtù* poetic life was Alberti's achievement. In the symbolic figures of his four major dialogues, he presented some of the diverse shapes this humanistic ideal could take, each of them a way of life "grato a te stesso, accetto agli altri, e utile a molti."[48] For Alberti himself,

---

The topic of Florentine civic humanism has received its finest treatment thus far in the works of Hans Baron: "Cicero and the Roman Civic Spirit in the Middle Ages and the Early Renaissance," *Bulletin of the John Rylands Library,* 20 (1938): 72–97; "Franciscan Poverty and Civic Wealth in Humanistic Thought," *Speculum,* 13 (1938): 1–37; *The Crisis of the Early Italian Renaissance.*

46. *Op. volg.,* 3: 223. The social import of *Theogenius* is evident in its subtitle: "Della republica, della vita civile et rusticana."

47. *Op. volg.,* 1: 31–32.

48. "Agreeable to yourself, welcome to others, and useful to many." *Ibid.,* p. 19.

however, these works were successive moments in the development of a single idea, a development which culminated in *De Iciarchia*.[49] In this dialogue of 1469, written three years before he died, Alberti discourses on the new cultural type who led neither the "active" nor the "contemplative" life in the medieval sense of these terms: the humanist, as Alberti ultimately came to understand him and to know himself.

The dialogue is once again set in Florence. Returning from his favorite walk to San Miniato across the Arno, the height from which he used to overlook his beloved city, an ageing Alberti meets two of his friends on the bridge. One is a *podestà* of Pisa, the other a member of the Florentine *Priori*. As they watch the threatening Arno, swollen by the winter rains, they reflect upon the harm caused by excess or by any departure from the "measure" which is proper to all things. Then they go indoors, and Alberti begins to instruct these magistrates in the fundamental art of self-government. Three youths who listen to the conversation give another biographical note to the work. Alberti had written a number of treatises throughout his lifetime for the young members of the Alberti family, generally exhorting them to live up to the excellence of their forefathers. Two of these nephews now sit by the fire in *De Iciarchia*, attending to what turned out to be his final words on learning and virtue—a discourse on what Alberti here calls "*iciarchia*."

The term Iciarco comes from the Greek, he explains, and it means "the man of excellence and ruler of his family."[50] As Alberti uses it, Iciarco comes to stand for another ideal type, a model comparable to Adovardo Alberti of *De Familia* and Agnolo Pandolfini of *Profugiorum ab aerumna*. Iciarco's distinctive excellence arises from his goodness and learning, and the main point of the dialogue is to persuade the reader (in the work, the three young men) that this superiority makes Iciarco a kind of "Prince" as well. He exercises his pre-eminence as a form of public duty; but he does so as a private person, not as a magistrate.[51]

Iciarco's "work," as we soon begin to see, makes this dialogue something of

49. In Grayson *Op. volg.*, 2: 187–286. My references are to Bonucci's *Op. volg.*, 3: 7–151.

50. *Ibid.*, p. 132.

51. *Ibid.*, p. 121–22: "Il governo e moderazione degli altri si porge in due modi, l'uno circa molti, come chi fusse proposto rettore d'una città, di uno esercito, di una provincia, e simili pubblici magistrati; l'altro quando fusse primo e superiore a pochi, come sarebbe a un numero d'uomini couniti per confederazione, conversatione, consanguinità e simile. E questo sarà magistrato sì, non però pubblico; ma sarà officio composto della cura domestica colla sollectitudine pubblica."

It is a mistake to view Iciarco's private "principate" as Lauro Martines does in *The Social World of the Florentine Humanists, 1390–1460*, pp. 294–98, as representing a withdrawal on Alberti's part from public affairs. On the contrary, the theme and emphasis of the work is that even the scholarly life is a public one, with distinctive social responsibilities.

The Humanistic Mode of Thought: Letters and Virtue

229

a companion piece to *Momus,* the allegorical satire which was intended to convey a serious political lesson. Subtitled "The Prince," *Momus* was an inverted image of the *Republic,* demonstrating how a willful and vacillating Jove who is himself governed by passion, vanity, and caprice can destroy the rational order of society (and the cosmos) which it is his duty to maintain. Iciarco, like the prince or public magistrate, also strives to bring about the right order of reason in his own person; and like them, he tries to direct society to this same end. But his social responsibility arises not from any poltical postion which he holds, but rather from his humanity and understanding: he guides society not as a political ruler but as a teacher and man of letters. Iciarco is the voice of reason, and hence the voice of the social conscience. In any gathering or community of which he is a member, and especially among his close associates (his *famigliari*), his task is to work in his "private" way, by word and example, to guide others toward that right order in which the "health" of human nature and society consists. This is why Alberti calls him the "father" of his "family":

> The papa of the little-one born in his house says: he is my son. And I reply, true; but you have made him like all other animals born with two legs. I have made him like an earthly god by virtue. . . . To whom would you say one who has been so ennobled is more indebted? To the papa (*babbo*) or to me, his true and best father (*padre*)?[52]

This new kind of *padre,* this Platonic doctor of the soul, owes his primary allegiance to the Idea of virtue as self-rule by reason, and his commitment to society springs from his recognition that reason is the true source of responsibility in the person and in the group. "His goods, his toil, his blood and life itself" are at the service of the well-being, the right order, of society, for Iciarco, the intellectual qua humanist, is made an integral part of society by his knowledge that "it is wicked not to resist evil where you can; and whoever permits injustice in others is not just himself."[53]

There is no mistaking the fact that *iciarchia* describes the way of life Alberti had shaped for himself. "I have here described the task of this man of excellence and guide of others," he says at the end of *De Iciarchia,* "which, I confess, from the time this head was blond down to the present when it is white with age, I have always sought to fulfill . . . not so much to make myself a leader, as to do what I could for you."[54] If Alberti was not torn between the claims of the spirit and the demands of the world as Petrarch had been, it is because he had achieved a union of the two in this humanistic conception of the work of reason, an idea which he progressively developed and carried out in the course of his own life. This is the ethical insight that he sought to clarify in his major humanistic writings; and in the various cultural tasks he undertook, he genuinely

52. *Ibid.,* p. 134; see also pp. 147, 148.
53. *Ibid.,* p. 150.
54. *Ibid.,* p. 151.

"sought to fulfill" it, to be of use to the artist, the builder, the map maker, the astronomer, the secretary in a Chancery, to poets, humanists, and to his *non litteratissimi cittadini.* The many facets of Renaissance culture that bear the traces of Alberti's "work" were unified in his life by a basic ethical conviction: that in such activities he served as guide and teacher of his age, and that this social function was but the obverse of the life of thought.

Even the last glimpse we have of Alberti finds him in his chosen role of Iciarco. In September 1471, Lorenzo de' Medici and a party of orators came from Florence to congratulate Sixtus IV on his elevation to the Papacy. It was Alberti, then living in Rome, who met them and conducted them around he Roman Forum, still acting as guide, introducing them to the remains of the ancient civilization that opened up a new conception of life and learning for him. He died the following spring at the age of sixty-eight, "content and tranquil" Vasari claims, having won "a most honorable name" for himself: a name, Alberti would have added, won by unremitting *adoperarsi.*

> Oh what a sweet thing is the glory we acquire by our labor! And worthy are the labors which give us a sign other than age to show that we have lived, and which leave for those who are to come some trace of our life and name other than the inscribed stone of a sepulchre.[55]

Epilogue: The Measure of the Man

As a tribute to Alberti's career, his younger friend, Cristoforo Landino, had him appear as a major personage in a dialogue he wrote in the rhetorical Ciceronian style which Alberti had popularized. Landino was one of the leaders of Florentine culture in the generation that succeeded Alberti's; he was a tutor of Lorenzo de' Medici and an associate in the Platonic Academy of Ficino, Pico della Mirandola, Politian, and Botticelli. His reflections upon the good life in his *Disputationum Camaldulensium* take the form of discussions held around the year 1468 among certain members of this group.[56] By including Alberti among them, having him as an older "private prince" uphold the merits of the contemplative life as the young Lorenzo de' Medici argues for the active life, Landino acknowledged the continuity between Alberti's interests and those of his own generation. For Alberti had been one of Ficino's auditors; and his own literary achievements, ethical ideas, and aesthetics all contributed to the outlook and interests of late fifteenth-century Florence. His conception of man's rational development, as growing into a kind of earthly god, foreshadows Pico della Mirandola's famous oration which

55. "Della tranquillità" (*Profugiorum ab aerumna*), *Op. volg.,* 1: 48.
56. *Disputationum Camaldulensium Libri IV.*

grounds human dignity in the spiritual activity of self-formation. His theory of art as a symbolic embodiment of Nature's intelligible forms is likewise caught up in Ficino's idealistic theory of man who "recognizes" the Divine Ideas and reconstitutes them in art as well as in thought. At several critical points, however, Florentine Neoplatonism diverged sharply from Alberti's position, and this fact Landino unwittingly obscured. Much as Alberti had made Agnolo Pandolfini and Adovardo Alberti expositors of his own ideas, so Landino's "contemplative" Alberti represents not Alberti's views but certain intellectual tendencies of the Academy.[57]

One fundamental feature of Alberti's thought was his avoidance of overtly philosophical issues and metaphysical speculation, but Florentine Neoplatonism was first and foremost "philosophy." It drew its inspiration from Marsilio Ficino (1433–99), and Ficino's ideas about culture and society were systematically bound to a metaphysical theory of man. Ficino found cosmological significance in the logical act by which the mind draws together the concrete and the abstract in its syntheses of thought and art. As artist and thinker, man links the disparate orders of things, his Divinely implanted ideas corresponding harmoniously to the actual structure of the world. He is a bridge between the Divine and the world, the intelligible and the sensible, placed quite literally at "the center of the universe" where he forms its dynamic bond and tie:

This [Man] is the greatest wonder in nature. All other things under God are always in themselves of one certain kind of being; this [human] essence is at once all of them. It possesses in itself images of the divine things upon which it depends. It also possesses the reasons and models of the inferior things which it in a sense brings forth. Since it is the mean of all things, it possesses the powers of all; hence it transforms itself into all things. And because it is itself the true bond of the universe, in passing into some things it does not forsake the others, but enters into individual things, and at the same time preserves all things. Therefore it can with justice be called the center of nature, the middle point of all that is, the chain of the world, the face of all, and the knot and bond of the universe.[58]

The force of genius, which Alberti had been so ready to acknowledge, here acquired an exalted metaphysical function. Its acts spring from the necessary central role which man has been assigned in the universal scheme of things. But

57. This is the root of Martines' misinterpretation of Alberti (above n. 51). He takes Landino's Alberti as a biographical portrait rather than a personification of certain of Landino's ideas. There are two excellent short essays on the Platonic Academy and Ficino in Paul Oskar Kristeller's *Renaissance Thought II*. For more detailed works, see his *The Philosophy of Marsilio Ficino*; A. Della Torre, *Storia dell'Accademia Platonica di Firenze*; Giuseppe Saitta, *La filosofia di Marsilio Ficino*.

58. "Platonic Theology" (Book 3, ch. 2), translated by Josephine L. Borroughs, *Journal of the History of Ideas*, 5 (1944): 227–39.

the price that Renaissance Neoplatonism had to pay for "explaining" mind in these ontological terms was high: it was no less than a restoration of the hierarchical mode of thought. The human functions of creation and love bind what were for Ficino two separate "realms": that of the world and that of the Divine. Thus the physical world once again became a mere region within the total hierarchy of being; Spirit was reified and given its "superior" place in the cosmic scale; and the idea of ascent from one to the other—from corporeal to spiritual beauty, from love of another person to love of God—once again came to dominate aesthetic and ethical thought.

To effect the unification between the two "realms" of being, Ficino renewed the bond between Beauty and Goodness, a bond which survived in the ideas of Platonic love which Castiglione, Michelangelo, and the later Renaissance drew from him. From the point of view of aesthetics, this meant that the ideas of proportion which Alberti had restored to their classical fullness tended to be engulfed once more by ideas of light.[59] Light and the Good it makes manifest stand in a real opposition to matter; and in the higher reaches of being, this kind of Beauty ultimately liberates itself from a physical medium altogether, something which harmonious proportions can never do. In ethics the same motif appears as a mystical yearning for the fullness of the Ideal. Drawn by love to the Divine Source of Beauty and the Ideas, man withdraws from the other end of the scale, from the corporeal world, from sense, imagination, and the concerns of society. His spiritual life becomes a movement toward a Good which he can attain only in the "next world," but contemplation of the Good will reward him even here, by way of confirmation and promise, with rare transports of ecstasy.[60]

Alberti may form a link between the Neoplatonism of the latter part of the century and the humanism and artistic-scientific developments of early quattrocento Florence, but clearly he belongs no more to the one than to the other phase of fifteenth-century thought. He really stands between the two, theoretical yet nonetheless experiential in outlook. Because of the role the a priori Ideas of virtue and beauty played in his thought, he gave a consistently idealistic turn to the practical, didactic and technical issues he treated; but on the other hand, his ethical and artistic ideas never lost their attachment to the world of social and sensory experience which absorbed Florentine civic humanism and

59. On the aesthetic ideas of Ficino and Renaissance Neoplatonism, see André Chastel, *Marsile Ficin et l'Art;* Erwin Panofsky, "The Neoplatonic Movement in Florence and North Italy" and "The Neoplatonic Movement and Michelangelo," *Studies in Iconology,* (New York: Evanston, London, 1962), pp. 129–230; also the relevant chapters in Panofsky's *Idea.*

60. "Now, in the body the soul is truly far more miserable, both because of the weakness and infirmity of the body itself and its want of all things and because of the continual anxiety of the mind; therefore, the more laborious it is for the celestial and immortal soul continually to follow its happiness, while fallen into an intemperate earthly destructible body, the more easily it obtains it when it is either free from the body or in a temperate immortal celestial body. . . .

artistic practice. For this reason, too, the empirical and ideal moments in his thought cannot be said to belong to two successive stages in his development. There never was a positivistic Alberti pure and simple, followed by a Neoplatonic one who succumbed in later years to Ficino's influence.[61] The course of Alberti's thought shows, rather, a steady clarification of one intellectual perspective, an outlook in which the theoretical and the experiential penetrate each other. It was the logic of his own technically grounded ideas in *Della pittura* which led him to the more speculative, Pythagorean-Platonic position of *De re aedificatoria;* and even here, the *rules* of artistic "imitation" remained his central concern, not its metaphysical implications. He developed his theory of beauty only to the point where it could ground and guide practice. How the

"When, indeed, the soul attains the infinite end, it certainly attains it without end, for it attains it in the same manner in which it is influenced, drawn along, and led by it [the end]. If the soul has been able at some time to rise up again to immensity from a certain finite condition infinitely distant from immensity, then certainly it can remain infinitely steadfast in immensity itself. This must indeed be true, for the same infinite power which attracted the soul to itself from afar will, when close by, hold it fast within itself with indescribable power. Finally, in the infinite good nothing evil can be imagined, and whatever good can be imagined or desired is most abundantly found there. Therefore, at that place [shall be found] eternal life and the brightest light of knowledge, rest without change, a positive condition free from privation, tranquil and secure possession of all good, and everywhere perfect joy." Marsilio Ficino, translated by Josephine L. Burroughs, "Five Questions Concerning the Mind," *The Renaissance Philosophy of Man,* edited by Ernst Cassirer, Paul Oskar Kristeller, John Herman Randall, Jr., pp. 211-12.

61. W. Flemming (*Die Begründung der modernen Aestetik, und Kunstwissenschaft durch L. B. Alberti*), who concentrated upon *De re aedificatoria,* drew attention to the idealistic strain in Alberti's aesthetic thought. Panofsky (in *Idea*) and Julius von Schlosser ("Ein Künstlerproblem der Renaissance: L. B. Alberti *Akademie der Wissenschaften in Wein, Sitzungberichte,* 210, vol. 2.), who were mainly concerned with *Della pittura,* disputed this interpretation and emphasized Alberti's so-called positivistic tendency. Lionello Venturi tried to reconcile these two views by maintaining that Alberti's thought developed from the earlier, positivistic position to the later, idealistic one: "Ragione e Dio nell'estetica di Leon Battista Alberti," *L'Esame,* 1 (1922). Chastel discusses this dispute in *Marsile Ficin,* pp. 107-11 and adopts Venturi's position. (In so doing, Chastel clarifies the historical relation between Alberti's Pythagorean-Platonic ideas and the aesthetics of the Academy by pointing out that it was Alberti who influenced the Academy rather than the other way around: "Il n'en faut pas conclure qu'Alberti fut sur tous ses points débiteur des doctrines néo-platoniciennes: c'est plutôt l'orientation du 'traité d'architecture' qui s'est imposée aux philosophes de l'Academie renaissante, comme l'une des principales références de leur 'pythagorisme'." P. 109.)

I should like to make just two points: (1) Alberti's thought does develop in the true sense of the word, i.e., it does not move from a positivistic to an idealistic position but gradually unfolds along its own distinctive lines (as I hope I have shown in this book); and (2) despite the fact that Ficino may have absorbed some of Alberti's ideas, the systematic differences between Alberti's aesthetics of proportion and the Academy's Neoplatonic aesthetics are irreconcilable because of the latter's dominant idea of transcendence. The same idea distinguishes Ficino's ethical position from that of Alberti.

Idea arises was the question he chose not to pursue, beyond asserting that it has its "seat" in reason and nature.

The same constancy of outlook distinguishes Alberti's ethical writings. Here his attention was focused upon the moral rather than the artistic "work"; but as early as *De Familia* that *adoperarsi* was directed by an ideal of *virtu,* and when this ideal received its full Platonic development in *Momus* and *De Iciarchia,* it retained its "seat" in human reason: the Idea of virtue is innate to reason which "by its very nature always urges the spirit toward excellence and restrains desire."[62] The ideal never transcended the actual in any "real" sense for Alberti. It remained logically transcendent only, to use the language of Kant, not because Alberti had worked out a critical epistemological theory as Kant did but because the Ideas functioned in his thought merely as rationally posited goals toward which activity should tend. "We make use of the same answer Plato made when he was asked where that perfect republic was to be found," he says in *De re aedificatoria,* justifying his definition of an "ideal" city:

> That, said he, was not the thing I troubled myself about. All I studied was how to frame the best that possibly could be, and that which deviates least from a resemblance to this ought to be preferred above all the rest.[63]

By confining himself to the creative processes of art and to the shaping of the moral life, in short, to experience, Alberti did more than merely avoid metaphysics. His concentration upon the "work" of reason also resolved for him the tension between world and spirit which reappeared in Ficino's metaphysical thought and in Landino's dialogue on the good life. Even in his last diaglogue, Iciarco still personifies the humanistic union of learning and virtue which belonged to Alberti's early days, and he voices the acceptance of society and culture to which that union inevitably led.

In its reconciliation with the world, Alberti's moral philosophy was diametrically opposed to the Neoplatonic ideal of contemplation and transcendence. It unified thought and action, as Florentine humanism did; but in his moral philosophy, as in his aesthetics, Alberti gave an idealistic significance to the ideas of the earlier part of the century. The synthesis of reason and practice in his humanistic writings had its source in a vital intuition of "spirit" as an immanent, creative force, an idea which was to become explicit in the thought of Ficino and Pico della Mirandola.

The Epicurean notion of a Deity, blissful in inactivity, was one that Alberti found disagreeable if not impossible. The Divine Spirit cannot rest in *il far nulla,* he maintained. God is eternally active, and active in the formation of rational order.[64] He and man are alike conceived not as "being" but as self-

62. "De Iciarchia," *Op. volg.,* 3: 66.
63. *De re aedif.,* bk. 4, chap. 2,
64. "A me qui non può dispiacere la sententia dell'Epicuro philosafo, el quale

235

directing process. The human spirit, too, "can never be idle"; it is "never without movement," and in its unfolding, reason orders its products and its course.[65] Thus it is not in artistic creativity alone that man participates in the Divine. If the artist comes to imitate *natura naturans* in *De re aedificatoria*, in *Momus* the social man imitates the rational, creative activity of Jove by the formation of a just social order. Where reason is conceived as an immanent, formative power, all its works "hanno in sè molta parte di divinità."[66] They all partake of divinity, and by them God is both imitated and served:

> Above all, I praise that just and true saying, that man has been created to please God, to recognize one true principle in the multiplicity of things. . . . Add to this . . . how man ought to render his gifts to God, to satisfy him with good works for the endowment of so many talents which he gave to the human soul, making it greater, more excellent, than all the other earthly creatures. Nature, that is, God, formed man in part heavenly and divine, in part more beautiful and nobler than any mortal thing. . . . Be certain, then, that man was not born to waste away in idleness (*otio*) but to work (*adoperarsi*) at great and magnificent tasks by which he can, first of all, please and honor God, and also bring about within himself the habit of virtue and thereby the fruit of happiness.[67]

The immanent, dynamic conception of "spirit" which was here taking form led Alberti to make new distinctions between the kind of conduct which truly serves and pleases God, and observances which seemed, from this vantage point, formalistic and superstitious. In these matters, his ethical and religious thought points in the direction of Pico and Erasmus. There are a number of notions in his writings (as in theirs) which the Reformers would later advocate, but in Alberti these ideas express that early deistic tendency which the Reformation would check but which would come to fruition after the religious wars. Thus he bitterly criticized the ambition and venality of the clergy;[68] he contrasted the charity and simple ceremonies of the primitive Church with the pomp of the

---

reputa in Dio somma felicità el far nulla. Sia lecito a Dio, quello che forse non è a'mortali volendo, far nulla; ma io credo ogni altra cosa potere essere a Dio di sé stessi forse meno ingrata e agli uomini, dal vitio in fuori, più licita che starsi indarno." *I primi tre libri della famiglia*, p. 192.

65. "Gli animi nostri fece la natura atti ad eternità, semplici, nulla composti, non da altri mossi che da sè stessi. . . . Quello che fu prima conguinta e ascritto alla vita si prova essere 'l moto; . . . l'animo può mai starsi ozioso, sempre si volge, e avvolge in sè qualche investigazione o disputazione o apprensione di cose." "Della tranquillità," *Op. volg.*, I: 28–29. Also "De Iciarchia," *Op. volg.*, 3: 28.

66. *Op. volg.*, 3: 90.

67. I have condensed this passage; it covers pp. 194–97 in *I primi tre libri della famiglia*. See also *Op. volg.*, I: 32; *Op. volg.*, 3: 24–25.

68. In "Pontifex" and "Nummus" in particular, *Op. ined.*, 67–121; 172–74. Also, *Op. volg.*, 2: 401, 403.

contemporary Papacy and the mindless multiplication of "altars and masses";[69] but most characteristically, he argued against passivity and reliance upon prayer.

Prayer cannot affect a constant Deity, Alberti tirelessly pointed out. Prayer presupposes that God serves human ends and will bring harm upon one person or group so as to serve the wishes of another;[70] but Jove, too, falls under rational law. He is responsible for the eternal order of the universe and will be moved neither by pity nor anger to alter the regular course of events. Man alone can do good and prevent evil—and therefore ought to do so: "In adversity, you may invoke the aid of God, but you should not abandon yourself in this and lead yourself to believe that you cannot by your own powers do that which you surely can do."[71] Man has to rectify by his own efforts the evils he once urged the gods to avert. The fundamental sin could therefore no longer be pride in human power. *Otio*, inactivity, is the source of every evil and vice: the spiritual torpor, the apathy and irresponsibility that holds man back from *lo adoperarsi*.

This is not to say that Alberti ever repudiated traditional forms of devotion and dogma. As far as his life and writings indicate, the devout and orthodox attitude he attributes to himself in *Profugiorum ab aerumna* was genuinely felt: "I praise you Battista," he has Agnolo Pandolfini say as they meet in the Duomo, "and I am pleased that in this, your faithful attendance at this church, as in other things, I find you most religious."[72] This sentiment agrees not only with Alberti's vocation as a churchman but with many pious statements scattered throughout his writings and with his explicit reflections upon God and religion.[73] Religion retained its place in his thought, but its mystical, sacramental, and sacerdotal features were eclipsed by the new, radiant conception he held of both the Divine and the human spirit.

It is the cosmic God, not Jesus, who appears in Alberti's writings. The man-God and all the concrete Catholic imagery of sin and redemption were forced into the background as the idea of God, the great Artificer of Nature

69. *De re aedif.*, bk. 7, chap. 13.
70. "Religio," *Op. ined.*, pp. 130–31.
71. *Op. volg.*, 1: 113. See also *ibid.*, p. 15; *I primi tre libri della famiglia*, 190–91; *Op. volg.*, 3: 24, 87, 165. This refashioning of the traditional religious-ethical outlook has been rightly appreciated in what I regard as the two most faithful interpretations of Alberti's moral philosophy: Valeria Benetti-Brunelli's *Leon Battista Alberti e il rinnovamento pedagogico nel quattrocento* and Saitta's pages on Alberti in *Il pensiero italiano nell'umanesimo e nel rinascimento*, 1: 393–424 (although I find no evidence for the "anguish of doubt" through which Saitta believes Alberti passed in his early years). As Benetti-Brunelli rightly says, "il culto si esplica, secondo l'Alberti, con l'esercizio: l'omaggio più genuino dell'uomo a Dio è il coltivarsi. Dio è in noi: ma nel nostro dinamico, che è in quanto si realizza." P. 109; see pp. 109–15 in particular.
72. *op. volg.*, 1: 7–8.
73. There are two works of a purely devotional nature by Alberti: An "Epistola consolatoria," Grayson *Op. volg.*, 2: 289–95; and "Psalmi precationum," *Op. ined.*, 31–35, five Latin psalms modeled upon those of Jerome which praise the omnipotence and mercy of God.

emerged, and the idea of man, made in his likeness, achieving his proper dignity, even his divinity, in the rational formation of his life and works. Agnolo Pandolfini's demand that the self and its talents be developed by continuous work clearly springs from this dynamic apprehension of the nature of God and man: "This intellect, this cognition, reason, and memory, so infinite and immortal, whence do they come if not from one who is infinite and immortal? .... Shall I not deem it my duty, by exercising myself in important and noble undertakings, to cultivate my 'self'?" The traditional notions of Grace and Providence had no role left to play in this outlook. They were sapped of vital meaning by the force with which the notion of spirit as creative process came to be conceived. With God revered as the formative principle of Nature, man had to assume control of his own sphere of creative activity.

Man's creative work thus constituted the very nature of the human spirit, for Alberti as for Ficino; but for Alberti, it also constituted the supreme form of "being." The idea that man should seek anything "above" or "beyond" his continuous, rational work is implicitly rejected in Alberti's thought. It is not simply that he never states that contemplation of God and a mystical union with him is the proper end of the human spirit; it is that "spirit" as he conceived it cannot logically find its end, its "rest" as Augustine and Ficino put it, in a cessation of its essential, formative activities. The rationally directed work which it undertakes in life is its only possible goal. This is "complete and divine beatitude," this "doing good and working in virtue which," Alberti says, "I can only call supreme happiness."[74] This glimpse of an immanent rather than a transcendent end of the spirit never attained the level of conscious, discursive reflection in Alberti's ethical thought. It never stood in open opposition to the traditional Christian notion of immortality, but it did find expression in one of his "stories." In his *Apologue of the Lion,* Alberti created a vivid image of the life-bound, Aristotelian conception of human destiny, an image which was so significant to him that he took his adoptive name, Leone, from it. Leone heard that a lion (Leo) had gained a place in heaven for himself by means of his outstanding works:

> Burning with desire for a like glory, he set himself the most arduous tasks so as to excel among lions.
>
> 'Why drive yourself like this?' asked Envy. 'The place in heaven which the other lion won has already been awarded.'
>
> 'It is enough, then,' Leone replied, 'simply to be worthy of it.'[75]

---

74. "Questa compiuta e divina beatitudine, quale tu virtuoso contribuisci a te stessi, facendo bene e adoperandoti in virtù, potrò io chiamarla altro che somma felicità." "De Iciarchia," *Op. volg.,* 3 : 95.

75. *Opusc. morali,* p. 393.

The view of human destiny which emerges from Alberti's writings is one in which man acknowledges "no other arbiter of his life and deeds than himself."[76] Man is thrown back entirely upon his own resources, yet in this lonely independence he comes once again into his own kingdom. Once again he is restored to the order of "reason and society" for which he alone is responsible and which alone constitutes the realm of his endeavors, his world. At this point, Alberti's ethical position broadens into a general theodicy, if not a theory, of culture. If he has often been treated as a contributor to educational theory,[77] even though he never wrote a treatise on the subject, it is because his writings suggest a new, and distinctively rational conception of the limits and powers of the human spirit. His idea of *adoperarsi* incorporates all the cultural "works" in which he was personally engaged, making them as constitutive of man's proper activity as his moral conduct. Man was born "to work at that which is proper to man": to him alone was it given "to investigate the reasons of things, to examine the truth of his thoughts and the goodness of his deeds; and this is nothing other than to exercise that faculty by which we acquire knowledge."[78] Science, art, morality—all are fruits of that power of reason which, in its continuous activity, makes man *un altro iddio,* another god.

"Man was born to be useful to himself and others; and our primary and proper use is to turn the powers of the soul toward virtue, to recognize the causes and order of things, and thereby to venerate God."[79]

As practice and theory were combined in his artistic, technical, and humanistic writings, so the practical and theoretical aspects of Alberti's life found their unity in this general orientation. His life and works alike reflect a theoretical vision of the immanent, law-giving spirit and the practical will to exercise its creative, rational powers. Even the mores, the life style, that emerged as the ideal of *humanitas* developed in the Renaissance were grounded by Alberti in this comprehensive intuition of a rationally formed, harmonious pattern of life and being. For him, as for Renaissance thought generally, the person, too, was a work of art and reason. Man was not merely to be *ben composto,* which is the inner work of virtue; he must also appear so. The style of the man—in manner, bearing, dress and speech—manifests his moral

76. "Della tranquillità," *Op. volg.,* 1: 71.
77. Benetti-Brunelli placed Alberti within the context of "il rinnovamento pedagogico" of the title of her book, and Woodward considered Alberti "a major figure in the educational movement" of humanism: *Studies in Education,* pp. 48–64. Actually, Alberti had very little to say about formal education, and this little had to do with his typically humanistic rejection of medieval abridgements in favor of a direct study of the ancient authors. See *I primi tre libri della famiglia,* p. 102; Grayson, " 'Cartule e grecismi' in L. B. Alberti," *Lingua nostra,* 13 (1952) : 105–6; and Giuseppe Billanovich, "Leon Battista Alberti, il *Graecismus* e la *Chartula,*" *Lingua nostra,* 15 (1954) : 70–71.
78. "De Iciarchia," *Op. volg.,* 3: 47–48; also pp. 55, 56.
79. *Ibid.,* pp. 24–25.

equilibrium. The proper outer "form" corresponds to the right order within, *i buon costumi* to *virtù*.[80]

Alberti's Platonic ideas on the rational order among the powers of the soul, and the fundamental conception of the "outer" world which he developed in his artistic and scientific works, completely penetrated each other here. In the notion of the "measure" of human behavior which appears in his writings and in humanistic writings on education and mores in general, aesthetic ideas of proportion were drawn into the realm of conduct. Thus Castiglione's Courtier would have to learn "to compose his entire life": no gesture or deed could be "discordant" with the rest, for life, like art, had come to demand a perfect correspondence of "the whole with the parts."[81] The aesthetic ideal of decorum, understood as a visible reflection of an "apt" proportion among the powers of the soul, was turned into a principle of conduct by the humanists; and conversely, the visual, artistic image of man was transformed at the same time by the ideal of *humanitas*.

The "new race of men" that Wölfflin found in Renaissance painting is a "race" restrained in gesture and movement, controlled in the expression of feeling. They exhibit a "classic repose" and an exaltation of human nature"[82] which is a direct pictorial translation of the humanistic ideas of the age. Alberti had pointed out that the painter makes known "the movements of the spirit by the movements of the body."[83] In his writings on mores and morality, describing how "the gestures, expressions, movements, and entire figure of the person are to be moderated,"[84] he produced a wealth of literary images which express the sense of personal style that Renaissance painting captured. He says in one place that man should conduct himself with the control of Aeneas who, through all his perils and ill fortune, *solum ingemuit, et palmas ad sidera tollit* (merely sighed, and raised his hands to the skies)."[85] The unmistakeable sign of the rule of reason which he so prized was found in such attitudes of noble restraint—attitudes which Raphael's figures would fully possess. Indeed, Wölfflin's faithful description of Raphael's "Pietà" is so like Alberti's characterization of this *dolce gravità* (the phrase he had Pandolfini use to describe the Duomo) that Alberti himself could have written it as a model for either the painter or the man: "At the moment of the most intense emotion,

---

80. "That moral worth and uncouthness are compatible was not readily intelligible to the man of the Renaissance." Woodward, *Studies in Education*, p. 247. Alberti's concern with manners is most fully developed in *De Iciarchia*, but even in an early work like *Efebie* he writes that one's bearing and gestures should conform "all'onestà e al decoro che la natura ha dato alla composizione della forma umana." *Op. volg.*, 5: 301. Remarks like this can be found throughout his writings.

81. *Il Cortegiano*, book 2, chap. 7.

82. *The Art of the Italian Renaissance*, pp. 299, 301, 306ff.

83. *Della pittura*, p. 93.

84. "De Iciarchia," *Op. volg.*, 3: 73.

85. "Della tranquillità," *Op. volg.*, 1: 108.

when Mary sees her Son dead before her, she does not scream, nor even weep. Calm and tearless, her features undistorted by grief, she stretches out her arms and gazes upwards."[86]

Here, too, in the bearing of the person, we meet a restraint of feeling based upon a norm of fittingness which has its roots in the general theory of proportion, a theory which underlies all the strands of Renaissance life and thought which Alberti's works have enabled us to trace. Measure in art and in conduct, in science, cosmology, and aesthetics—this is the outer manifestation of the vital, inner impulse of the Renaissance toward the discovery of rational, proportional norms and their re-creation in art and all of humanity's works. Understanding this, we can see how the spatial schema which Alberti did so much to bring about in Renaissance art produced a classic "mode of beholding" which befits the humanism of the age. The "humanism" of Renaissance art, as Geoffrey Scott saw it in *The Architecture of Humanism,* consists in its projection of ways of feeling into the forms of art. The masses, lines, and spaces of Renaissance art convey images of the qualities and rhythms of human feeling, its intensities, its tensions and their resolutions, its movements and their direction.[87] Yet this is the case with all artistic form, as Susanne K. Langer has shown in her studies of art and biology.[88] The symbolic projection of forms of feeling constitutes the nature of art in any age, regardless of its style or moral outlook. From this more general standpoint, all art can be called "humanistic"; and yet, in some special sense, classic art is humanistic as no other style has ever been.

The formal devices of classic art pure and simple—the perspectival arrangement of the scene, the anatomically correct figure, the architectural orders—cannot alone be responsible for its special humanistic import, because these conventions were bent to many different expressive uses in post-Renaissance Europe, from the Baroque aim of fusion with the other-worldly to the primitive, propagandistic aims of twentieth-century official art. But if the particular symbolic import of the art work cannot be found in these stylistic conventions themselves, it can be sought in the pattern of space which they organize. The imaginal or "virtual space" of the visual art work, as Susanne Langer describes it, is "organized by forms (be they lines, or volumes, or intersecting planes, or shadows and lights) that reflect the pattern of sentience and emotion."[89] What characterizes the imaginal space of the classic art of

86. *Art of the Italian Renaissance,* p. 303.
87. Geoffrey Scott, *The Architecture of Humanism,* pp. 157, 159.
88. As she says on p. 490 of *Feeling and Form,* "it is only when nature is organized in imagination along lines congruent with the forms of feeling that we can understand it, i.e., find it rational (this was Goethe's ideal of science and Kant's concept of beauty)." In *Feeling and Form,* Professor Langer presents this theory of the art work as a "non-discursive" symbol of the forms of feeling (not of nameable feeling-states or emotions), and she has recently developed the biological and psychological implications of the theory in *Mind: An Essay on Human Feeling.*
89. *Feeling and Form,* p. 83.

Hellenic Greece and its successful renaissances is its proportionality. The pattern of its pictorial, sculptural, and architectural space is one which Wölfflin termed a "multiple unity"; it is an order which leads to a distinctive perception of the whole in its parts, a relational "wholeness," a lawful unity, in which each of the parts still remains distinct. This proportional spatial schema—which is evident in Raphael's "School of Athens," Donatello's second "Feast of Herod," and Alberti's Sant' Andrea in the arrangement of their visual elements—creates the image of organicity which the aesthetic ideal of *concinnitas* was intended to denote.

To be sure, every work of art seems "organic" insofar as its forms are expressive of feelings of life, conveying an impression of vitality, movement, rhythm. To be an effective symbol of dynamic forms, the art work must be such that feelings seem to "inhere" in it. But over and above this general illusion of vitality displayed by all styles of art, classic art uniquely aspired to express the *kind* of feeling which attends "organic" balance. Whereas rhythms of quiescence are projected in the nonetheless "vital" forms of Egyptian art, and those of spiritual longing and liberation in the Gothic, the proportional forms of classic art, in painting, in the human figure, and in the edifice, aimed at a dynamic equilibrium, "the image of perfection at rest with itself."[90] A sense of completeness, and of a vital, perfectly organized activity at the same time, arises from the proportional spatial schema in which nothing seems to be wanting or to be superfluous, in which all parts of the work appear as distinctive members of it by virtue of their necessary, lawful place within the balanced whole they compose.

The formal characteristics of harmony, regularity, and variety-in-unity achieved and conveyed by the pattern of imaginative space created by classic art are definitive of the Renaissance sense of order. They define the theoretical vision and capture the very tone of life of an age dominated by the intuition of a strictly human and fully human function: the creative, law-giving function of reason.[91] In this sense, Renaissance art still teaches us how it feels to be an Alberti, striving to "exercise" our rational powers in a manifold of works and

90. Heinrich Wölfflin, *Principles of Art History,* p. 9.
91. For the "organic" character of Renaissance art, see Wilhelm Worringer, *Form in Gothic,* pp. 106, 134 *et passim.* Worringer regards this as an expressive as well as a formal feature of Renaissance art. Wölfflin, on the other hand, does not: he was so intent upon defending the a priori character of the spatial schema of the art work, that he considered its formal features to be "in themselves inexpressive, and belong[ing] to a development of a purely optical kind." *Art of the Italian Renaissance,* p. 429; see also the Introduction to *Principles of Art History.* I concur with Wölfflin (and Kant) that visual perceptions are organized by the forms of spatial intuition, and that these forms of experience, i.e., of perception and representation, are therefore not logically derivable from the data of experience. However, they must, in the *artistic* organization of perceptual elements, serve an expressive purpose; otherwise, the formal "values" of art have nothing to evaluate, and the "formed symbol" is symbolic of nothing.

ordering the appearances of things, and life itself, in accordance with an ideal of harmony.

> In the ordering of life, in ideas, desires, projects, and works . . . know how to hold to that mean which the Peripatetics advocated, so that there will be nothing wanting and nothing in excess, nothing that is not fitting.[92]

92. "Amicitia," *Op. volg.*, 2: 420.

Bibliography

Works by Leon Battista Alberti

Opere volgari di Leon Battista Alberti. Edited by Aniccio Bonucci. 5 vols. Florence, 1843–49.

Leon Battista Alberti. Opere volgari. Edited by Cecil Grayson. 2 vols. to date. Bari: Laterza, 1960–.

Opera inedita. Edited by Girolamo Mancini. Florence, 1890.

Opuscoli morali di Leon Battista Alberti, Gentil'huomo Firentino. Edited by Cosimo Bartoli. Venice, 1568.

Opera. Edited by Girolamo Massaino, Florence, 1500?

Della pittura. Edited by Luigi Mallè. Florence: Sansoni, 1950.

On Painting. Translated with introduction and notes by John R. Spencer. New Haven: Yale University Press, 1956.

L'architettura (De re aedificatoria). Latin and Italian. Edited by Giovanni Orlandi. 2 vols. Milan: Edizioni Il Polifilio, 1966.

De re aedificatoria libb. X. Florence, 1485.

Ten Books on Architecture. Translated by James Leoni. Edited by J. Ryckwert. London: Alec Tiranti, 1955.

I primi tre libri della famiglia. Edited by F. C. Pellegrini and R. Spongano. Florence: Sansoni, 1946.

Momus o del principe. Latin and Italian. Edited by Giuseppe Martini. Bologna: Nicola Zanichelli, 1942.

Opuscoli inediti: "Musca," "Vita S. Potiti." Edited by Cecil Grayson. Florence: L. S. Olschki, 1954.

"Una intercenale inedita di L. B. Alberti, Uxoria." Edited by Cecil Grayson. *Italia Medievale e Umanistica* 3 (1960): 291–307.

"Leon Battista Alberti: Alcune intercenali inediti." Edited by Eugenio Garin. *Rinascimento* 4 (1964): 125–258.

Leon Battista Alberti. La prima grammatica della lingua volgare. Edited by Cecil Grayson. Bologna: Casa Carducci, 1964.

245

*An Autographed Letter from Leon Battista Alberti to Matteo de' Pasti,
November 18, 1454.* Edited by Cecil Grayson. New York:
Pierpont Morgan Library, 1957.

Secondary Works

Almagià, Roberto. *Monumenta Italiae cartographica dal secolo XIV al XVII.*
Florence: Istituto geografico militare, 1929.
————. *Monumenta cartographica Vaticana.* Vol. 1. Vatican City:
Biblioteca apostolica vaticana, 1929.
Almagia, Roberto, and Destombes, Marcello. *Monumenta cartographica
vetustioris aevi, A.D. 1200–1500.* Vol. 1, *Mappaemundi.*
Amsterdam: N. Israel, 1964.
Altamura, Antonio. *Il certame coronario.* Naples: Silvio Viti, 1952.
Apianus, P., and Frisius, Gemma. *Cosmographia.* Antwerp, 1584.
Argan, Giulio Carlo. "The Architecture of Brunelleschi and the Origins of
Perspective Theory in the Fifteenth Century." *Journal of the Warburg and
Courtauld Institutes* 9 (1946): 96–121.
Armitage, Angus. *The World of Copernicus.* New York: New American
Library, 1951.
Badt, Kurt. "Drei plastische Arbeiten von Leone Battista Alberti." *Mitteilungen
des Kunsthistorischen Institutes in Florenz* 8 (1958): 78–87.
Baron, Hans. "Cicero and the Roman Civic Spirit in the Middle Ages and the
Early Renaissance." *Bulletin of the John Rylands Library* 20 (1938):
72–97.
————. "Franciscan Poverty and Civic Wealth in Humanistic Thought."
Speculum 13 (1938): 1–37.
————. "Towards a More Positive Evaluation of the Fifteenth-Century
Renaissance." *Journal of the History of Ideas* 4 (1943): 21–49.
————. *The Crisis of the Early Italian Renaissance.* Princeton: Princeton
University Press, 1955.
Bartoli, Cosimo. *Del modo di misurare.* Venice, 1564.
Bazeries, Commandant. *Les chiffres secrets dévoilés: Étude historique sur les
chiffres.* Paris: Librairie Charpentier et Fasquelle, 1901.
Beazley, C. R. *The Dawn of Modern Geography.* 3 vols. London: J. Murray,
1897–1906.
Behn, Irene. *Leone Battista Alberti als Kunstphilosoph.* Strassburg:
Heitz and Mündel, 1911.
Benetti-Brunelli, Valeria. *Leon Battista Alberti e il rinnovamento pedagogico
nel quattrocento.* Florence: Vallecchi, 1925.
Billanovich, Giuseppe. "Leon Battista Alberti, il *Graecismus* e la *Chartula*."
Lingua Nostra 15 (1954): 70–71.

Blunt, Anthony. *Artistic Theory in Italy, 1450–1600*. Oxford: Clarendon Press, 1956.

Boffito, Giuseppe. "Intorno alla più antica veduta di Firenze e al suo autore." In *Atti dell'VIII Congresso Geografico Italiano* 2 (1921): 243–54. (Also in Appendix, Boffito and Mori, below, pp. 139–46).

Boffito, Giuseppe, and Mori, Attilio. *Piante e vedute di Firenze: Studio storico, topografico, cartografico*. Florence: L. Franceschini, 1926.

Bosanquet, Bernard. *A History of Aesthetics*. 2d ed. London: George Allen and Unwin, 1934.

Breed, Charles B. *Surveying*. New York: John Wiley & Sons, 1942.

Brunschvicg, Léon. *Les étapes de la philosophie mathématique*. Paris: Librairie Félix Alcan, 1912.

Bruyne, Edgar de. *Etudes d'esthétique médiévale*. 3 vols. Bruges: De Tempel, 1946.

Bunim, Miriam Schild. *Space in Medieval Painting and the Forerunners of Perspective*. New York: Columbia University Press, 1940.

Burckhardt, Jacob. *The Civilization of the Renaissance in Italy*. 3d ed. London: Phaidon Press, 1950.

Burtt, Edwin Arthur. *The Metaphysical Foundations of Modern Physical Science*. Rev. ed. Garden City, N. Y.: Doubleday & Co., 1955.

Calabi, A., and Cornaggia, G. *Matteo dei Pasti: La sua opera medaglistica*. Milan: G. Modiano, 1927.

Cantor, Moritz. *Vorlesungen über Geschichte der Mathematik*. Vol. 2. Leipzig: B. G. Teubner, 1913.

Cassirer, Ernst. *Das Erkenntnisproblem*. Vol. 1. Berlin: Bruno Cassirer, 1906.

———. *Individuum und Kosmos in der Philosophie der Renaissance*. Leipzig and Berlin: B. G. Teubner, 1927. (*The Individual and Cosmos in Renaissance Philosophy*. Introduction and English translation by Mario Domandi. New York: Harper & Row, 1964).

———. "Some Remarks on the Question of the Originality of the Renaissance." *Journal of the History of Ideas* 4 (1943): 49–56.

———. *Philosophie der Symbolischen Formen*. 3 vols. 2 ed. Oxford: Bruno Cassirer, 1954.

Cassirer, Ernst; Kristeller, Paul Oskar; Randall, John Hermann, Jr., eds. *The Renaissance Philosophy of Man*. Chicago: University of Chicago Press, 1948.

Castiglione, Baldesar. *Il Cortegiano*. Florence: Sansoni, 1929.

Cataneo, M. Girolamo. *Dell'arte del misurare, libri due*. Brescia, 1583.

Cennini, Cennino. *Il libro dell'arte*. 2 vols. New Haven: Yale University Press, 1932.

Ceschi, C. "La Madre di Leon Battista Alberti." *Bollettino d'Arte* (1948): 191–92.

Bibliography   Chabod, Federico. *Machiavelli and the Renaissance*. London: Bowes & Bowes, 1958.

Chastel, André. *Marsile Ficin et l'art*. Geneva: Librairie E. Droz, 1954.

Cian, Vittorio. *La Satira*. Vol. 1. Milan: Vallardi, n.d.

Ciapponi, Lucia A. "Il 'De Architectura' di Vitruvio nel primo umanesimo." *Italia Medioevale e Umanistica* 3 (1960): 59–99.

Clark, Arthur Bridgman. *Perspective: A Textbook and Manual for Artists, Architects, and Students*. Stanford: Stanford University Press, 1936.

Clark, Kenneth. *Leon Battista Alberti on Painting*. Proceedings of the British Academy, Vol. 30 (1944).

Colombo, Carmela. "Leon Battista Alberti e la prima grammatica italiana." *Studi Linguistici Italiani* 3 (1962): 176–87.

Copernicus, Nicholas. *Three Copernican Treatises*. Translated and with an introduction by Edward Rosen. New York: Columbia University Press, 1939.

Crone, G. R. *Maps and Their Makers*. London and New York: Hutchinson House, 1953.

Danfrie, Philippe. *Declaration de l'usage du Graphometre*. Paris, 1597.

Dehio, Georg. "Die Bauprojekte Nicolaus V." *Repertorium für Kunstwissenschaft* 3 (1880) 241–57.

Du Fresne, Raphael. "The Life of Leone Battista Alberti." In *Ten Books on Architecture,* edited by J. Ryckwert. London: Alec Tiranti, 1955.

Duhem, Pierre. *Etudes sur Leonard de Vinci: Ceux qu'il a lus et ceux qui l'ont lu.* 3 vols. Paris: A. Hermann et fils, 1906–13.

———. *Le système du monde.* 7 vols. Paris: A. Hermann et fils, 1913–56.

Durand, Dana Bennett. *The Vienna-Klosterneuburg Map Corpus of the Fifteenth Century*. Leyden: E. J. Brill, 1952.

Eckert, Max. *Die Kartenwissenschaft*. 2 vols. Berlin and Leipzig: Vereinigung Wissenschaftlicher Verleger, 1921.

Eden, W. A. "Studies in Urban Theory: The *De re aedificatoria* of Leon Battista Alberti." *Town Planning Review* 19 (1943): 10–28.

Edgerton, Samuel Y., Jr. "Alberti's Perspective: A New Discovery and a New Evaluation." *Art Bulletin* 48 (1966): 367–78.

Ettlinger, L. D. "Pollaiuolo's Tomb of Pope Sixtus IV." *Journal of the Warburg and Courtauld Institutes* 16 (1953): 239–74.

Ferguson, Wallace K. *The Renaissance in Historical Thought: Five Centuries of Interpretation*. Boston: Houghton Mifflin Co., 1948.

Ficino, Marsilio. "Platonic Theology," bk. 3, chap. 2, translated by Josephine L. Burroughs. *Journal of the History of Ideas* 5 (1944): 227–39.

Filarete (Antonio di Piero Averlino). *Treatise on Architecture*. Translated and with an introduction by John R. Spencer. 2 vols. New Haven and London: Yale University Press, 1965.

248   Finaeus, Orontius. *De re et praxi geometrica*. Paris, 1556.

Fischer, J. *Claudii Ptolemaei Geographiae.* Vol. 1, *Tomus Prodromus.* Leyden and Leipzig: O. Harrassowitz, 1932.

Flaccavento, Giorgio. "Per una moderna traduzione del 'De Statua' di L. B. Alberti." *Cronache di Archeologia e Storia dell'arte* 1 (1962): 50–59.

———. "Sulla data del 'De Statua' di Leon Battista Alberti." *Commentari* 16 (1965): 216–21.

Flemming, W. *Die Begründung der modernen Aestetik und Kunstwissenschaft durch L. B. Alberti.* Berlin and Leipzig: B. G. Teubner, 1916.

Foullon, Abel. *Descrittione et uso dell'holometro.* Venice, 1564.

Francesca, Piero della. *De prospectiva pingendi.* Edited by G. Nicco Fasola. Florence: Sansoni, 1942.

Frankl, Paul. "The Secret of the Medieval Masons." *Art Bulletin* 27 (1945): 46–60.

———. *The Gothic: Literary Sources and Interpretations through Eight Centuries.* Princeton: Princeton University Press, 1960.

Frey, Dagobert. *Gotik und Renaissance als Grundlagen der modernen Weltanschauung.* Augsburg and Baden bei Vienna: B. Filser Verlag, 1929.

Frutaz, Amato Pietro. *Le piante di Roma.* 3 vols. Vatican City: Biblioteca apostolica vaticana. 1962.

Garin, Eugenio. *L'umanesimo italiano.* Bari: Laterza, 1952.

Gioseffi, Decio. *Perspectiva artificialis.* Trieste: Istituto di storia dell'arte antica e moderna, 1957.

Goldstein, Thomas. "Geography in Fifteenth-Century Florence." In *Merchants and Scholars.* Minneapolis: University of Minnesota Press, 1965.

Grayson, Cecil. "Notes on the Texts of Some Vernacular Works of Leon Battista Alberti." *Rinascimento* 3 (1952): 211–44.

———. "'Cartule e grecismi' in L. B. Alberti." *Lingua Nostra* 13 (1952): 105–6.

———. "Studi su Leon Battista Alberti." *Rinascimento* 4 (1953): 45–62.

———. "A Portrait of Leon Battista Alberti." *Burlington Magazine* 96 (1954): 177–79.

———. "L. B. Alberti: Traduttore di Walter Map." *Lettere italiane* 7 (1955): 11–12.

———. "Alberti and the Vernacular Eclogue in the Quattrocento." *Italian Studies* 11 (1956): 16–29.

———. "The Humanism of Alberti." *Italian Studies* 12 (1957): 37–56.

———. "Note sulle rime dell'Alberti." *Rassegna della Letteratura italiana* 63 (1959): 76–78.

———. "The Composition of L. B. Alberti's 'Decem Libri De re aedificatoria.'" *Münchner Jahrbuch der Bildenden Kunst,* ser. 3, vol. 11 (1960): 152–61.

———. "Alberti." Article in *Dizionario biografico degli Italiani.* Rome: Enciclopedia italiana, 1960.

———. "L. B. Alberti's 'costruzione legittima.'" *Italian Studies* 19 (1964): 14–27.

Gunther, Robert T. *The Astrolabes of the World.* 2 vols. Oxford: Oxford University Press, 1932.

Harvey, John H. "Four Fifteenth-Century London Plans." *London Topographical Record* 20 (1952): 1–8.

Haswell, John H. "Secret Writing: The Ciphers of the Ancients, and Some of Those in Modern Use." *Century Magazine* 85 (1912–13): 83–92.

Helton, Tinsley, ed. *The Renaissance.* Madison: University of Wisconsin Press, 1961.

Heydenreich, Ludwig H. *Leonardo Da Vinci.* 2 vols. New York: Macmillan, 1954.

———. "Die Cappella Rucellai von San Pancrazio in Florenz." In *De artibus opuscola XL: Essays in Honor of Erwin Panofsky,* edited by Millard Meiss. New York: New York University Press, 1961.

Hill, George Francis. *A Corpus of Italian Medals of the Renaissance before Cellini.* 2 vols. London: British Museum, 1930.

Hinks, Roger. *Myth and Allegory in Ancient Art.* London: Warburg Institute, 1939.

Holtzmann, Walther. "Der älteste mittelalteriche Stadtplan von Rom." *Archäologisches Institut des Deutschen Reiches, Jahrbuch* 41 (1926): 56–66.

Honnecourt, Villard de. *The Sketchbook of Villard de Honnecourt.* Translated and edited by Theodore Bowie. Bloomington, Ind.: Indiana University Press, 1959.

Hubala, Erich. "L. B. Albertis Langhaus von Sant Andrea in Mantua." In *Festschrift Kurt Badt zum siebzigsten Geburtstage.* Berlin: Walter de Gruyter & Co., 1961.

Ivins, William M. Jr., *On the Rationalization of Sight.* New York: Metropolitan Museum of Art, 1938.

Jacobs, Emil. "Cristoforo Buondelmonti: Ein Beiting zur Kenntnis seines Lebens und seiner Schriften." In *Beiträge zur Bücherkunde und Philologie August Wilmanns.* Leipzig, 1903.

———. "Neues von Cristoforo Buondelmonti." *Archäologisches Institut des Deutschen Reiches, Jahrbuch* 20 (1905): 39–45.

Janitschek, Hubert. "Leon Battista Albertis Kleinere Kunsttheoretische Schriften." *Quellenschriften für Kunstgeschichte* 11 (1877).

Janson, H. W. *The Sculpture of Donatello.* 2 vols. Princeton: Princeton University Press, 1957.

———. *History of Art.* Englewood Cliffs, N. J.: Prentice-Hall, 1962.

Jungingen, Conrad von. *Geometria culmensis.* Latin edition and German translation by H. Mendthal. Leipzig, 1886.

Kahn, David. *The Codebreakers.* London: Weidenfeld & Nicolson, 1967.

Katzenellenbogen, Adolf. "The Representation of the Seven Liberal Arts." In *Twelfth-Century Europe and the Foundations of Modern Society,* edited by Marshall Clagett and others. Madison and London: University of Wisconsin Press, 1966.

Keuning, Johannes. "The History of Geographical Map Projections until 1600." *Imago Mundi* 12 (1955): 1–24.

Kimble, G. H. T. *Geography in the Middle Ages.* London: Methuen and Co., 1938.

Klein, Robert, "Pomponius on Perspective." *Art Bulletin* 42 (1961): 211–30.

Klibansky, Raymond. *Ein Proklos-Fund.* Heidelberg: Philosophisch-historische Klasse, 1929.

———. "Plato's Parmenides in the Middle Ages and the Renaissance." *Medieval and Renaissance Studies* 1, 2 (1943): 281–331.

———. *Plato Latinus.* Vol. 3, *Parmenides.* London: Warburg Institute, 1953.

Koyré, Alexandre. *Etudes galiléenes.* Paris: A. Hermann et fils, 1939.

———. *From the Closed World to the Infinite Universe.* New York: Harper and Row, 1958.

Krautheimer, Richard, and Krautheimer-Hess, Trude. *Lorenzo Ghiberti.* Princeton: Princeton University Press, 1956.

Krautheimer, Richard. "Alberti's Templum etruscum." *Münchner Jahrbuch der Bildenden Kunst,* 3d ser., vol. 12 (1961): 65–72.

———. "Alberti and Vitruvius." *Acts of the Twentieth International Congress of the History of Art* 2 (1961): 42–52.

Kretschmer, Konrad. "Die italienische Portolane des Mittelalters." *Veröffentlichung des Instituts für Meereskunde und des geographischen Institut an der Universität Berlin* 13 (1909).

Kristeller, Paul Oskar. *The Philosophy of Marsilio Ficino.* New York: Columbia University Press, 1953.

———. "The Place of Classical Humanism in Renaissance Thought." *Journal of the History of Ideas* 4 (1943): 59–63.

———. "The Modern System of the Arts: A Study in the History of Aesthetics." *Journal of the History of Ideas* 12 (1951): 496–527; 13 (1952): 17–46.

———. *The Classics and Renaissance Thought.* Cambridge, Mass.: Harvard University Press, 1955.

———. *Studies in Renaissance Thought and Letters.* Rome: Edizioni di Storia e Letteratura, 1956.

———. *Renaissance Thought: The Classic, Scholastic, and Humanistic Strains.* New York: Harper & Row, 1961.

———. *Renaissance Thought II: Papers on Humanism and the Arts.* New York: Harper & Row, 1965.

Kuhn, T. S. *The Copernican Revolution.* Cambridge, Mass.: Harvard University Press, 1957.

Landino, Cristoforo. *Disputationum Camaldulensium libri IV.* Venice [1507?].

Lang, Ruth. *Leon Battista Alberti und die Sancta Masseritia.* Saint Gall: Rapperswil, 1938.

Langer, Susanne K. *Feeling and Form.* New York: Charles Scribner's Sons, 1953.

——. *Mind: An Essay on Human Feeling.* Vol. 1. Baltimore: Johns Hopkins Press, 1967.

Lee, Rensselaer W. "Ut pictura poesis: A Humanistic Theory of Painting." *Art Bulletin* 30 (1940): 197–269.

Lehmann-Brockhaus, O. "Albertis 'Descriptio urbis Romae.'" *Kunstchronik* 13 (1960): 345–48.

Leibnitz, Gottfried Wilhelm. *Oeuvres philosophiques de Leibnitz.* Edited by P. Janet. Vol. 3. Paris, 1866.

Lemoine, Jean-Gabriel. "Brunelleschi et Ptolemée: Les origines géographiques de la 'boite d'optique.'" *Gazette des beaux-arts* (1958): 281–96.

Libri, Guillaume. *Histoire des sciences mathématiques en Italie.* 4 vols. Paris, 1838–41.

Magnuson, Torgil. "The Project of Nicholas V for Rebuilding the Borgo Leonino in Rome." *Art Bulletin* 36 (1954): 89–115.

Mâle, Emile. *Religious Art in France: Thirteenth Century.* Translated by Dora Nussey. New York: E. P. Dutton & Co., 1913.

——. *L'art religieux de la fin du Moyen Age en France.* Paris: Librairie Armand Colin, 1922.

——. *Religious Art from the Twelfth to the Eighteenth Century.* New York: Pantheon Books, Inc., 1949.

Malfatti, V. "Le navi romane del lago di Nemi." *Rivista marittima* (1926): 693–700.

Mancini, Girolamo. *Vita di Leon Battista Alberti.* 2d ed., rev. Florence: G. Carnesecchi e Figli, 1911.

Mariani, Valerio. *Incontri con Roma nel Rinascimento: L. B. Alberti, Donatello, A. Mantegna, Raffaello.* Rome: Istituto di studi romani, 1960.

Martines, Lauro. *The Social World of the Florentine Humanists, 1390–1460.* Princeton: Princeton University Press, 1963.

Meister, Aloys. *Die Geheimschrift im Dienste der Päpstlichen Kurie.* Paderborn: F. Schönergh, 1906.

Mendelsohn, Charles J. "Cardan on Cryptography." *Scripta Mathematica* 6 (1939): 157–68.

——. "Bibliographical note on 'De Cifris' of Leon Battista Alberti." *Isis* 32 (1940): 48–51.

Mesnil, Jacques. *L'art au nord et au sud des Alpes à l'époque de la Renaissance.* Brussels-Paris: G. Van Oest and Co., 1911.

——. *Masaccio et les débuts de la Renaissance.* The Hague: Martinus Nijhoff, 1927.

Michel, Paul-Henri. *Un idéal humain au XVe siècle: La pensée de L. B. Alberti.* Paris: Sociéte d'Editions "Les Belles Lettres," 1930.

Miller, Konrad. *Die ältesten Weltkarten.* Part 4: *Die Herefordkarte.* Stuttgart,
1896.

Nordenskiöld, A. E. *Facsimile-Atlas to the Early History of Cartography.*
Translated by J. A. Ekelöf and Clements R. Markham. Stockholm, 1889.

Oberhummer, Eugen. "Leonardo da Vinci and the Art of the Renaissance in Its
Relation to Geography." *Geographical Journal* 33 (1909): 540–69.

Olschki, Leonardo. *Geschichte der Neusprachlichen Wissenschaftlichen Literatur.*
3 vols. Heidelberg, Leipzig, and Halle: Carl Winters'
Universitätsbuchhandlung, 1919–27.

Omont, H., ed. *Géographie de Ptolémée. Traduction latine de Jacopo d'Angiolo
de Florence. Reproduction réduite des cartes et plans du manuscrit latin
4802 de la Bibliothèque nationale.* Paris [1926?].

Ossat, Guglielmo De Angelis d'. "Enunciati euclidei e 'divina proporzione'
nell'architettura del primo Rinascimento." In *Atti del V convegno
internazionale di studi sul Rinascimento.* Florence, 1958.

Pachter, Henry M. *Paracelsus: Magic into Science.* New York: Crowell-Collier
Publishing Co., 1961.

Panofsky, Erwin. "Das perspektivische Verfahren Leone Battista Albertis."
Kunstchronik 26 (1915): 504–16.

———. *Idea.* Leipzig and Berlin: B. G. Teubner, 1924.

———. "Die Perspektive als 'Symbolische Form.'" *Vorträge der Bibliothek
Warburg* (1924–25): 258–330.

———. *The Codex Huygens and Leonardo da Vinci's Art Theory.* London:
Warburg Institute, 1940.

———. *Abbot Suger on the Abbey Church of St. Denis and Its Art Treasures.*
Princeton: Princeton University Press, 1946.

———. "Postlogium Sugerianum." *Art Bulletin* 29 (1947): 119–287.

———. *Early Netherlandish Painting: Its Origins and Character.* 2 vols.
Cambridge, Mass.: Harvard University Press, 1953.

———. "Artist, Scientist, Genius: Notes on the 'Renaissance-Dämmerung.'" In
The Renaissance: Six Essays. New York: Harper & Row, 1953.

———. *Meaning in the Visual Arts.* New York: Doubleday & Co., 1955.

———. *Gothic Architecture and Scholasticism.* New York: Meridian Books,
1957.

———. *Renaissance and Renascences.* Uppsala: Boktryckeri Aktiebolag, 1960.

Parronchi, Alessandro. "Il *punctum dolens* della 'costruzione legittima.'" In *Studi
su la dolce prospettiva.* Milan, 1964.

———. "La 'costruzione legittima' è uguale alla 'costruzione con punti di
distanza.'" *Rinascimento* 4 (1964): 35–40.

———. "Il Filarete, Francesco di Giorgio e Leonardo su la 'Costruzione
legittima.'" *Rinascimento* 5 (1965): 155–67.

Parsons, William Barclay. *Engineers and Engineering in the Renaissance.*
Baltimore: Williams & Wilkins Co., 1939.

Passerini, Luigi. *Gli Alberti di Firenze: Genealogia, storia, e documenti.* 2 vols. Florence, 1869–70.

Petrini, Mario. "L'uomo di Alberti." *Belfagor* 6 (1951): 665–74.

Pirenne, M. H. "The Scientific Basis of Leonardo da Vinci's Theory of Perspective." *British Journal for the Philosophy of Science* 3 (1952): 169–85.

Pittaluga, M. "Masaccio e L. B. Alberti." *Rassegna italiana d'arte* (1929): 779 ff.

Ponte, Giovanni. "La datazione del 'Teogenio' di L. B. Alberti." *Convivium* 23 (1955): 150–59.

———. "Il petrarchismo di Leon Battista Alberti." *Rassegna della letteratura italiana* 62 (1958): 216–22.

Pope-Hennessy, John. *Italian Renaissance Sculpture.* London: Phaidon Press, 1958.

Pozzetti, Pompilio. *Leo Baptista Alberti.* Florence, 1789.

Procacci, Ugo. *Sinopie e affreschi.* Milan: Electra editrice, 1961.

Ptolemy, Claudius. *Geography.* Translated and edited by Edward Luther Stevenson. New York: New York Public Library, 1932.

Ragghianti, Carlo L. "Tempio Malatestiano." *Critica d'Arte,* vol. 12, fasc. 71 (1965): 23–31; fasc. 74 (1965): 27–40.

Randall, John Hermann, Jr. *The School of Padua and the Emergence of Modern Science.* Padua: Editrice Antenere, 1961.

Ricci, Corrado. *Leon Battista Alberti Architetto, cinquanta tavole con introduzione.* Turin: E. Celanza, 1917.

Ritscher, Ernst. *Die Kirche S. Andrea in Mantua.* Berlin, 1899.

Rossi, Giovanni Battista de. *Piante iconografiche e prospettiche di Roma anteriori al secolo XVI.* Rome, 1879.

Rossi, Vittorio. *Il quattrocento.* Milan: F. Vallardi, 1933.

Ruggiero, Guido de. *Rinascimento, riforma e controriforma.* 2 vols. Part 3 of *Storia della filosofia.* Bari: Laterza, 1950.

Sabbadini, R. *Le scoperte dei codici latini e greci ne' secoli XIV e XV.* 2 vols. Florence: Sansoni, 1905–14.

Sacco, Luigi. *Un primato italiano: La crittografia nei secoli XV e XVI* (extract from *Bollettino dell'Istituto di cultura dell'arma del genio* 26 [1947]). Rome, 1954.

Saitta, Giuseppe. *La filosofia di Marsilio Ficino.* Messina: Principato, 1923.

———. *Il pensiero italiano nell'umanesimo e nel rinascimento.* 3 vols. Bologna: Cesare Zuffi, 1949–51.

Santinello, Giovanni. *Leon Battista Alberti. Una visione estetica del mondo e della vita.* Florence: Sansoni, 1962.

Sarton, George. *Introduction to the History of Science.* Vol. 3. Baltimore: Williams & Wilkins Co., 1948.

———. *The Appreciation of Ancient and Medieval Science during the Renaissance (1450–1600).* Philadelphia: University of Pennsylvania Press, 1955.

Schlosser, Julius von. "Ein Künstlerproblem der Renaissance: L. B. Alberti." *Akademie der Wissenschaften in Wein, Sitzungberichte 210.* Vol. 2. Vienna and Leipzig, 1929.

———. *La letteratura artistica.* Translated by Filippo Rossi. 2d ed. Florence: La Nuova Italia; Vienna: Anton Schroll, 1956.

Schöne, Wolfgang. *Über das Licht in der Malerei.* Berlin: Gebrüder Mann, 1954.

Scott, Geoffrey. *The Architecture of Humanism.* 2d ed. Garden City, N. Y.: Doubleday & Co., 1954.

Simson, Otto von. *The Gothic Cathedral.* New York and Evanston: Harper & Row, 1964.

Singer, Charles; Holmyard, E. J.; Hall, A. R.; and Williams, Trevor I. *A History of Technology.* Vol. 3. New York: Oxford University Press, 1957.

Soergel, Gerda. "Die Harmonien in Leone Battista Albertis Tempio Malatestiano." In *Untersuchungen über den theoretischen Architekturentwurf von 1450–1550 in Italien.* Inaugural dissertation, Philosophical Faculty of the University of Cologne, 1958, pp. 8–22.

Stefanini, L. "La prospettiva tolemaica." *Rivista di estetica* (1956): 97–106.

Stokes, Adrian D. *Art and Science: A Study of Alberti, Piero della Francesca, and Giorgione.* London: Faber & Faber, 1949.

Straub, Hans. *A History of Civil Engineering.* Translated by E. Rockwell. London: Leonard Hill, 1952.

Theuer, Max. *Zehn Bücher über die Baukunst. Ins Deutsche übertragen, Eingeleitet und mit Anmerkungen und Zeichnungen versehen.* Vienna, 1912.

Thorndike, Lynn. *Science and Thought in the Fifteenth Century.* New York: Columbia University Press, 1929.

———. *A History of Magic and Experimental Science.* Vols. 4 and 5. New York: Columbia University Press, 1934.

———. "Renaissance or Prenaissance?" *Journal of the History of Ideas* 4 (1943): 65–74.

Tigler, Peter. *Die Architekturtheorie des Filarete.* Berlin: W. De Gruyter, 1963.

Tiraboschi, Girolamo. "Vita di Leon Battista Alberti." In *Della pittura e della statua di Leon Battista Alberti.* Milan, 1804.

Toffanin, Giuseppe. *History of Humanism.* Translated by E. Gianturco. New York: Las Americas Publishing Co., 1954.

Torre, A. della. *Storia dell'Accademia Platonica di Firenze.* Florence: Carnesecchi, 1902.

Toulmin, Stephen, and Goodfield, June. *The Fabric of the Heavens.* New York: Harper & Row, 1961.

Uccelli, Arturo. *Storia della tecnica dal Medio Evo ai nostri giorni.* Milan: Ulrico Hoepli, 1945.

Ueberweg, Friedrich. *History of Philosophy.* 2 vols. New York, 1893.

Usher, Abbott Payson. *A History of Mechanical Inventions.* Rev. ed. Cambridge, Mass.: Harvard University Press, 1954.

Uzielli, Gustavo. *La vita e i tempi di Paolo dal Pozzo Toscanelli.* In *Raccolta di documenti e studi, R. Commissione Colombiana,* Pt. 5, vol. 1. Rome, 1894.

Vansteenberghe, Edmond. *Le Cardinal Nicolas de Cues.* Paris: Edouard Champion, 1920.

Vasari, Giorgio. *Vite cinque annotate da Girolamo Mancini.* Florence: G. Carnesecchi e Figli, 1917.

Venturi, Adolfo. "Un opera sconosciuta di Leon B. Alberti." *L'arte* 17 (1914): 153–56.

———. "Intarsi Marmorei di Leon Battista Alberti." *L'arte* 22 (1919): 34–36.

———. *Leon Battista Alberti, Ventisei Riproduzioni.* Rome: Biblioteca d'arte illustrata, 1923.

Venturi, Lionello. *History of Art Criticism.* Translated by Charles Marriott. New York: E. P. Dutton & Co., 1936.

Vignola, Giacomo Barozzio. *Le due regole della prospettiva pratica.* Rome, 1611.

Vincent, A. J. H. "Le traité de la dioptra d'Heron d'Alexandrie." *Notices et extraits des manuscrits de la Bibliothèque impériale* 19 (1858).

Vinci, Leonardo da. *The Literary Works of Leonardo da Vinci.* 2 vols. Edited by Jean Paul Richter. London, 1883.

———. *Problèmes de géométrie et d'hydraulique.* 3 vols. Paris: Edouard Rouveyre, 1901.

———. *I libri di meccanica.* Edited by Arturo Uccelli. Milan: Ulrico Hoepli, 1942.

Vitruvius. *De Architectura.* Translated by Frank Granger. London: William Heinemann, 1931.

Wallerstein, Victor. *Die Raumbehandlung in der oberdeutschen und niederländischen Tafelmalerei der ersten Hälfte des XV Jahrhunderts.* Strassburg: Heitz & Mündel, 1909.

Ware, William R. *Modern Perspective.* Boston, 1882.

Waterhouse, James. "Notes on the Early History of the Camera Obscura." *Photographic Journal,* May 1901.

———. "Camera Obscura." Article in *Encyclopaedia Britannica.* 11th ed. 1910–11.

Watkins, Renée. "The Authorship of the Vita Anonyma of Leon Battista Alberti." *Studies in the Renaissance* 4 (1957): 101–12.

———. "L. B. Alberti's Emblem, the Winged Eye, and His Name, Leo." *Mitteilungen des Kunsthistorischen Institutes in Florenz* 9 (1960): 256–58.

Weber, Max. *The Protestant Ethic and the Spirit of Capitalism.* New York: Charles Scribner's Sons; London, George Allen and Unwin, 1950.

White, John. "Developments in Renaissance Perspective." *Journal of the Warburg and Courtauld Institutes* 12 (1949): 58–79.

————. *The Birth and Rebirth of Pictorial Space*. London: Faber & Faber, 1957.

Wind, Edgar. *Pagan Mysteries in the Renaissance*. New Haven: Yale University Press, 1958.

Winterberg, Dr. "Leon Baptista Alberti's technische Schriften." *Repertorium für Kunstwissenschaft* 11 (1883): 326–56.

Wittkower, Rudolf. *The Artist and the Liberal Arts*. London: H. K. Lewis & Co., 1952.

————. "Brunelleschi and 'Proportion in Perspective.'" *Journal of the Warburg and Courtauld Institutes* 16 (1953): 275–91.

————. *Architectural Principles in the Age of Humanism*. Rev. ed. London: Alec Tiranti, 1962.

Wolff, Georg. "Leon Battista Alberti als Mathematiker." *Scientia* 60 (1936): 353–59.

————. "Zu Leon Battista Alberti's Perspektivlehre." *Zeitschrift für Kunstgeschichte* 5 (1936): 47–54.

Wölfflin, Heinrich. *Principles of Art History*. 7th ed. Translated by M. D. Hottinger. New York: Dover Press, n.d.

————. *The Art of the Italian Renaissance*. Translation of *Die Klassische Kunst*. New York and London: G. P. Putnam's Sons, 1928.

Woodward, William Harrison. *Vittorino da Feltre and other Humanist Educators*. Cambridge, 1897.

————. *Studies in Education during the Age of the Renaissance 1400–1600*. Cambridge: Cambridge University Press, 1924.

Worringer, Wilhelm. *Form in Gothic*. New ed. London: Alec Tiranti, 1957.

Zoubov, V. "Léon Battista Alberti et les auteurs du Moyen Age." *Medieval and Renaissance Studies* 4 (1958): 245–66.

————. "Léon Battista Alberti et Léonard de Vinci." *Raccolta vinciana* 18 (1960): 1–14.

Index

Acqua Vergine (Rome), 94

Aeneas, 240

Aesop, 220

Albergati, Cardinal (Bishop of Bologna), 5

Alberti, Adovardo (*De Familia*), 215, 229, 232

Alberti, Bernardo (cousin), 11 n.16

Alberti, Carlo (brother), 3, 4,

Alberti, family, 5, 22, 168, 215, 227, 229

Alberti, Gianozzo (*De Familia*), 215

Alberti, Leon Battista: art theory, architecture, 9, 55–56, 98–100, 104–8, 108–17, 122–24, 133–35, 140–42; art theory, painting, 7, 28, 40, 55–56, 67, 87–91, 131–32; art theory, sculpture, 55–56, 76–81, 84, 87–91; astronomy, 195–98; beauty, theory of, 9, 14, 70, 81–82, 84, 85, 87–89, 104–17, 128–41, 201, 214, 233–35; cartography, 6, 15, 71–76, 166–95; cryptography, 10, 12, 14, 15, 207–11, 219; early life, 3–4; education, 4–5; engineering, 94, 203–4; humanism, 7, 12, 69, 167, 203, 213–43; in Bologna, 4, 5, 7, 93; in Ferrara, 7, 93, 118, 196 n.68; in Florence, 5, 6, 7, 9, 10, 22, 73, 196 n.67 and n.68, 217, 218, 229; in France, 5, 6; in Genoa, 3, 168; in Germany, 5; in Low Countries, 5; in Padua, 4, 168, 196 n.68; in Rome, 5, 6, 7, 8, 9, 71–74, 93 n.1, 93–98, 167, 196 n.68, 215 n.7; in Urbino, 9; in Venice, 168; instruments, 6, 10, 12, 38, 39, 72, 75, 76, 77, 168–75, 198, 205–6, 208–9; Italian language, 6, 7, 9, 12, 14, 22, 215, 217–20, 228–31; as Latinist, 220 n.26, 220–21; literary pursuits, 4–5, 7–8, 12, 14; moral philosophy, 4, 7, 10, 14, 214–39; as papal secretary, 5, 9; perspective theory, 2, 6, 7, 9, 14, 21, 26,

30, 34 n.19, 35, 38, 40–44, 45–54, 63–65, 67, 68, 75–76; religious thought, 235–39; Renaissance views of, 3, 10–11, 21, 66, 75, 84, 99, 117, 119, 131 n.56, 195, 202, 202 n., 203, 216, 218, 220, 231; scientific ideas, 201–7; self-portait 8, 69; surveying, 6, 9, 12, 40–41, 72–74, 167–79. Architectural Projects: adviser to Nicholas V, 8, 93–94; Annunziata Rotonda (Florence), 117 n.38; Arco del Cavallo (Ferrara), 8, 118; Holy Sepulcher (Florence), 124–26; Palazzo Venezia (Rome), 117 n.38; Rucellai Chapel and Loggia (Florence), 117 n.38, 124 n.49; Rucellai Palace (Florence), 9, 91, 124, 126–28; San Martino, apse (Gangalandi), 117 n.38; San Sebastiano (Mantua), 9, 117 n.38, 138 n.64; San Stefano Rotondo (Rome), 117 n.38; Santa Maria Novella (Florence), 9, 23, 91, 112–14, 120–21, 124, 128; Sant' Andrea (Mantua) 9, 135–40, 242; Tempio Malatestiano (Church of San Francesco, Rimini), 9, 95–98, 111, 112 n.32, 117, 118–20, 121. Writings: *Amator*, 5 n.6; *Amicizia*, 215 n.7, 218; *Apologi*, 7, 220, 223, 238; *Canis*, 7, 220; *De componendis cifris*, 10, 12, 15, 207–11; *De equo animante*, 8; *De familia*, 4, 6, 7, 10, 215, 217, 218, 219, 223, 225, 227, 229, 235; *De Iciarchia*, 10, 223, 229–30, 235; *Deiphira*, 5 n.6; *Della pittura*, 6, 7, 8, 12, 13, 14, 21, 22, 26, 28, 34 n.19, 37 n.21, 45 n.28, 46 n.29, 47, 49 n.31, 49 n.34, 55, 55 n.1, 62, 63 n., 67, 68, 74 n., 75, 76 n.29, 80 n.35, 81, 82, 84, 87, 88, 91, 104, 110, 131, 170, 214, 234; *Della statua*, 7, 13, 14, 76, 77 n., 80, 81, 82, 84, 87, 104, 116; *De*